Mrs. Lincoln Phelps

Our Country, in Its Relations to the Past, Present and Future

A national book, consisting of original articles in prose and verse, contributed by

American writers

Mrs. Lincoln Phelps

Our Country, in Its Relations to the Past, Present and Future
A national book, consisting of original articles in prose and verse, contributed by American writers

ISBN/EAN: 9783337386559

Printed in Europe, USA, Canada, Australia, Japan

Cover: Foto ©ninafisch / pixelio.de

More available books at **www.hansebooks.com**

OUR COUNTRY,

IN ITS RELATIONS TO THE PAST, PRESENT AND FUTURE.

A NATIONAL BOOK,

CONSISTING OF ORIGINAL ARTICLES IN PROSE AND VERSE, CONTRIBUTED BY AMERICAN WRITERS.

EDITED BY
MRS. LINCOLN PHELPS,

UNDER THE SANCTION OF THE STATE FAIR ASSOCIATION OF THE WOMEN OF MARYLAND, FOR THE BENEFIT OF THE U. S. CHRISTIAN AND SANITARY COMMISSIONS.

BALTIMORE:
PRINTED BY JOHN D. TOY.

1864.

ENTERED, according to the Act of Congress, in the year 1864.
BY ALMIRA LINCOLN PHELPS,
In the Clerk's Office, of the District Court of Maryland.

DEDICATION.

To the MOTHERS, WIVES and SISTERS of the Loyal States, whose SONS, Husbands, and Brothers are periling their lives in the cause of the Country, in the Armies and Navies of the United States, with the prayer that the objects of their affection may, in God's good time, be restored to them, crowned with triumph, and rewarded with the blessings of their grateful fellow-citizens, this volume is affectionately DEDICATED by the women of Maryland, through their State Fair organization.

PREFACE.

This volume goes forth freighted with the loyal sentiments of many good and gifted Authors, who have freely given their offerings for "Our Country;" a talisman which, while it touches the heart, inspires the genius. The Editor has not sought for assistance among men in office, active politicians, or the leaders of cliques or parties. The opinions of such might have less weight than of those who regarding the great national questions from the quiet shades of retirement, or under circumstances which leave the judgment unbiased and the principles uninfluenced, may be supposed better qualified to act as judges. True patriotism demands the renouncing of self-interest, of tastes, habits and opinions; it leads to a higher and purer atmosphere, where truth, which the mere politician often sees with disordered vision, appears in its proper lineaments and proportions.

It has been the object of the Editor to consolidate in the "National Book," a body of thought and sentiment which permeating the floating mass of crude or erroneous political principles pervading society, might induce the wavering or the indifferent to renew their fidelity to their Country, and soften that asperity of feeling which would condemn every attempt to win back our erring brethren of the South to their allegiance—at the same time yielding nothing of the stern requisitions of law and government, such as the Fathers of the Country enjoined us to maintain.

Every article from a living writer which appears in this volume has been presented by its Author, and, in almost every instance, prepared expressly for this Book. The Editor would return grateful thanks to the many distinguished writers and kind friends, who have aided and encouraged her in the arduous enterprise, which, by their help and God's blessing, is, after much anxiety brought to a successful termination in the finishing of this volume, now ready to go forth on its mission of *love, duty* and *patriotism*.

EUTAW-PLACE,
BALTIMORE, MD., March 28th, 1861.

CONTENTS.

	PAGE.
INTRODUCTION,	xiii

RESTORATION OF THE UNION.
    Hon. Edward Everett, Massachusetts, 13

SONG OF THE SOUTHERN LOYALISTS.
    J. H. Alexander, LL.D., Maryland, 44

THE REBELLION.
    Rt. Rev. T. M. Clark, Bishop of Rhode Island, 45

STARS OF MY COUNTRY'S SKY.
    Mrs. L. H. Sigourney, Connecticut, 52

OUR MARCH TO GETTYSBURG.
    Col. James Wallace, late of 1st Reg. E. S. Vols., Maryland, 54

THE FLAG.
    Rev. Thomas Hill, D.D., Pres. Harv. Un., Massachusetts, 70

CONSEQUENCES OF THE DISCOVERY OF AMERICA.
    Rev. John Lord, Connecticut, 72

THE AMERICAN ENSIGN.
    Rev. A. Cleveland Coxe, D.D., New York, 87

THE NAVAL ACADEMY IN SECESSION TIMES.
    Allan D. Brown, U. S. N., Vermont, 90

NATIONAL HYMN............*Mrs. Emma Willard, New York,* 99

TO WHAT PURPOSE IS THIS WASTE?
    Rev. Prof. A. P. Peabody, D. D., Harv. Un., Massachusetts, 101

CONTENTS.

THE THREE ERAS OF THE UNITED STATES.
J. H. Alexander, LL.D., Maryland, 109

AN EPISODE OF THE FLORIDA WAR.
Maj. Brantz Mayer, U. S. A., Maryland, 110

THE MISSISSIPPI.........*Mrs. Sarah Josepha Hale, Pennsylvania,* 133

THE WOMEN OF SEVENTY-SIX ....*Mrs. E. F. Ellet, New York,* 140

SONNET—ANTIETAM.
Rev. A. Cleveland Coxe, D.D., New York, 148

DRUM-HEAD NOTES FROM CAMP AND FIELD.
Col. Charles E. Phelps, 7th Reg. Vols., Maryland, 149

THE BLUE COAT OF THE SOLDIER.
Rt. Rev. George Burgess, Bishop of Maine, 182

ON THE NAME AMERICA........*Mrs. Emma Willard, New York,* 186

A TALE OF EAST TENNESSEE.
Mrs. Anna H. Dorsey, Washington, D. C., 192

WHAT OUR COUNTRY WANTS.
Ex-Gov. E. Washburn, LL.D. Law Prof. Harv. Un. Mass. 206

A VOICE................*Mrs. Sophia May Eckley, Massachusetts,* 212

BALTIMORE LONG AGO.......*Hon. John P. Kennedy, Maryland,* 214

FLOWER AND LEAF INTERPRETED.
Lieut. E. Thornton Fisher, 139th Reg. Vols., New York, 243

TRUE BOND OF UNION.
Charles Eliot Norton, Ed. N. Am. Rev., Massachusetts, 246

"THY WILL BE DONE."..............*Mrs. Celia M. Burr, Ohio,* 251

WOMEN OF THE TIMES....*Mrs. C. B. W. Flanders, New York,* 253

THE OPPORTUNITY; OR THE APOTHEOSIS OF PAN.
Rev. Thomas Hill, D.D. Pres. Harv. Un. Massachusetts, 261

THE FOUR RELICS.....*Thomas E. Van Bebber, Esq. Maryland,* 263

CONTENTS.

PAGE.

A BATTLE EVE..................*Mrs. E. J. Ellicott, Maryland,* 292

REMINISCENCES OF THE HANCOCKS.
    Miss Martha A. Quincy, Massachusetts, 295

THE SPIRIT OF MARYLAND IN 1794.
 An unpublished poem of the late Chancellor Kilty, Maryland, 316

FIELD LILIES..............*Mrs. C. A. Hopkinson, Massachusetts,* 319

NEEDED REFORM......................*Mrs. E. F. Ellet, New York,* 326

AIME DE MON CŒUR............*Miss C. G. de Valin, Maryland,* 329

THE MORAL STRENGTH OF OUR COUNTRY'S CAUSE.
    Rev. F. D. Huntington, D D., Massachusetts, 332

THE PRESIDENT'S THANKSGIVING HYMN.
    Rev. W. H. Muhlenberg, D.D., New York, 344

UNIVERSAL PEACE................*Mrs. Emma Willard, New York,* 347

SYMPATHY.....................*Mrs. L. H. Sigourney, Connecticut,* 357

HISTORICAL SKETCH—WITH THOUGHTS ON THE PRESENT AND
 FUTURE ....*Mrs. Lincoln Phelps, Maryland,* 359

APPENDIX.

ON THE CHRISTIAN COMMISSION.
    Rev. J. N. McJilton, D.D., Maryland, 387

ON THE SANITARY COMMISSION,
 *John Ordronaux, M.D., Prof. Medical Jurisprudence,
    Columbia College, New York,* 406

INTRODUCTION.

THOUGH DEAD, THEY YET SPEAK.

There was a time in the History of our Country when the question of Union or Disunion was fully discussed by the master minds of that period. It would seem as if the Almighty Ruler of Nations permitted discontent to rise up against the Government, in order to elicit the incontrovertible arguments which must ever stand out, against all attempts to sever the Union of the States.

As time goes on, we are in danger of forgetting first principles. Let us then briefly retrace the events which attended the formation of our National Government, as introductory to some quotations from the great Advocates of the Constitution, Washington, Hamilton, Jay and Madison.

In the second year after the Independence of America, delegates from the thirteen original States assembled at Philadelphia, agreed upon the original Articles of Confederation, known as the "Old Constitution." After ten years had elapsed, there was a general call for a stronger National Government; and on the 17th of September,

1787, after much deliberation, the present Constitution was adopted. It was agreed that the ratification of the Convention by *nine* States, should be sufficient for the establishment of the Constitution between the States so ratifying the same—all other States were to be treated as foreign powers by the United States.

Here was an opportunity without war or bloodshed, for secession, which was then freely offered. "Either consent to this stronger government, which we find necessary to uphold our nation, or withdraw from us." After some argument upon *"State-Rights,"* every member of the old family entered the new, under the provisions of that Constitution, which in all its essential features, is the same as the loyal people of the country now contend for.

"The Father of his Country," VIRGINIA'S WASHINGTON, in his address as President of the Convention, to the Governors of the different States, asking each to call a State Convention to deliberate on the adoption of the Constitution, in his plain and energetic language thus argues:

"The friends of the Country have long seen and desired that the power of making war, peace, and treaties: that of levying money and regulating commerce; and the correspondent executive and judicial authorities, should be fully and effectually vested in the general government of the Union. * * * * It is obviously impracticable in the Federal government of these States, to secure all rights of independent sovereignty to each, and yet provide for the interest and safety of all. Individuals entering into society must give up a share of liberty to preserve the rest. The magnitude of the sacrifice must depend as well on situation and circumstance, as on the object to be obtained. It is at all times difficult to draw with precision the line between those rights which must be surrendered, and those which may be reserved; and on the present occasion, this difficulty was increased by a difference among the several States as to their situation, extent, habits, and particular interests.

"In all our deliberations on this subject, we kept steadily in our view that which appears to us the greatest interest of every true American, the CONSOLIDATION OF OUR UNION, *in which is involved our prosperity, felicity, safety, perhaps our national existence.* This important consideration, seriously and deeply impressed on our minds, led each State in the Convention to be less rigid on points of inferior magnitude, than might have been otherwise expected; and thus the Constitution, which we now present, is the result of a spirit of amity, and of that mutual deference and concession which the peculiarity of our political situation rendered indispensable. That it will meet the full and entire approbation of every State, is not perhaps to be expected: but each will doubtless consider, that had her interests been alone consulted, the consequences might have been particularly disagreeable or injurious to others: that it is liable to as few exceptions as could reasonably have been expected, we hope and believe: that it may promote the lasting welfare of that country so dear to us all, and secure her freedom and happiness, is our most ardent wish."

If the dead have cognizance of what is passing in this lower world, how must the "Father of his Country" regard the action of his own State, in this day of national calamity. Land of Washington, how hast thou degenerated! If Virginia had remained true to his teachings, what horrors would she have spared her own people, and the nation at large! North Carolina would have remained loyal—for she has had no especial cause to love her pretentious neighbor on the South, who never affected to conceal her contempt for the more honest but plain old North-State. Without Virginia, the Southern Confederacy would have died away, as did the rebellion in South Carolina, in the days of Jackson. But, thank God, the flood waters of rebellion met with a check in Maryland. Like a rock on the ocean, she has breasted the shock, gaining strength as she resisted!

Voices from the dead! Washington has spoken of the value and absolute necessity of the Union. Let us hear what other great statesmen of that period have to say that may strengthen our patriotism at this evil day, when sectional interests (the interests of slavery) have caused States to set aside our solemn national compact, and to destroy that Union on which Washington solemnly declared, "depended the safety and welfare of every individual in the whole country."

ALEXANDER HAMILTON! a statesman of clear intellect, endowed with almost superhuman prescience in respect to political events. He speaks—let us listen:

"On the existence of the UNION, depends the safety and welfare of the parts of which it is composed; the fate of an empire, in many respects, the most interesting in the world. Among the most formidable obstacle which the new Constitution will have to encounter, we may reckon *the perverted ambition of men, who will either hope to aggrandize themselves by the confusions of their country, or will flatter themselves with fairer prospects of elevation from the subdivision of the empire into several partial confederacies, than from its Union under one Government.* * * * * * The vigor of Government is essential to the security of liberty."

JOHN JAY, the intimate friend of Washington, was associated with Hamilton and Madison in the attempt to influence the people of the country to adopt the new Constitution. In a publication called "The Federalist," these three great statesmen, jointly put forth the results of their deliberations. The North and the South through them met, and amicably united in the noble work of influencing the country at large to act for their own common interest. To Jay was assigned the office of setting forth the dangers which would accrue to a disunited country from "foreign force and influence." He says:

"It has until lately been a received and uncontradicted opinion, that the prosperity of the people of America depended on their continuing firmly united, and the wishes, prayers, and efforts of our best and wisest citizens have been constantly directed to that object."

Mr. Jay then comments on the new and extraordinary opinions of some who advocate a division of the States, and calls on the people to examine into these dangerous political tenets.

"It has often given me pleasure," he remarks, "to observe, that independent America was not composed of detached and distant territories, but that one connected, fertile, wide-spreading country, was the portion of our Western sons of liberty. Providence has, in a particular manner, blessed it with a variety of soils and productions, and watered it with innumerable streams, for the delight and accommodation of its inhabitants. A succession of navigable waters forms a kind of chain round its borders, as if to bind it together; while the most noble rivers in the world, running at convenient distances, present them with highways for the easy communication of friendly aids, and the mutual transportation and exchange of their various commodities.

"With equal pleasure I have as often taken notice, that Providence has been pleased to give this one connected country to one united people; a people descended from the same ancestors, speaking the same language, professing the same religion, attached to the same principles of government, very similar in their manners and customs, and, who, by their joint counsels, arms and efforts, fighting side by side throughout a long and bloody war, have nobly established their general liberty and independence.

"This country and this people seem to have been made for each other, and it appears as if it was the design of Providence that an inheritance so proper and convenient for a band of brethren, united to each other by the strongest ties, should never be split into a number of unsocial, jealous, and alien sovereignties.

"They who promote the idea of substituting a number of distinct confederacies in the room of the plan of the Convention, seem clearly to foresee that the rejection of it would put the continuance of the Union in the utmost jeopardy: that certainly would be the case: and I sincerely wish that it may be as clearly foreseen by every good citizen, that whenever the dissolution of the Union arrives, America will have reason to exclaim, in the words of the Poet, 'FAREWELL! A LONG FAREWELL, TO ALL MY GREATNESS.'" * * * * * *

Another voice from the Shades of the Past! JAMES MADISON was a son of Virginia, and one of whom the State, in her days of honest integrity, was justly proud. After triumphantly meeting the various objections to the Union from the great extent of country, the Virginian Statesman says:

"I submit to you, my fellow citizens, these considerations, in full confidence that the good sense which has so often marked your decisions, will allow them their due weight and effect, and that you will never suffer difficulties however formidable in appearance, or however fashionable the error on which they may be founded, to drive you into the *gloomy* and *perilous scenes into which the advocates* for disunion would conduct you. Hearken not to the unnatural voice, which tells you that the people of America, knit together as they are by so many chords of affection, can no longer live together as members of the same family; can no longer continue the mutual guardians of their mutual happiness; can no longer be fellow citizens of one, great, respectable and flourishing empire. * * * * No, my countrymen, shut your ears against this unhallowed language. Shut your hearts against the poison which it conveys. *The kindred blood which flows in the veins of Americam citizens, the mingled blood which they have shed in defence of their sacred rights, consecrate their Union, and excite horror at the idea of their becoming aliens, rivals, enemies."*

Want of space has compelled us to abridge, (injuriously for the effect,) the testimony of these our venerated Statesmen and patriots; but enough is given to prove their horror and detestation of *Secession, disunion, and defiance of that Constitution* which the united wisdom of our Fathers transmitted to us to Love, Honor and Maintain.

THE

RESTORATION OF THE UNION.

Every good citizen and good patriot looks forward to the earliest possible termination of the war, by an honorable and durable peace, as a consummation devoutly to be wished for. It is, however, a conviction not less universal, on the part of the loyal people of the country, that this object can only be attained by the complete prostration of the military power of the rebellion, and the reestablishment of the authority of the General Government over the seceded States. Originally there were persons of various shades of political opinion in the free States, who, recoiling from the evils of civil war, were willing that the cotton-growing States should try the experiment of separation, of course on admissible conditions as to boundaries, the possession of the national fortresses, and the command of the great inlet into the interior of the continent. But no person, whose authority is of any considerable weight in the country, has expressed the opinion, that any concession can *now* be honorably or safely made to the rebel leaders of those States, who avowedly plunged the country into this desolating war, not from any military necessity, but for the sake of drawing the Border States into the conspiracy. Looking forward to a future of indefinite extent, and contemplating the relation in which the two sections of the country would stand to each other, if the dominant oligarchy of the South should be permitted to carry their point and come out of the struggle triumphantly, it may be said to be the unanimous sentiment of loyal men, that the rebellion must be put down. A peace on any other basis would be but a precarious truce, and hold out a standing encouragement to the leaders of the revolt and their successors, to decide all future controversies by the sword.

We must never forget, in this connection, the purely unprovoked and aggressive manner in which the war was commenced. The United States occupied a fort in Charleston harbor with a single company of soldiers; far too few even to man the imperfect armament of the place. There were no guns in Sumter by which the city could be reached; the President of the United States had distinctly stated, that he did not propose to re-inforce the garrison; and, notwithstanding the outrage of firing upon the provision ships, sent with supplies of food,—acts themselves of overt treason and war,—no measure of retaliation or punishment was threatened or contemplated. Nay more, it was admitted by General, then Major, Anderson, in conference with the Confederate General that, unless supplied with provisions, (which the rebels had shown themselves fully able to prevent,) he could not hold out more than forty-eight hours. It was under these circumstances, that General Beauregard commenced a cannonade from eleven batteries on a fortress built by the United States, on an island which had been ceded by South Carolina to the General Government, and which was lawfully occupied by an officer in their service, in obedience to his orders. This, of course, was an act of aggressive war, as flagrant and unprovoked, as it was, in the absence of all urgency and the monstrous disproportion of forces, mean and cruel. Had any of Major Anderson's men been killed, it would not have been a casualty of honorable war, but it would have been, both by the law of the land and the law of nations, a murder at the door of General Beauregard and his confederates in crime. If the United States, in addition to all the other outrages they had endured during that dismal winter of 1861, had tamely submitted to this last intolerable insult, they would have shown themselves utterly destitute of self-respect; and would not only have stood disgraced in the eyes of the nations, inviting encroachments from every foreign power, but they would have taught the rebellious States, in what way all future controversies were to be settled.

If these remarks required any illustration, it might be found in the conduct of Great Britain in the case of the "Trent." That steam-packet, a private neutral vessel, was, in the exercise of the undoubted belligerent right of search, detained on the high seas by an American frigate, and two persons taken from her. If, in addition to this, half her ship's company had been transferred for safety to the San Jacinto, if a prize crew had been placed on board the "Trent," and she had then been sent to a port of the United States for adjudication, the whole proceeding would have been within the undisputed limits of belligerent right under the law of Nations. The disposition to be made of the vessel would have been a question for a Court of Admiralty, and the disposal of the persons captured in her a fair subject for discussion between the two governments. On the ground that this formality was neglected, (which was done in part from regard to the convenience of the passengers on board the "Trent,") the detention of the vessel and the arrest of the rebel emissaries were regarded by the British Government as a cause of war. Formidable military preparations were instantly set on foot for its declaration, unless satisfactory atonement should be made for "the affront." Such were the views entertained, all but, unanimously, by the Government and people of Great Britain, as to what constitutes a just cause of war.

But contrast this provocation, under any view of the affair of the "Trent," with that given by the rebel leaders in the attack on Fort Sumter. The actual violence done to that vessel consisted in a detention of three hours, without a harsh word on the part of the boarding officer,* a gentleman as courteous and mild as he is firm and fearless, a model of a Christian officer, holding a commission under a Government, recognized by every other civilized nation, and in the exercise of an indisputable belligerent right. Sumter was cannonaded for thirty-six hours with red hot cannon balls, by men, who held commissions from no acknowledged authority, and whose pretended Government had not yet even been recognized as belligerents by any power on earth. The American officer who detained the "Trent," acted in good faith, without instruction from his superiors, but in what he believed to be the discharge of his duty, and the exercise of his right under the law of nations, as expounded and enforced by the British Government and British Tribunals. The officers who bombarded Sumter, knew that the validity of the ordinance of secession, under which they were proceeding, was utterly denied by the Executive, the Legislative, and Judicial authorities of the United States, and that they were com-

---

* Lieutenant, now Captain, Fairfax.

2*

mitting acts that would be regarded by the Government, which they had themselves sworn to support, not only as acts of war, but as acts of treason. Finally, instead of being an unpremeditated and a solitary affair like that of the "Trent," it was but one of a series of outrages on the forts, custom-houses, arsenals, mints, and other establishments and property of the United States, any one of which, if unatoned for, would have been regarded by every Government in Europe, as a justification of war. In this state of things, no English statesman or citizen, who regarded the affair of the "Trent" as a justifying cause of hostilities, could entertain any different opinion of the attack on Sumter.

To make this a little clearer, let us put a case, as nearly as may be parallel. Granting, for the sake of argument, the right of South Carolina to secede, (which however, is of course utterly denied;) although in virtue of that right, she might take herself out of the Union, she could not take with her the forts, nor the islands upon which they were built; for the islands had been formally ceded to the United States, and at their expense and by their authority, the forts had been constructed. It is, therefore, saying little, to say, that they belonged to the United States, as much as Gibraltar belongs to England. Now suppose that Spain, feeling as she does keenly that this encampment of a foreign power upon her soil is a standing reminder of her weakness and decline,—in fact a great territorial and political eyesore,—should first propose to buy Gibraltar of the British Government, and send Commissioners to London to negotiate the purchase, as South Carolina sent agents to Washington in 1860-'61, to negotiate the purchase of Moultrie and Sumter. England, would of course, reject the offer; she would as soon sell to Spain, the harbor of Plymouth, or the dock-yard at Woolwich. Spain disdains to prolong the negotiation; recalls her Commissioners in disgust; lays siege to Gibraltar by land and sea; fires upon an unarmed supply-ship sent by England, to provision the fortress; and at length, in a time of profound peace, without a shadow of provocation, and for no other reason than that she wants Gibraltar for her own purposes, bombards it, and, more successful than in 1782, reduces and captures it. How many hours would elapse, after the news reached London, before every available ship in the British navy would be ordered to the coast of Spain, and every available soldier in the British army would be embarked, to wash out this intolerable insult in blood? But this is the precise counterpart of the bombardment of Sumter, except that the outrage, instead of being confined to one Gibraltar, was followed up by the surprise and seizure of half a dozen other Gibraltars, belonging to the American Government, and scattered along our coasts and at the mouths of our rivers.

So far then, is the war from being a war of aggression, on the part of the United States, as is pretended by the South and its sympathizers, it is a war forced upon us; which could not, without an entire sacrifice of manhood and national honor, have been avoided; and any other end of it than the utter prostration of the military power of the rebel leaders, instead of conducing to perfect harmony and peace, would result either in the establishment of two rival and hostile powers engaged in eternal border war with each other, or in the breaking up of both sections into groups of petty States, forever flying at each other's throats. We may, without being uncharitable, believe that the foreign writers and speakers who dwell, at one moment, on the overgrown magnitude and strength of this country as a menace and a danger to other powers; and at the next, denounce the injustice of the present war on the part of the United States, desire that it should end in one or the other of these two forms of national ruin. It is enough to say here, that the cause of humanity and peace is the last, which would be benefitted by either result.

But it is objected, that eventual harmony and reconciliation cannot be produced by the continuance of the war, even if it is successfully prosecuted by the United

States; that all the victories gained by the Union arms, and all the disasters suffered by the Confederates, instead of tending toward the restoration of a good understanding, embitter and exasperate those who thus suffer by the operations of the war, and so tend to render a reconciliation hopeless. This however, though a plausible, is a superficial view of the subject, without foundation in reason, history, or experience. There are various grounds on which the precisely opposite view can be maintained conclusively.

One great cause of the readiness of the Southern leaders to rush into the present war, was their entire misapprehension of the character both of the South and of the North. The social system of the slave-holding States, the temper and habits engendered by the exercise from the cradle of irresponsible power, often over large numbers of fellow-men; the idleness and dissipation of plantation life; the practice of wearing concealed arms, and the exaggerated code of false honor, all united to produce a corrupting influence on the Southern character. It was largely tinctured with the conceit of a fancied superiority over the laborious, ingenious, and frugal North. Forgetting the most notorious facts in their early history and ours, they imagined themselves to be cavaliers, and derided us as round-heads; not bearing in mind, even if that comparison were better founded in fact, that it was not, in the light of history, a very safe ground, on which to lay claim to a greater aptitude for statesmanship or arms. By the side of great courtesy in private life, (not without an occasional tinge of condescension on the part of individuals,) there was, almost from the foundation of the Government, an arrogant and masterful tone in the political intercourse of the South with the North, which, long indulged, led too many of the former to think themselves at last, wiser, better, and braver than their Northern brethren. There were, of course, wise and good men at the South, who did not share this delusion; but they themselves, for more than thirty years, have been, on account of their liberality and moderation, too often discredited and set aside. The genuine Southern aristocracy, that of morals, manners, and culture has, for a full generation, been to a considerable degree, ostracized and kept in private life by the gentry of the race-course, the jurists of the County Court, and the statesmen of the cross roads.

This state of things had at length become an intolerable evil. Under the arrogance and self-conceit of the popular leaders of the South, the Government was degenerating. That mutual respect of the different sections of the country, which is so essential to the harmony of a family of States, was rapidly disappearing, and dictation and menace on the one side, and acquiescence on the other side were passing into an angry and irritable antagonism.

It is doubtful whether any milder discipline than war would have sufficed to take the conceit out of our Southern brethren; and even that will fail of the beneficial effect, it would otherwise produce, if remitted before the military power of the rebels is utterly broken. They must be effectually taught once and forever, that we are in all respects their equals, and that a "few disappointed aspirants to office" are not to be allowed now, or at any time hereafter, to destroy the life of a great nation, because they cannot continue to monopolize the Government.

The North, in her turn, required a lesson. She had allowed the busy round of her pleasant and gainful pursuits; the varied agriculture of her small farms, owned by those who tilled them; her matchless manufactures and her commercial enterprise, moving with the mighty force of voluntary and amply compensated labor; the thousand forms of her material prosperity and refinement; her successful cultivation of science and the arts; her vast educational system; the distribution and employment of her life-giving capital throughout the length and breadth of the land;—she had allowed these objects of absorbing interest, and the occupations connected with them, to engross her time and thoughts. The vulgar wranglings of the Capitol, and the tawdry splendors and tasteless dissipation of Washington life, were unattractive to her. There she allowed the South, who found it an agreeable change from the dreary solitude of her plantations, to bear a scarcely disputed sway, to play off the factions of the free States against each other, and thus to monopolize the control of the Government. With a little greater moderation in wielding this somewhat invidious power, it might have been submitted to for an indefinite period. But the intelligence of the free States was fatigued by the audacious theoretic absurdity of the doctrines of nullification and secession, (intended only when proposed, to frighten the North into continued compromise,) and its patience was exhausted by the abrogation of the Missouri line and the alternate frauds and outrages in Kansas. Accordingly a President was at length chosen without the aid of Southern votes. This was the unpardonable sin, the *crimen læsæ majestatis australis*, which is now undergoing expiation by the best blood of both sections of the country. They will come out of the struggle better acquainted with each other. The South, probably with a radical change in her social system, will have learned to respect the North; and the North to vindicate her proportionate share in the government of the country.

The idea that a civil war, in consequence of the supposed embittering effects of its ravages, must necessarily terminate in the dismemberment of a country, is preposterous, and without any foundation in the teachings of history. If it were so, there never could be for any great length of time, an extensive Empire or a powerful Government, inasmuch as a civil war, in some stage of its progress, will be found in the annals of every nation. Those who hold the opinion in question, are probably misled by the analogy of the American Revolution, which was in some sense a civil war, and which did end in separation. But the separation was induced by great physical and political causes which prevented the mother country from prolonging the contest; such as the vast distance and the intervening ocean, which threw difficulties almost insuperable in the way of military expeditions, and the superadded burden of war with France, Spain and Holland, under which England was compelled to succumb. In addition to this, the United States had manifestly outgrown the limits of Colonial Government as then understood and practised.

When it is passionately declared that the South in consequence of the injuries inflicted upon her, by the operations of the war, will never consent to a re-union with the North, it is forgotten, that in many respects the North has suffered at the hands of the South, as much as the South has suffered at the hands of the North. In any just view of the subject, the North has infinitely the most to forgive. It is true her pride has not been so deeply wounded by the capture of her ports, the blockade of her coasts, and the occupation of her territory; but the loss which outweighs all others, by the side of which no other form of suffering deserves a name,—the loss of her children whom she has sent to the wars,—is, to the full, as great as that of the South. The South indeed claims that it is far greater. To punish the free States for choosing a President without their votes, the South has levied a war, which has cost the North largely over a hundred thousand precious lives. Again there has been a large destruction of private property, at the seat of hostilities in the rebel States. This is a deplorable, but I fear, an unavoidable incident of war. Neither Governments nor Commanders are able wholly to prevent it. But on the other hand, the Union men in the Border States have suffered the same losses wherever the Confederate armies have penetrated, while in the rebel States to be loyal to the Government of the Union has been to insure imprisonment and confiscation, and in many districts the most cruel personal outrage. Then, too, there are the ravages of the rebel corsairs. It is probable that the destruction of private property by these sea-rovers, is quite equal to that which has been caused in the Confederate States, by the direct operations of the war. In addition to this, it is calculated that the South was indebted to the North at the outbreak of the rebellion, from four to five hundred millions of dollars. In fact, the repudiation of this debt was one of the inducements for plunging into the contest. In consequence of the rebellion, the North has suffered this heavy pecuniary loss, as it will long have to suffer the burden of debt, which the war has thrown upon the country.

In these various ways, it is plain, as I have observed that the North has as much to forgive to the South, as the South has to forgive to the North. The evils they have inflicted upon us, as we think without a cause, are as great as those which we have inflicted upon them, as they think without a cause, and this relation of the two parties to each other, is, by the very constitution of our natures, a practical basis of reconciliation. The leaders of the rebellion indeed, are in no condition to take a sober view of the state of affairs. Originally spurred by ambition to the commission of the most aggravated crimes, of which men in civil society can be guilty; with the fearful responsibility upon their consciences of all the sufferings and sorrows of the war, an avenging demon drives them forward. They cannot retrace their steps. The restoration of peace to their bleeding country would, probably, be at best to them, ignominious and life-long exile from its shores. But no such frenzy possesses the body of the people. It is not in human nature, that they should not feel the folly and the wickedness of the contest; and the unutterable madness of persevering in it. There is not the least reason to doubt, that the bold utterances of the "Raleigh Standard" express the real sentiments of the great majority of the Southern people. They will feel more and more that they are by no means the passive victims of Northern violence, as they are told by their profligate leaders. They know that they have been and are inflicting on us evils analogous to those which they suffer; and that the time has come, when as Christians it is their duty to throw off the yoke of the bold bad men who have brought these measureless calamities upon all parts of the country. The entire adult generation among them knows full well, that under the Government of the United States, in which the South at all times was clothed with power far beyond her proportionate share, she enjoyed a degree of prosperity never before vouchsafed to the children of men; while they know equally well, that the rebel government has been from its inauguration a burden, a scourge, and a curse. How can this comparison fail to produce its natural effect, not upon the minds of infuriated leaders, but upon the masses of a people endowed with average intelligence? Much as we have suffered by the war, there is no bitterness or exasperation on the part of the North; why should we suppose the angry passions are forever to rage at the South?

There are many interesting facts connected with the progress of the war, which show that there is no bitterness on the part of the people, North or South, notwithstanding the pains taken by the rebel leaders, in their proclamations and addresses, and the rebel press in its editorial columns, to inflame the minds of the South. There are Union citizens of the highest social position on the Mississippi river, who have been reduced from affluence to straitened circumstances, and in some instances to absolute poverty, by the desertion of their slaves, or their enlistment in the Union armies. Instead of being shaken in their loyalty, they know that these results are unavoidably incident to war carried on in regions burdened with slavery. They do not even allow the abuses which occasionally take place on the part of the authorities, civil and military, in the present necessarily confused and abnormal state of things, to swerve them from their attachment to the Union. We could give the names of noble and patriotic citizens, to whom this remark applies. They do not, because the war has prostrated their own fortunes, throw the blame of its existence on the Government of the United States. They know too well the insidious arts, by which the Southern mind was deluded and prepared for secession, and the ambitious motives, on the part of the leaders, for which the war has been levied, and they prefer exile and poverty in the free States to the iron sway of the selfish chiefs of the Confederacy.

Take another most significant fact in the State of North Carolina. The entire seaboard of that State, (with the exception of one rigorously blockaded port), has been occupied by the Union forces. Her ancient capitol of Newbern, the home of the Gastons and Stanleys, has been for more than two years in our possession. All its prominent inhabitants were necessarily compelled by the rebel armies to fall back with them into the interior, and immense losses have consequently accrued upon the deserted estates alike of the loyal and disloyal. But in no one of the States in secession, has the old Union sentiment been more boldly uttered than in North Carolina. The press at Raleigh might be advantageously taken as a model, by many a journal in the loyal States. Men whose plantations near the coast have been desolated, and whose old family mansions are occupied as barracks by the Union armies, are, at this moment, denouncing the leaders of secession, and demanding the restoration of peace. The mountains on the western border of North Carolina are filled with Union men who have fled from the conscription, where from their fastnesses, they defy the rebel government. A similar state of things still further developed, exists in Arkansas, notwithstanding its sufferings by the war.

It was claimed by the rebels, as boldly as falsely, that Maryland is in heart with the Confederacy. Two invasions by armies of one hundred thousand men have failed to receive the slightest aid from the masses of the people. Notwithstanding the attempts, throughout the South, to enlist the people, as in a common cause, in what is truly called "the slaveholders' war;" Maryland is marching with rapid strides toward emancipation. Missouri, Tennessee, and Louisiana are moving steadily toward the same goal; more earnestly since the emancipation proclamation than before. So little foundation is there for the idea, industriously propagated, that this measure would render the restoration of peace impossible.

In the conduct of the war itself, there has been a remarkable absence of bitterness. With armies of such magnitude on both sides, acts of violence are unavoidable. It is impossible to restrain the outrages of stragglers, and deserters, and the lawless banditti, who always hang upon the skirts of a camp or a moving column. Some atrocious cruelties have been committed by *guerillas*, for which the rebel government is justly responsible, in consequence of the countenance it insists upon extending to this unprincipled description of force. But even Quantrell is not wholly inaccessible to the pleadings of humanity. He spared one cottage in Lawrence because it was "too pretty to be burned." In Calabria, French prisoners were roasted alive. In Spain, *guerillas* placed their captives between boards and sawed them asunder. In the Spanish

American States, on every turn of their wretched politics, the leaders who fall into the hands of the enemy are taken out and shot through the back. In India, rebellious Sepoys are blown from the cannon's mouth. No such enormities have marked the progress of our war.

Southern prisoners of war are treated with the utmost humanity in the free States. I visited Camp Douglas near Chicago, at a time when eight thousand Confederate prisoners were confined there. They had an area of fifteen or twenty acres, where they were allowed to take such recreation as they thought best, and their food in quantity and quality was equal to that of the Union regiments which guarded them. The best of Western hams were emptied by the wagon load into their barracks. They were unquestionably faring better than before their capture. The same is the case at Johnson's Island on Lake Erie. I have lately conversed with an officer of rank just returned from that Island, and he assures me that ample provision is made for their health and comfort. Mr. Jefferson Davis, in his last annual message, endeavors to make a grievance of the confinement of Southern prisoners on an Island so far to the North. He may not be aware, that St. Pauls, in Minnesota, which was a favorite resort for invalids from the South, summer and winter, is three and one-half degrees further North than Johnson's Island. It might possibly also occur to him that the climate of Columbia, S. C. may be as trying in summer to the Northern prisoners confined there as Johnson's Island is to the Southern prisoners in winter. But the most curious fact in this connection is, that, owing to the greater provision against cold in the North, twice as many persons are reported in the census returns as freezing to death in the Southern, as in the Northern States. Of the prisoners confined at Johnson's Island, it is beyond question that fewer die there than would have died, summer or winter, had they remained at home in the Gulf States.

The accounts differ as to the treatment of Northern prisoners at the South, especially at Richmond. Many that have been exchanged return to the North wasted to shadows, and dropping into the grave. Mr. Foote in the Rebel Congress denounced the manner in which they were treated as cruel; and one officer at least, employed to superintend the prisoners at Richmond, was discharged for "irregularity," meaning defrauding them of their pittance of food. The charge of ill-treatment is, however, indignantly repelled by the Confederate Government and press, and as a sufficient refutation of the charge, it is passionately maintained, that they are fed as well as the soldiers of the rebel army. But the same nominal ration may differ greatly in the quality of the article, the time and manner of distribution, and the means of preparation as food. Besides, if the allowance is not adequate for the healthful support of the prisoner, it is no excuse that their own soldiers fare no better. That argument would equally justify an enemy in slaughtering prisoners which he could no longer feed. The belligerent who cannot afford to give his prisoners a fair allowance of wholesome food, is bound by the law of nations, not less than by the dictates of common humanity, to release them on parole.

There is one class of prisoners at the South, with respect to whom there are grave apprehensions of the most cruel and atrocious wrong. There is much reason to fear, that quarter has, in some instances at least, been refused to colored soldiers, and that, when captured, they have been mercilessly scourged, shot or hung. If this charge against the rebel government and rebel leaders is well founded, it is but another illustration how completely the moral sentiments may be stifled in the hearts of men, and the feelings of humanity crushed, by "damned custom." If it were possible that we could, for any reason, derive satisfaction from the perpetration of inhuman acts by the enemy, we might remember, that nothing will so effectually put the European sympathizers with rebellion to shame, and lead them to abandon the cause of the South, as this denial of the rights of war to colored prisoners.

The conduct of the opposing forces in the field is, I am

happy to say, by no means indicative of the bitterness and ferocity which usually characterize civil wars. Soldiers on picket duty, it is said, have generally given up the murderous practice of firing upon each other. When not expressly forbidden, they exchange good natured banter, newspapers, and small stores. The wounded in battle, as they lie side by side, forget that they are enemies, and remember only that they are brothers in suffering. Many a poor youth from the South has found in our hospitals the tender care of mother and sister, replaced, if such a thing were possible, by the ministering angels of charity that know no distinction of friend or foe. The records of the Sanitary and Christian Commissions afford the most touching illustrations of this remark, as far as concerns the wounded prisoners from the South, who have fallen into our hands. That similar kindness has been shown to our wounded at the South has been sometimes reported. I am not aware of any sufficient evidence that this is generally the case, though willing to believe and hope that it is so.

That the experience of mankind everywhere proves the transient nature of the feuds engendered by civil war, will be admitted by every diligent student of history. On this subject, I venture to add a few paragraphs from the address delivered by me at the consecration of the Soldiers' Cemetery at Gettysburg. In that discourse, I tried to show that the gracious Providence which overrules all things for the best, from seeming evil still educing good, has so constituted our natures, that the violent excitement of the passions in one direction is generally followed by a reaction in an opposite direction, and the sooner for the violence. If it were not so—if anger produced abiding anger, if hatred caused undying hatred, if injuries inflicted and retaliated of necessity led to new retaliations, with forever accumulating compound interest of revenge,—then the world, thousands of years ago, would have been turned into an earthly hell, and the nations of the earth would have been resolved into clans of furies and demons, each forever warring with his neighbor. But it is not so. All history teaches a different lesson. The wars of the Roses in England lasted an entire generation, from the battle of St. Albans, in 1455, to that of Bosworth Field, in 1485. Speaking of the former, Hume says: "This was the first blood spilt in that fatal quarrel, which was not finished in less than a course of thirty years; which was signalized by twelve pitched battles; which opened a scene of extraordinary fierceness and cruelty; is computed to have cost the lives of eighty princes of the blood; and almost entirely annihilated the ancient nobility of England. The strong attachments which, at that time, men of the same kindred bore to each other, and the vindictive spirit which was considered a point of honor, rendered the great families implacable in their resentments, and widened every moment the breach between the parties." Such was the state of things in England under which an entire generation grew up; but when Henry VII., in whom the titles of the two houses were united, went up to London after the battle of Bosworth Field to mount the throne, he was everywhere received with joyous acclamations, "as one ordained and sent from Heaven to put an end to the dissensions" which had so long afflicted the country.

The great rebellion in England of the seventeenth century, after long and angry premonitions, may be said to have begun with the calling of the Long Parliament, in 1640, and to have ended with the return of Charles II., in 1660,—twenty years of discord, conflict, and civil war; of confiscation, plunder, havoc; a proud hereditary peerage trampled in the dust; a national church overturned, its clergy beggared, its most eminent prelate put to death; a military despotism established on the ruins of a monarchy which had subsisted seven hundred years, and the legitimate sovereign brought to the block; the great families which adhered to the king proscribed, impoverished, ruined; prisoners of war—a fate worse than confinement in Libby—sold to slavery in the West Indies;—in a word, everything that can imbitter and madden contending factions. Such was the state of things for twenty years, and yet, by no gentle transition, but suddenly, and "when the restoration of affairs appeared most hopeless," the son of the beheaded sovereign was brought back to his father's blood-stained throne, with such "unexpressible and universal joy," as led the merry monarch to exclaim, "He doubted it had been his own fault he had been absent so long, for he saw nobody who did not protest he had ever wished for his return." "In this wonderful manner," says Clarendon, "and with this incredible expedition, did God put an end to a rebellion that had raged near twenty years, and had been carried on with all the horrid circumstances of murder, devastation, and parricide, that fire and sword, in the hands of the most wicked men in the world [it is a royalist that is speaking] could be instruments of, almost to the desolation of two kingdoms, and the exceeding defacing and deforming of the third. . . . By these remarkable steps did the merciful hand of God, in this short space of time, not only bind up and heal all those wounds, but even made the scar as undiscernible as, in respect of the deepness, was possible, which was a glorious addition to the deliverance."

In Germany, the wars of the Reformation and of Charles V. in the sixteenth century, the thirty years war in the seventeenth century, the seven years war in the eighteenth century, not to speak of other less celebrated contests, entailed upon that country all the miseries of intestine strife for more than three centuries. At the close of the last named war, which was the shortest of all, and waged in the most civilized age, "An Officer," says Archenholz, "rode through seven villages in Hesse, and found in them but one human being." More than three hundred principalities, comprehended in the empire, fermented with the fierce passions of proud and petty States; at the commencement of this period the castles of robber counts frowned upon every hill-top; a dreadful secret tribunal, whose seat no one knew, whose power none could escape, froze the hearts of men with terror throughout the land; religious hatred mingled its bitter poison in the seething caldron of provincial animosity; but of all these deadly enmities between the States of Germany, scarcely the memory remains. There is no country in the world in which the sentiment of national brotherhood is stronger. There are controversies in that country, at the present day, but they grow mainly out of the rivalry of the two leading powers.

In Italy, on the breaking up of the Roman Empire, society might be said to be resolved into its original elements;—into hostile atoms, whose only movement was that of mutual repulsion. Ruthless barbarians had destroyed the old organizations and covered the land with a merciless feudalism. As the new civilization grew up, under the wing of the Church, the noble families and the walled towns fell madly into conflict with each other; the secular feud of Pope and Emperor scourged the land; province against province; city against city; street against street waged remorseless war against each other from father to son, till Dante was able to fill his imaginary hell with the real demons of Italian history. So ferocious had the factions become, that the great poet-exile himself, the glory of his native city and of his native language, was by a decree of the municipality, ordered to be burned alive, if found in the city of Florence. But these deadly feuds and hatreds yielded to political influences, as the hostile cities were grouped into states under stable governments; the lingering traditions of the ancient animosities gradually died away, and now Tuscan and Lombard, Sardinian and Neapolitan, as if to shame the degenerate sons of America, are joining in one cry for an united Italy.

In France, not to go back to the civil wars of the League in the sixteenth century, and of the Fronde in the seventeenth,—not to speak of the dreadful scenes throughout the kingdom which followed the revocation of the edict of Nantes,—we have, in the great revolution which commenced at the close of the last century, seen the bloodhounds of civil strife let loose as rarely before in the history of the world. The reign of terror established at Paris, stretched its bloody Briarean arms to every city and village in the land, and if the most deadly feuds which ever divided a people had the power to cause permanent alienation and hatred, this surely was the occasion. But far otherwise the fact. In seven years from the fall of Robespierre, the strong arm of the youthful conqueror brought order out of this chaos of crime and woe; Jacobins, whose hands were scarcely cleansed from the best blood of France, met the returning emigrants whose estates they had confiscated and whose kindred they had dragged to the guillotine, in the Imperial antechambers; and when, after another turn of the wheel of fortune, Louis XVIII. was restored to his throne. he took the regicide Fouché, who had voted for his brother's death, to his cabinet and confidence.

These illustrations could be greatly multiplied, and all history warrants the grateful conclusion, that, when the authority of the General Government shall be happily re-established over the States in rebellion, an era of good feeling will return, and the different sections of the country, now so sadly estranged from each other, will be bound together more strongly than ever, by the ties of mutual respect and affection.*

---

* It was on the 19th of November, 1863. that Mr. Everett, ever prompt to respond to the call of his country, having come from his distant home to assist in the consecration of the National

Cemetery, delivered the address here alluded to, and which is destined to live in the National archives. It was a day, (we quote from our Diary of that date,) calm and glorious. From the second story of our friend's house, we had a full view of the grand procession as it moved towards Cemetery Hill. After an imposing military array, appeared the Executive and Legislative branches of our National and State Governments with a grand military escort; then came various delegations and associations from the most remote, as well as nearer, portions of our great empire. But no part of this grand display was so touching as the sight of a band of invalid and maimed soldiers, remnants of different brigades of the army, clad in their blue overcoats, and slowly following the immense and brilliant cavalcade, to the plaintive air of "When this cruel war is over"—Ah! and what then, my suffering braves? to you, there remains but a life of decrepitude and suffering. May your country see to it that poverty too shall not be in your future lot! After the entire procession had passed, accompanied by Mr. B., we drove to the Cemetery. As carriages were not allowed to enter the enclosure, we walked in, directing our course towards the table-land in the centre, but the crowd was so dense as to forbid our progress, and we returned to our carriage, where, upon a commanding eminence, we had a panoramic view of the scene around us. A solemn stillness pervaded the immense assemblage, broken only by the sound of the speaker's voice, which was occasionally borne to our ears by a favoring breath of air. What a contrast to the roar and thunder of battle of July 2d, when the possession of Cemetery Hill was so hotly contested by the contending armies! From the sight of the thousands of living men who had come together to do honor to those who had so lately died for their country, the imagination turned to that Thursday (for this too was Thursday) when the dead and dying lay strewed around the hill sides, the valleys and the open fields, like leaves scattered by the autumn blast. These are events too momentous for language to express; the imagination fails before the awfully moral sublime,—and such we felt to be the scene before us, in its relation to the past, present and future of our country. EDITOR.

SONG OF THE SOUTHERN LOYALISTS.

Up with the Old Flag; fling out its folds:
   Stand by to witness it wave once more:
Gather round readily, lift it up steadily;
   Braver it looks than ever before.

Not a Star vanished,—each one is there;
   Not a Stripe faded, no where a stain:
Welcome it merrily, speak of it cheerily;
   God bless the day for the Old Flag again!

Sad was the season when it was struck;
   Darker, still darker, days languished on;
Trampled down forcefully, touch it remorsefully;
   Love it the more, because lost and won.

Up with the Old Flag; long may it float,
   Never a Pleiad lost from its plain;
Lift it up lovingly, shout all approvingly,
   God bless the day for the Old Flag again!

THE REBELLION.

We have experienced a strange revolution in our habits, during the last three years. Before this time, there was not a nation on the face of the earth in which there was so little to remind one of military power. Our standing army consisted of some twelve or fifteen thousand men, scattered here and there on the outposts; in our navy-yards, unfinished ships had been rotting on the ways for more than forty years; our military musters had become such a farce, that the militia were every where disbanded. War was regarded as a thing of the past; we read the histories of old time and wondered at the infatuation which led the men of those days to settle their disputes by arms; the farmer, plodding behind his plough, sometimes found in the sod a blackened musket-ball, and then he thanked God that the days of bloodshed were over forever; the artisan stood by the anvil, and with a song on his lips of "the good time coming," beat the swords into plough-shares; the merchant sent his vessel off upon the seas, thankful that there were no more pirates or privateersmen to obstruct the highway of nations; ministers of the Gospel denounced all war as unchristian; Carlylean philosophers ridiculed the notion of settling points of equity with lead and saltpetre; political economists figured up the awful cost of war, and startled the world by their arithmetic; Peace Congresses held their sessions and scattered abundant rose-water as a sovereign disinfectant; Non-Resistants met in council and protested against the contest of arms with a horrible strife of tongues; West Point Cadets by scores entered the ranks of the Christian ministry—some of them have gone back to the old ranks now; and our poets sang jubilantly of the reign of universal amity and concord.

They tune their harps to a wilder song to-day. For, what a change! The drum rattles in our ears from morning till midnight; ponderous cannon rumble in our streets; all around our cities, acres of tents whiten the sward; the nation has been decimated to furnish soldiers; the only news that we care to read is that which comes from the seat of war; every where our tool-shops are making rifles and our foundries casting cannon; the basement of our Capitol has been turned into a mammoth bakery;—better use, perhaps, than it was put to, when loyal and rebel Senators became fraternal there, over the cup which inebriates as well as cheers. How strange it is to walk over the beautiful Arlington Heights, and see the cultivated grounds cut up into streets, labelled by the New

York boys, Broadway, Bowery, Wall Street, Fifth Avenue; and then, entering the house, to find a U. S. Quarter-Master sitting at General Lee's writing-desk, with the old family portraits looking down reproachfully upon him. Strange associations were quickened at finding a venerable spinnet still standing in a dark corner, cob-webbed, mouldy and silent, which made music after its fashion years ago, touched in the evening twilight by fair fingers that have long since lost their cunning.

But darker shadows crowd upon the picture. A hundred thousand men now lie upon their beds in our hospitals, or crawl out into the sun to see if the fresh breath of heaven will give them any new life; thousands upon thousands are sleeping, where the morning reveille will waken them no more; children ask every evening when their father will come home, who will never feel the warm pressure of his hand again; and "there is not a house, where there is not one dead."

What does it all mean? What has happened, to bring all this misery upon us? What is it, which has called into being the largest army in the world, revolutionized all our habits, deranged our currency, burdened us with taxation, arrayed father against son, brother against brother, broken the ties of ancient friendships, and converted the land into an Aceldama of blood? We are in a state of civil war. Of *civil* war?

Between whom? Men of the same lineage, the same interests, the same religion.

A little more than eighty years ago, the New Englander and the Georgian stood side by side in the battle field, fighting to achieve for themselves one, free and independent nationality. When they fell, the child of the South pillowed his aching head on the bosom of his Northern brother; heart to heart, hand in hand, they grappled with the stern agonies of death, and passed away together to the land of spirits.

To-day. the children of those men stand face to face on the bloody field, and each drives his bayonet in the other's heart.

Three years ago, and one flag floated at the mast-head of every American vessel on the seas; on every fortification in the land, the morning breeze kissed the glorious old stars and stripes, under which our fathers made us free; and whenever or wherever in foreign lands, an American saw that banner given to the winds, he felt that he was safe, and his heart bounded with loyal pride.

To-day, that flag lies trailing in the dust, torn and dishonored; and in many of our States, another banner, which our fathers knew not, with ten of the old stripes gone, and most of the stars blotted from the escutcheon, droops over the national forts, which rebels have stolen, the badge of sedition and infamy.

What is the stake at issue, in this awful civil war? The question to be determined is, shall we henceforth and forever cease to be a nation? Shall our past history, with all its sacrifices and all its heroic deeds, of which we have been so proud, go for nothing? Shall the great experiment of constitutional freedom, with which God has charged us, come to a miserable and disgraceful end?

If we fail in this contest, it will be because we deserve to fail; because we are not in earnest. But we must not fail. The nation must not die so soon. "Our fathers' blood cries to us from the ground." I hear the war-worn veterans of the Revolution, speaking *out* of the depths of eternity, and they say, "Remember us! remember what we endured; remember our sad defeats and our dear-bought victories; remember the long dreary days of discouragement, defection, disorder, secret and open treason, through which we passed, to make you a nation; and now will you suffer all this to be lost? Shall a wretched faction, which has for its one main object, the everlasting perpetuation of human bondage, be allowed to destroy the noblest political fabric ever erected on earth?"

There are those amongst us who plead for peace; for peace, on almost any terms. Sometimes they hang out their *white* flags, when the Stars and the Stripes ought to be waving in the breeze,—and there they droop ingloriously, winding-sheets, pale shrouds, emblems of national death. They say, humanity calls upon us to put an end to this hideous war. And so it does; it calls upon us to end the war, by *conquering* a peace. They say, it is a political war: and so it is, but not a party war. What question is there before the nation to-day, but that of life or death! They say, we never can subjugate the South. We do not wish to subjugate the South, but only to crush this wicked rebellion. We wish to give the *loyal men of the South* freedom to utter their real sentiments; freedom to act in behalf of a cause, which is still dear to their hearts, although there is a padlock of steel on their lips.

These men want peace. God knows we all want it. We long for peace, as the sick man longs for the light of the morning. We are weary of strife; weary of sending our brave boys to the war, and having them returned to us sick, maimed and dying. Our hearts are very weary of this work of death; weary of all the ghastly horrors of the battle-field; our children lying there, with their pale faces turned to the pitiless moon, and no man to bury them; gray hairs brought down in sorrow to the grave; mothers refusing to be comforted; the first-born, whom they once rocked in his little cradle and who used to put his arms around their neck and nestle in their bosom, as he slept so sweetly through the long winter nights,—now, these winter nights, sleeping the sleep which knows no waking, under the cold shroud of snow,—O, it is too awful, will there never be an end of this horrible butchery? Shall we never have peace?

Yes, we can have peace whenever we say the word; on the condition of *national suicide*. We can have peace, on the condition that all the sacrifices we have already made, shall be naught. We can have peace, by consenting to national dismemberment; the end of which none can foresee,—which cuts the arteries of the land, and allows the life-blood to flow, till there is nothing left but a corpse. We can have peace for a year, on the condition of border wars, that will last for generations. For, wherever you draw the line, which divides the two nations, there must be a hundred miles of territory on both sides that will be a perpetual waste. We can have peace, on conditions that will put back the progress of the world for a century. We can have peace, by surrendering every thing that we have fought for, and giving our destiny into the hands of demagogues and tyrants. Is such a peace desirable? Is it not better, that we should suffer a little longer, if then we can *win* a peace, for which our posterity will have no cause to curse us.

STARS OF MY COUNTRY'S SKY.*

Are ye all there? Are ye all there?
  Stars of my country's sky;
Are ye *all* there? *Are ye all there*,
  In your shining homes on high?
"Count us!" "Count us!" was their answer,
  As they dazzled on my view,
In glorious perihelion,
  Amid their fields of blue.

"I cannot count ye rightly,
  There's a cloud with sable rim;
I cannot make your number out,
  For my eyes with tears are dim.
O, bright and blessed Angel,
  On white wing floating by,
Help me to count and not to miss
  One star in my country's sky."

    * Written in the Summer of 1860.

Then the Angel touch'd my eye-lids,
    And touch'd the frowning cloud,
And its sable rim disparted,
    And it fled with murky shroud.
There was no missing Pleiad,
    'Mid all that sister race;
The Southern Cross shone radiant forth,
    And the Pole Star kept its place.

Then I knew it was the Angel,
    Who woke the hymning strain;
That at our dear Redeemer's birth,
    Flow'd out on Bethlehem's plain.
And still its echoing key-tone,
    My listening country held,
For all her constellated stars
    The diapason swell'd.

OUR MARCH TO GETTYSBURG

AND THE

BATTLE OF JULY 3, 1863.

The evening of the 19th day of June, found our Regiment, the 1st Eastern Shore of Maryland Volunteers, scattered along the eastern Peninsula of Maryland and Virginia: Some on Provost duty in the important towns; some on the shores of the beautiful Chesapeake, while others were on the islands, lagoons, and extensive bayous that line the Atlantic coast, where the deep blue ocean rolls—

"Dark, heaving, boundless, endless and sublime."

An orderly dashed up to head-quarters with a despatch from the General Commanding, directing immediate concentration of the Regiment, and its embarkation for the City of Baltimore. The news spread, there was a stir in camp; the soldier understood there was an end to his inactivity, and that he was soon to enter upon the sterner duties of military life. Orderlies were despatched in every direction, the fast sailing canoe was put in requisition, and flew like a gull over the waters, with the hurried despatch summoning these men of Maryland, to meet the enemy on the border.

On the 23d of June, our scattered detachments had coveyed together, and were encamped on the environs of Baltimore. There we found great anxiety, and extensive preparations being made to meet the threatened advance of the enemy. It was known that General Lee was moving rapidly northward with his entire force, and it was believed that Baltimore was his goal. General Ewell had crossed the Potomac on the 22d, and was marching up the valley towards Hagerstown. General Hill crossed on the 27th, and was soon followed by Longstreet, and the entire rebel forces of northern Virginia. Chambersburg, Gettysburg, York and Hanover, were rapidly occupied by the enemy. These operations naturally created great alarm in the Monumental City. The enemy was within two days march, and there was no defence. The army of the Potomac seemed to be lost, and the distracted people knew not which way to look for succor. In this extremity, with the spirit of 1814, they set to work in their own defence. The citizens volunteered by thousands; business was partially suspended, and drill was the order of the day. In the midst of this excitement we arrived in the city, and for a few days assisted in garrisoning one of the numerous forts which had so suddenly sprung into existence.

On the 28th June, we received marching orders, and were directed to join the army of the Potomac, and report without delay, to Brigadier General Lockwood, at Monocacy Bridge. By 11 o'clock, A. M., tents were struck, wagons packed, and we were off. As we filed through the streets the band struck up some martial air, and with a shout, we bade farewell to our homes and to the dear ones left behind. As the soldier stepped gaily forward, little did he dream that he might never return, but deeming "all men mortal but himself," with a firm and steady gait, we all went "marching along."

Without incident, we rapidly passed over the beautiful country that lies each side of the Frederick turnpike, and entered the village of Ellicotts Mills, as the sun was going to rest. The excitement of the city had spread to the village. The whole population turned out to give us welcome, and cheer us on. National banners were displayed from every house we passed. Loyal-hearted men gathered in groups, and gave loud expression to their sympathies, while beautiful ladies clapped their hands for joy, and loaded us down with choice flowers. The heart of this loyal village was stirred, and we were deeply grateful for this sudden and unexpected ovation. We encamped near by, serenaded the ladies, and enjoyed the substantial hospitalities of our new made friends until a late hour of the night.

The morning of the 29th dawned upon us bright and beautiful. The *reveille* started me from my slumbers at the first grey of the morning. Preparations were made for a speedy departure, and with the rising of the sun, we resumed our march. Before leaving, I could but linger, and admire the beautiful scenery that lay around me—we had encamped upon the summit of a lofty hill. In front was the thriving village, just beginning to stir with life; at the foot of the hill lay the smiling valley of the Patapsco, dappled all over with elegant homesteads of a wealthy and refined population. The cattle were just rising from their dewy beds; the sheep were going forth to pasture; the mists of the river were floating over the meadows, while the rich red rays of the sun were gleaming over the hill tops and waking all nature into newness of life. For a few moments, I was enraptured with the delightful vision. The command had gone and left me, but spurring my horse, I soon regained my comrades.

This was the Sabbath-day, but it was no day of rest to us. Our orders and the exigencies of the public service demanded that we should press forward. So, onward we marched under the burning rays of a harvest sun, and after passing twenty-eight to thirty miles, weary and way-worn, we encamped in a beautiful grove at "Poplar

Springs." Before our arrangements for the night were complete, darkness was upon us. A hasty supper was prepared, the camp-fires were dying out, many sore-footed soldiers had retired to rest; but the sound of the *tattoo* roused them from their slumbers. A cavalry-man rode hurriedly into camp with the startling intelligence that our communications were cut off, that the enemy was in strong force between us and Baltimore, but a short distance down the road, and would probably move upon us before morning. As evidence of the truth of his story, he brought with him a prisoner who proved to be a very intelligent young fellow, and upon examination, stated that he belonged to Stewart's Cavalry, that his General had crossed the Potomac the night before at Seneca Creek, that he was encamped down the road about two miles with five brigades of Cavalry and Artillery, and had been informed by his scouts that we were in the vicinity. Had a thunderbolt descended from the heavens, in a cloudless sky, it would not have been more startling than this intelligence. No one imagined that there was an enemy within forty miles. It was supposed that the army of the Potomac and the two mountain ranges were between us and the foe; but when it became evident that we were face to face with so overwhelming a force, and liable to be attacked and cut to pieces at any moment, our condition assumed a very serious aspect. Retreat was out of the question. To move forward seemed equally dangerous, for from all that was known to us, it was fair to presume that the rebels were in front as well as rear. It was a moment of intense solicitude and fearful responsibility. Not knowing which way to go, it was determined, as our position was naturally strong and well taken, to stay where we were and hold our ground at all hazards. In the meantime, Duvall's Cavalry had encountered the enemy down the road, and a section of Rhode Island Artillery had fallen back and joined their fortune to ours. A short reconnoisance determined the best disposition to be made of our little force. The artillery-men were placed on the summit of the hill commanding the road that led to our camp The infantry were marched up to support our battery, and so placed as to enfilade the approaches to our position. A cavalry picket was thrown down the different roads to watch the movements of the enemy. While the residue of our mounted men were placed to the rear, the wagons were parked, and a strong picket line placed entirely around our camp. With these dispositions we lay upon our arms, determined not to be surprised, and awaited an attack. As the hours of night passed away. all nature become quiet; not a sound was heard save the low whispers of the men at arms, giving evidence that they were on the alert. About two o'clock in the morning, the noise of approaching horsemen was heard thundering down the pike. The clattering of many hoofs floating along the still morning air, gave tidings that our pickets were returning with speed. "What is the matter?" "what is the matter?" whispered each one to his neighbor. All thought the enemy were upon us. Every man looked at his weapon and received perfect assurance that all was in order. Eyes gleamed into the dark to catch the outlines of the approaching foe, while every ear caught up the slightest sound that might explain the tumult on the road. It was the return of our outer picket—some misunderstanding having caused them prematurely to fall back. Another cavalryman came into camp from the rear. It was one of the bold scouts of the brave Kilpatrick, and he gave us the pleasing intelligence that his Chief, with five thousand men, lay encamped five miles in front. He was immediately despatched with a note to his General, giving intelligence of the presence of the enemy and our position. He soon returned with advice that we should march to Ridgeville, and take shelter under the batteries and strong legions that lay encamped at that place. Knowing the enemy would be astir at early dawn hoping to catch us asleep; with the first streak of light, we called in our outposts and marched quietly away. We passed the advanced guard of Kilpatrick moving down the road, and with the rising sun, we stacked our arms upon a commanding hill that overlooked the village of Ridgeville. Scarcely had our camp fires been kindled, when the guard we had passed, came flying down the road; the old Ringgold battery dashed into our lines—unlimbered, loaded, and trailed their pieces. The enemy was at hand. Twenty minutes from the time we left our camp, he was after us; but we had gone. A hand to hand fight took place with the advanced guard we passed; they were overpowered and chased back into our midst.

A bugle was sounded, and then was witnessed one of the most magnificent scenes I ever beheld. Kilpatrick's Cavalry was in motion. In a moment they deployed as skirmishers, and like wild Tartars, went bounding over fields and fences, meadows and woodlands. They disappeared behind the hills and forests in eager hunt for the foe. Stewart, finding his prey had escaped, and his old enemy was upon his heels, beat a hasty retreat, and fled towards Westminster. Again the bugles of Kilpatrick sounded the recall. The echo had hardly died away over the hills, before the daring horsemen were seen pouring out of the forests, over the fields, and down the roadways, until the hillsides and summits were black with their thousands. In a moment more the advance was sounded—and away they went, rushing dashing, plunging down upon the retreating enemy. The rumbling of artillery, the tramping of thousands of horses, the wild shout of excited men reverberated over hill and valley, and died away in the distance like the roar of old ocean thundering against its rock-bound shore.

About noon we resumed our march, but had not passed the town before we encountered two corps of the noble, war-worn, battle-tried army of the Potomac, pushing on in an impetuous torrent to meet their old enemy on a field far to the north of their former battle grounds.

Here we received an order from General Lockwood, changing our destination, and ordering us to cut across the country, and make for Taneytown by the shortest route, and report at that place. It now became evident that our fortunes were to be joined to those of the Grand Army of the Potomac, and we were to share with them the glory of some hardly contested fight. Leaving them however, for the present, when they diverged to Westminster, we made for Liberty, thence to Middleburgh, and arrived at Taneytown, on the evening of July 1st. Here we met General Meade, whose headquarters were then there, and from whom we learned that our brigade of Marylanders had joined the 12th Army Corps, and were marching for Gettysburg, where a battle was then progressing.

On the morning of the 2d, we emptied knapsacks, abandoned all extra baggage, left behind the sick and disabled, and started on a rapid march for the field of conflict. Soon we met the usual stream flowing back from the field of battle. First, a long train of wagons hurrying out of the way; then a bearer of despatches; then a troop of cavalry dashing by; then a squad of fugitives skulking out of the way of danger; and each gave an account of the progress of the fight according to the heat of his imagination.

Excited by these reports, we quickened our pace, and mile after mile was rapidly passed, though occasionally obstructed, hindered, and stopped by the passing trains and troops moving to the rear, until about six o'clock in the afternoon we reached an elevated knoll—and there lay spread out before us the field of Gettysburg, the grandest battle-scene ever witnessed upon the continent of America.

A long line of blue resting upon a prominent ridge, and a succession of hill-tops sweeping from the Round-top mountain on the left, to Culp's hill on the right, indicated the army of the Potomac. While upon a corresponding range of hills, distant about one mile, circling round the position of General Meade, was stationed the Confederate army.

The valley between these two ranges of hills was the scene of the terrible struggle that was shaking the very earth beneath our feet. Large masses of troops were seen moving to and fro, leaving old and taking new positions. The pillars of white smoke and the flash of guns told where the enginery of death was at work. We descended into the plain just in time to witness the close of the terrible struggle between Sickles and Longstreet. After a furious cannonade from more than one hundred guns, the enemy had massed his forces, descended with loud shouts into the valley, and like an avalanche swept over the intervening plain, and charged up the opposite hill, where they met the Sixth Army Corps standing like a wall of brass. Twenty guns now opened upon the advancing columns of the enemy, mowing down great masses, and cutting wide lanes at every discharge through their staggering ranks; but still on they rushed, over dead and wounded that were falling like autumn leaves, until half the hill was gained. In an instant the long line of blue changed into a line of fire—the Round-top smoked like a volcano—the quivering masses of the enemy reeled, staggered, broke and fled. The bugles sounded the recall, the enemy retired to his lines on hills, and the conflict ceased for the day, while we marched away to join our brigade.

The dark shadows of the night overtook us ere we found our chief. We kindled our camp fires, and lay down on the ensanguined field; but the rumbling of ambulance trains, the hum of living, moving, excited masses of men, and the cries of the wounded, robbed me of sleep until the later watches of the night. As I lay at the root of a tree with my saddle for a pillow, and looking up at the starry heavens above, my spirit wandered homeward, and dwelt with the loved ones left behind. Memory recalled our parting scene; the image of the tearful, heart-broken wife, the weeping children, the innocent, curly haired little boy that clung around my neck and would not let me go—and the painful thought forced itself upon me, that the morrow—the unknown morrow—might part us forever. With a sad, yet confiding heart, I sank to rest, committing myself and the terrible events of the morrow into the hands of an all-wise and merciful God.

The early dawn of July 3d, 1863, was ushered in by salvos of artillery. One hundred and fifty thousand men responding to the sound, sprung to their arms and prepared for the most terrible conflict of this terrible war. General Lee had, during the night, collected his entire force, and marshaled near ninety thousand men for his last great effort to break our lines, and crush our army. General Meade, however, with the quick perception of a great leader, discovering our weakest points, strengthened them during the night, and presented in the morning a position well nigh impregnable. His centre, commanded by General Howard, was on Cemetery Hill, a lofty eminence overlooking the town of Gettysburg, and commanding the country for miles around. From this point ran a range of hills to the right and left, sweeping backwards for several miles on either side. Upon this ridge was the army of General Meade posted, with reserves between; thus giving to our position the form of a triangle, with the apex facing the town of Gettysburg. The enemy occupied a corresponding ridge about one mile distant, and part of the village, with a beautiful plain between. The right flank of Meade's army rested on Culp's and Wolf's Hills, and was commanded by General Slocum, while the left was held by the 2d, 6th, 3d and 5th Corps.

Our brigade of Marylanders, under Lockwood, having arrived about sunset the evening before, were moved to the right to reinforce Slocum, and aid in driving back the enemy who had penetrated our lines on the evening previous at "Spangler's Spring." These dispositions having been made, the ball was opened about 4 o'clock by a small battery on the left of the Baltimore Pike, throwing shell into the wooded slopes occupied by the enemy. At 5 o'clock Lockwood deployed his brigade and moved upon the enemy, and the action fairly commenced along the whole line.

The 1st Potomac, under Colonel Maulsby, gallantly supported by the 150th New York, under Col. Ketchum, pressed hard upon Early's left, and drove him back, step by step in a well contested fight over the ground gained from us the evening before, and retook our rifle pits.

At 7 o'clock orders came for our regiment to move to the front. In a moment we were off in quick time down the pike, through Spangler's Lane, and into the bloody field we plunged. Ah! here was a scene that beggars description. Over this ground the fight had raged for two hours before our arrival, and all around lay the dead and wounded, and to the novice in war as I was, the scene was truly appalling; but there was no time for sympathy or contemplation. Aids from General Williams were hurrying us up; the enemy had rallied for another assault, and we wheeled into line and marched up a small hill to relieve a Pennsylvania regiment. The enemy, taking advantage of these movements and the slackened fire, made a dash at our rifle pits, and as we gained the summit, they were seen rushing down an opposite slope, and through a wooded valley, yelling like wild Indians. A volley from our splendid rifles over the heads of some Pennsylvanians in the rifle pits, checked their headway, and two more sent them flying back. The enemy rallied again, and we advanced and took possession of the rifle pits and relieved the Pennsylvanians, whose ammunition was exhausted. For two hours the crack of rifles, and the rattle of musketry were incessant, varied occasionally by the explosion of shells. Thus the battle raged along our entire line. At $10\frac{1}{2}$ o'clock there was a lull—the enemy drew back, we stacked our arms and lay down to rest. But this lull was the awful silence before the bursting of the storm. The fight ceased for the day upon the right; but the enemy was gathering his forces for his final attack. At 2 o'clock the tempest came. Three hundred pieces of artillery shook the earth; shells went screaming through the air, like fiends from below; the hills echoed and re-echoed the sounds of strife, until the very air trembled, and all natured seemed in turmoil.

About $2\frac{1}{2}$ o'clock the enemy emerged from behind Seminary ridge, and moved across the plain in two massive columns towards our left centre, commanded by Gen. Hancock. The Emmitsburg road was gained; then our artillery opened, and the heads of columns fell like grass before the mower's scythe; but still on came the roaring, shouting, surging masses of the enemy, up to the very cannon's mouth. Ten thousand rifles flashed destruction in their face; whole ranks fell at every discharge—but still on they came, over piles of dead and martyred heroes; the fortunes of the day trembled in the balance; the destiny of our nation hung upon a hair—but the 2d Corps stood like a wall of adamant, and dealt out such blows that flesh and blood could not stand. Stannard and Webb seeing the enemy falter, threw their brave legions upon them, and the cold steel turned the tide of battle in our favor. The enemy broke and fled.

In the meantime, our brigade had been ordered up as a reinforcement, and in the midst of this tornado of battle we reached the foot of Cemetery hill in time to see the gallant charge of Stannard and Webb—to see the enemy stagger back, break and fly in wild confusion over the plains; just in time to hear and join in the shout of victory that burst forth from twenty thousand exultant hearts. Oh! it was a glorious shout. It was the triumphant outburst of joy and gladness from the hearts of victorious freemen. The refrain was caught up by thousands from the adjacent hills, and the glad tidings were spread from Wolf's hill to Round-top in one general, long, enthusiastic peal, that went ringing over the old Keystone State, and vibrating in every loyal heart in the land. Thus ended the great battle of Gettysburg.

THE FLAG.

Hail! all hail! to Columbia's flag,
    Flag of Liberty, Justice, and Truth;
She shall wave it forever and aye,
    Like an eagle renewing her youth.
        Then all hail to the Stars and the Stripes!
            To the flag of the brave and the free;
        And as long as the stars shall endure
            Shall it wave o'er the land and the sea.

The Pacific shall mirror its stars;
    With its stripes the Atlantic shall glow,
From the Gulf to the Lakes shall it wave
    Over hill, plain, and valley below.
        Then all hail, &c.

'Neath that flag was our liberty born,
    And our nation to greatness has grown;
For our banner on land and at sea
    Is the Star Spangled Banner alone.
        Then all hail, &c.

With its stripes is our history entwined,
  By its stars is our future illumed,
He who fails to defend it to day
  To the fate of the traitor is doomed.
    Then all hail, &c.

When our fathers their freedom maintained
  The Almighty himself was their friend;
And, whatever the foes that assail,
  May He, us and our children defend.
    Then all hail, &c.

Yellow Springs, *Ohio*, 1861.

CONSEQUENCES

OF THE

DISCOVERY OF AMERICA.

To a Genoese navigator was given the transcendent privilege of conferring the greatest boon on the human race that ever fell to the lot of a human being. Kings have bestowed laws, charters, and charitable endowments. Philanthropists have instituted great reforms. Philosophers have created systems and methods of inquiry. Religious enthusiasts have swept away the accumulated evils of centuries. Socrates, Aristotle, Constantine, Justinian, Charlemagne, Abelard, Luther, Bacon, Descartes, Galileo, Watts, Franklin, Washington, and others of immortal fame, have been the instruments of great movements which have resulted in the prosperity and happiness of mankind. They are benefactors of the race, and grateful nations will not let them die. But Christopher Columbus gave a new continent—added half a hemisphere to the enterprises of man, and made a new field of inconceivable activities, the greatness of which has only just began to be appreciated,—changing the currents of human thought and energies, and presenting boundless opportunities.

Like all great boons, it was providential, and brought about only by almost superhuman energy, patience, and fortitude. The fortunes of Columbus have an irresistible charm. His scheme is a marvel of genius. It was an inspiration. He inferred that the Atlantic was the common boundary of the eastern and western world—of the islands of Marco Polo, and the western shore of Europe. He did not dream of a new continent, but of a new way to reach India and China. He pondered day and night to solve a great geographical mystery. He collated charts and maps, read Ptolemy and Hipparchus, meditated on the travels of Polo and Mandeville, speculated on Plato's Atalantis, and studied the phenomena of the ocean. The more he meditated, the profounder were his convictions of unknown lands in the west. These were grounded on the rotundity of the earth, on travels to the east, and the strange plants and carved woods which had floated occasionally from the west,—as he supposed from the eastern shores of Asia.

He resolved to reach those distant shores, so full of mystery and dread—yea, so rich in gold and silver, in gems and spices, by sailing in ships directly west. He wished simply to avoid the almost impossible labor of crossing the eastern continent. He was inspired by a commercial idea. He would add to the wealth of the world, and aggrandise the mercantile powers of Europe. But enormous difficulties stared him in the face. He was without means, or credit, or influence. He had no ships or devoted followers. He had no charts. He did not know how distant were those eastern realms. The ocean was unexplored. He alone saw the end, but he could not inspire others with his faith. He appealed to various Courts. They were indifferent. He tried the Universities, but scientific men decided against him. Nobody believed in him. He was regarded as a dreamer and a visionary. I may not linger on the well known incidents of his residence in Spain—his deferred hopes—his unsatisfactory correspondence—his delays at Court—his disappointments—his poverty, and other obstacles which almost drove him to despair.

But help came, as is usual with great benefactions, from unexpected sources. It is seldom that the schemes of genius are comprehended by those from whom we expect sympathy. His aid came from a Saint, and a woman. Religion and love are the first to understand genius; and genius ever looks to Saints and woman for believers. Juan Perez, a monk, believes in him, as Ali did in Mohammed. He secured his introduction to Isabella, and she also believed, as Kadijah did in the Prophet. She felt an attraction which partook of affection. The great object of his life is furnished him in the benediction of an enlightened Saint, and the smile of a sympathetic woman. Never let genius despair when it is encouraged by piety and love. They are the divine voices of our world.

A munificent Queen, amid the doubts and jeers of nobles, furnishes the means. The ships are small. They have not even decks. The sailors are clamorous, mercenary and superstitious. No matter. Genius holds the helm. Faith inspires the soul. Providence assists those who trust in Him. The breezes are propitious. The sky is serene. The needle varies, but the variations are explained. Columbus sails onward. Deception follows deception. Mirages skirt the horizon. Amid murmurs and fears the land is reached. A new continent is added to the realm of civilization.

We will not dwell on the varied fortunes of the intrepid Admiral. What care we, whether rewarded or unrewarded—whether loved or hated—whether rich or poor—whether honored or persecuted? He has his reward. He is enrolled in the catalogue of the greatest benefactors. He is a favorite of heaven. All benefactors have varied fortunes. They contend with envy and hatred. That is their lot. And they are isolated men, like Dante and Galileo, and Michael-Angelo—from superior knowledge, finding that the increase of knowledge is the increase of sorrow. If this life were all, we should compassionate Columbus, when slandered, persecuted, robbed, and deprived of honors. But his great soul lives, and is marching on. Robed in immortal glory, we care nothing for the accidents of earth.

We are most interested in the gift itself, worthy of a deity, which he conferred—in the results of his great discovery. They suggest great inquiries. On this, it is good to meditate.

What are the consequences of the discovery of America? They may be classed under two heads—the impulse given to material forces, and the new theatre afforded for human experiments. Who can estimate the vast energies which have been directed to commerce, colonization, and material gains? Who can measure the enrichment of Spain and Portugal, Holland and England, from the precious metals which the adventurers found in Mexico and Peru? Commerce was immeasurably stimulated throughout the world; and the East Indies furnished spices, and silks and teas, as well as the West the precious metals. Asia and Europe were brought together, and comprehended each other. The islands of the sea revealed inexhaustible resources. New fruits, vegetables, and flowers were given to man. The rapid increase in arts and culture, in palaces and gardens, in statues and paintings—in all forms of material civilization received a mighty impulse—everywhere, especially in the maritime cities. What poetry in the voyage of Ojida, of Nino, of Pinzon, of Balboa, of Vespucci, of Cabot, of Raleigh? The coasts and rivers of the whole American continent are gradually explored. The riches of Brazil and Mexico, and Peru are revealed. Factories are established in distant cities on the shores of the Indian Ocean. More wealth flows to Spain than all the Eastern Countries of Asia afforded to Rome and mediaeval Europe. England gains fisheries and colonies. Portugal rivals the East. Holland becomes a first class power. The enterprise of all Europe is stimulated. And a field of enterprise and hope for the poor man, is opened in the West. He settles in the wilderness with his wife and children. He explores mountains and rivers. Everywhere he finds a rich soil and a genial climate. He can fly from oppression at home, to peace and competence abroad. On the banks of the Mississippi, he finds that he is still in the middle of the world. Every place is alike a new centre. The whole continent is colonized by ambitious and energetic races. Indians and wolves alike flee before them. New populations multiply with unexampled rapidity. No man need now starve or beg on the whole earth. A garden of Eden is found in the West, of virgin soil—productive beyond all the past precedents of the world. A population exceeding all Europe, can be

7*

fed. With the new scope for energies, all plants and fruits and animals are multiplied. Inventions keep pace with the field for enterprise. Machinery comes in as a mighty power, abridging the labors, while it multiplies the necessities of man. It is invested with the glories of ancient art. It accomplishes the most astonishing results, cutting through mountains, spanning rivers, filling up valleys, conquering nature, and even making the most powerful animals insignificant as aids in labor. It transports travellers forty miles an hour over mountains and plains, almost annihilates distances. It sends messages across a continent more rapidly than lightning passes from cloud to cloud. It batters down the grandest fortifications at a distance of five thousand yards. It moves ten thousand tons through surging billows, against wind and currents, with the speed of a race-horse. It borrows the unknown forces of nature to unite distant countries in complete and constant communications. It scans, and measures, and counts the stars. It finds agents in the bowels of the earth. It builds cities in a day. It illuminates them in the night, with the brightness of the sun. It garners in the harvest of the husbandman, and transports it one thousand miles at less expense, than horses could have carried it on level roads, a twentieth part the distance three hundred years ago. It can clothe more people in a week than all the looms of antiquity could do in a year. It has made every man a Briareus. It has filled the world with Titans. It outworks Hercules in labors and in heroisms. So, the new world is populated with men who fear nothing, and overcome everything, heat, cold, darkness, fire, water; for energies, have been so amazingly stimulated that they seem miraculous. A continent, howling, desolate, uninhabited, except by savages, is covered, in three hundred years, with cities, farms, palaces, churches, monuments, armies, everything pertaining to civilization, and surpassing the glories of ancient Rome and Greece. If Columbus could re-visit the wilderness he discovered, he would see more wonders in every direction, for thousands of miles, than ever Genoa and Venice, and Madrid afforded. He would see a material greatness absolutely astonishing; civilized nations more powerful than the Spaniards and Italians, and the English and Dutch together, when he set off on his daring voyage. These nations, he was instrumental in calling into being, and this wondrous civilization, he, more than any other man, promoted. Fortunate pioneer; how great are the blessings he has bestowed upon the race! He thought only to enrich Spain. He has enriched all nations and countries. And he has given a home to all the miserable and the oppressed upon the face of the earth. And they rise up and call him blessed. Some day, they will erect a monument to his memory, higher than the pyramids; more magnificent than St. Peter's Church. The gold and silver alone which he has given to man, would gild every palace and temple of the ancient world. The cotton which his colonists have planted, could clothe the human race; and the corn of the Indian, could feed them. No longer hunger and famine on the earth; America can supply all the starving nations. No longer poverty and nakedness; she can give a shelter and a garden. She has even converted the naked African, against his will, into a Christian, and his very slavery has proved his blessing. She even promises *him* liberty, and this wild child of burning deserts, is to rejoice in the new land, already his own magnificent heritage, purchased by suffering and tears.

We take, however, a very inadequate idea of the destinies of America, or the splendid boon conferred on civilization by Columbus, if we look merely to material progress. There was a magnificent civilization among the Greeks and Romans; but they were unable and unwilling to preserve it. Those nations passed away, like Assyrian and Egyptian monarchies; and the fruit of their labors was reaped by new races—mere barbarians from the German forests. Civilization did not perish, but entered into new combinations. Nothing which the genius of man creates is suffered to die. Yet men die, and nations perish. The Roman world, with all its proud trophies of dominion, passed away. No influences were sufficiently conservative to save it—neither art, nor science, nor literature, nor philosophy, nor jurisprudence, nor a remarkable mechanism of government. Nothing which comes from man's unaided genius can save man in the great crisis of misfortune or degeneracy. Higher influences are necessary. They came too late among the Romans. Their Empire was doomed long before the barbarian advanced to conquer and to reconstruct. No genius or good fortune, or propitious circumstances of soil and climate can save a nation when moral forces have fled. This is the uniform history of the world. As it has been, so it will be. It is a law of Divine Providence that prosperity will provoke luxury and pride, and thus lead to effeminacy and ruin, without the conservative influence which springs from Christian ideas. There will be everlasting circles in which society will run, unless man gains strength from supernatural aid. The Gospel is the only hope of the world, and the great principles which are to be deduced from it.

There is no reason drawn from reason, or experience, or Christianity why America will not share the fate of all the other nations, unless animated by higher principles than have had dominion in our world. It will be split up into rival States; it will be convulsed by anarchies; it will be formed into monarchies and tyrannies; it will degenerate, and be punished if there are not patriotism, virtue and intelligence among the people. Never yet have they proved their capacities for self-government. Self-government is still an experiment. Godless, and thoughtless and ignorant people will choose bad rulers,—there will be public and private corruption, dissensions, blunders, follies,—all leading to dissolutions and reconstructions. Ignorant and incapable rulers will run the ship ashore; and degenerate people will acquiesce in the ruin for the sake of change and spoils. There must be virtue and intelligence even here, in order to preserve our magnificent inheritance.

We fondly hope for the best. We do not trust in human nature: we trust in God and His religion. We are sanguine of an indefinite progress. We believe in truth—in regenerating ideas. We have faith in the final elevation of the race—in the restored Eden—in the reign of righteousness. We are warranted in this faith.

Now where can a new field be found so favorable as America for the trial of this last great experiment? Not in Europe, nor Asia, nor Africa. It must be tried here. We are Christians. We spring from noble races. We have accepted the great ideas which grow out of Christian equality. We annihilate slavery. We institute schools and colleges for the poor. We elevate the poor man. We give liberty to all. We have glorious witnesses of truth in every village and city. We approve the right. We execrate the wrong. We contend chiefly with inexperience. We believe in the future world. We merge the finite in the infinite, and in the majesty of man we adore the majesty of God.

Believing that America is the truest field for the development of virtue and intelligence, and, rejoicing in our past triumphs—our successive reforms—our educational institutions, our aspirations for happiness on a sound foundation, we consider that its real dignity and greatness consist in the opportunities for ever advancing light and peace. Her mission, we believe, is to civilize the world—to show that self-government is practicable, and that the normal corruption of society can be arrested by the great truths which we accept.

Hence it is the peculiar blessings which the people in this country enjoy pertaining to liberty and education and the worship of God, which constitute our birthright, and make America the hope and glory of the world. Columbus gave it a new theatre of action and passion. And the reformers of the older nations came here to try their experiments. We are to solve the problems of liberty, and the culture of the great mass. Our institutions are not copies: they are indigenous, as jurisprudence was to the Romans, and arts to the Greeks. Political liberty is born with us. It only exists in name in Europe. Popular education is American and not European. Schools, and colleges, and lyceums thrive here as in no other country, for they belong to the poor and not the rich. Every man can rise. Most men do rise. See what strides have been made by Irish and German emigrants! They have corrupted us, but we have raised them. The balance is in favor of liberty and happiness and knowledge. Our very war—so disastrous—so mournful—so dark a shade on American institutions, was yet a necessary event—like the melting away of Indian tribes incapable of civilization. And it will prove providential. If the Crusades—those execrable wars, resulted in the civilization of Europe, much more this war in defence of national unity. Slavery may be swept away; this is one of the issues; but is this a lasting calamity? National bankruptcy may come; but the credit system will give place to something better, even though it involves the annihilation of all the national debts of Europe. State rights may suffer, but the centralization of power, as desired by Hamilton, may promote national prosperity. The Constitution may be changed, but changed to suit the unalterable condition of human society. A million may die; their bones will not whiten the soil of the worn-out monarchies of the world, but will be an impressive lesson to all future generations of the blessing of peace. A million more may suffer from broken fortunes, but a hardy people will be trained to support the dignity and honor of the nation in the future struggles to which we may be doomed with the hostile powers of Europe. Out of the storm, above the clouds, beneath the depths, the voice, "I have loved thee with an everlasting love," will be heard to cheer the erring and the miserable. We have a magnificent mission to discharge for humanity, and it will be discharged in spite of the evil forces. Our laws, our schools, our popular legislation will remain. No revolution can destroy our literature, our village festivals, our boundless aspirations Give us the conservative influence of churches, of philanthropies, of schools, of lectures, of books, of town halls, of village gatherings to discuss the great problem of government—give us an educated and disinterested clergy, and learned teachers, and sympathetic and philanthropic women—all animated by the desire to raise the dignity of man—all looking to the Bible as the thesaurus of all vital truths—all bowing down to the majesty of its Author, and I am indifferent, comparatively, to those material glories in which we have put too great a trust, and which the older nations have in common with ourselves. It is only as we realize the expectations of Christian philosophers that I can see how our civilization will be permanent here, or re-act beneficially on the old world itself. Our brilliant future does not rest on works of art and science, grand as they may be, so much as on those conservative influences which elevate the soul of man, and send peace and hope to suffering millions in her favored lands.

These *must* be maintained, at any cost, or we share the fate of the older nations, and America will prove only an extension of what has been tried and failed. Columbus, great as he was, simply looked to the triumphs of science and the increase of wealth. Isabella had nobler views—she thought of the salvation of idolatrous nations. We have still higher aspirations. We hope for an indefinite elevation of the race itself, under the leadership of those men whose ancestors forsook their fatherland to try the grandest experiments of which this earth has been the theatre. If we are true to their principles, if we seek our welfare in the triumph of virtue and the spread of truth, then our experiment will not fail, and Columbus will have conferred a boon whose value all succeeding generations cannot over estimate—the glory and the hope of oppressed and miserable people in every corner of this earth.

THE AMERICAN ENSIGN.

It has been often objected to the National Flag of our Country, that it is meaningless to the Christian, and without moral beauty. Other nations have displayed the Cross, and gloried in Christian emblems; but young America, it is said, has no such token in her banner.

It does not seem, to the author of the following stanzas, that such an objection is well-founded. At all events, he has been accustomed to read its emblems with a Christian eye; and the verses, written several years ago, which are here presented, are an attempt to express in rhyme, the sacred associations, with which, to say the least, our National colors are not incapable of being ennobled.

See, from the rampart, how the freshening breeze
    Flings out that flag of splendors, where the Night
Mingles with flaming Day's, its blazonries,
    And spreads its wavy azure, star-bedight.

Thy flag, my country! Let those colors toss
    O'er wave or field, o'er steadfast hearts they fly:
But me delight memorials of the Cross,
    And thy diviner symbols to descry.

What though th' ignoble herd those tokens tell,
    Even as they tell of Heaven no star aright!
For me, high meanings in their broidery dwell,
    And Christ's five wounds each star displays to sight.

Let millions live beneath that flag enrolled:
    One shall they be, as heaven is one, above,
While faith is theirs to read, in every fold,
    Signs of their God and of Redeeming Love.

Thy Name is there, oh Thou of many scars,
    Whose many sons like stars shall ever shine;
Thy Name—oh Star of all the Morning-stars!
    For many crowns, bright starry crowns are thine.

And thine the crimson of that snowy field!
    Those bloody dyes, like scourgings all bespread,
Tell of the Stripes by which we all are healed,
    And plows that plowed those furrows deep and red.

Oft o'er the seaman's or the soldier's bier,
    Droops that dear banner for his glittering pall,
Where every star might seem an angel's tear,
    And every stripe Christ's mercy covering all.

Or streaming wildly, from the lifted lance,
   'Mid strife and carnage if that flag be borne,
Onward and upward, ever in advance,
   Rent, but unstooping—taintless all, though torn:

Still be it Mercy's ensign!—even there
   As over Ocean's Alps, or calmest bay,
A sign of promise, opening everywhere
   For Truth and Peace, a free and glorious way.

And by these tokens conquer! Let it fly
   For Christ a herald, over wave and field:
His Stars they are who for Mankind did die;
   His glorious Stripes, by which we all are healed.

THE NAVAL ACADEMY

IN SECESSION TIMES.

The political campaign of 1860 was not without its results at this Institution; for soon after the election of President Lincoln became a fixed fact, the agitation which pervaded the Southern States extended to those midshipmen in the School, who came from the disaffected regions. All through the fall, political discussion had waxed warmer and warmer, until the usual results attending such debates began to be very sensibly felt. There was a sort of a division into cliques, as is always the case, but at this time, agreement in politics was the foundation for all such. As is the case with all Southern youth, these midshipmen had become most thoroughly indoctrinated with State rights and State sovereignty, even to the extent of secession. The wiser of the pupils from all parts of the country avoided these political discussions, for the distance from a word to a blow is but very short. This feeling, existing so extensively throughout the School, led all to expect that the threatened secession of South Carolina would cause the withdrawal of those representing her. Soon came the news of the passage of the so-called secession ordinance; and "in obedience to the demands of their State," but in violation of their oaths to the United States, now followed the resignation of the South Carolinians. Then followed in rapid succession the beleaguering of Sumter, the cutting off of supplies, the firing upon the Star of the West—all which produced more discussion and more division of feeling; perhaps I should say more unanimity, for the Northern boys were bound more strongly together, leaving those of Southern birth to seek companions among those of their own sentiments.

One by one, the States seceded; one after another the midshipmen from those States resigned; though some desiring rather to remain, waited for positive commands from their parents, and they followed in the train of those who had preceded. Matters were finally coming to a crisis. There was strong talk of the secession of Maryland. Annapolis was by no means free from the taint of disloyalty; and it really became necessary to take means to prevent the seizure of the Government property.

Anchored a short distance from the buildings of the Academy, lay the School ship, "Old Ironsides;" to her were transferred all the heavy guns, save one left in the battery, bearing on the channel; then followed the ammunition and stores. The guns were cast loose day and night, ready for instant action. Upon the slightest symptoms of a movement, the town could have been laid in ashes. On shore, the midshipmen were nightly detailed for guard duty; the officers exercised the most sleepless vigilance; and yet, amidst all this turmoil and excitement, as if loth to yield to the power of Mars, Science kept on her steady way; recitations were heard as usual, and doctrines of loyalty were inculcated, only to be spurned and cast aside by the Southerners, and to be pressed closer to the hearts of the Northerners. On board the ship the same precautions were observed, the same vigilance exercised. The lamented Commander, George W. Rogers, one of the brightest ornaments of our own, or any service, was determined to give up the "Constitution" only with his life. The Superintendent, Captain George S. Blake, assisted by Commander C. R. P. Rodgers, was unceasing in his efforts to protect the honor of the flag, and through God's blessing he was successful. Night after night were "watch and ward kept," until at last came the news of the Baltimore riots, and then excitement was at a fever heat. Rumors of an expected attack came to the ears of those within the Academy walls, and all was prepared for the reception of the traitors.

At length, on board the Constitution, came the alarm, which soon extended to the shore. In less time than it takes to write it, the midshipmen and officers were at their posts, awaiting whatever should come next. A small vessel is seen coming down the river, gradually nearing the ship; closer and closer she approaches, and then the hoarse shout of "Boat Ahoy!" is answered by a friendly "Halloo!" and the little craft glides by—all thankful that the alarm was but a false one. Then words fell thick and fast from the lips of the actors in the scene; when suddenly comes a glare of light, and from the picket boat at the mouth of the river, up shoots a rocket, tracking its way through the air, and giving warning of an approaching vessel. Again all is hurry and excitement; but there is no confusion, as all stand awaiting the second rocket, which is to tell of the approach of the vessel seen. But it does not come, and then those not on duty return to their quarters, the rest remaining to watch with strained eyes the slightest indication of an approaching foe. Through the first gray dawn of morning, looms up a huge steamer, seemingly crowded with men. It is yet too dark to distinguish clearly, and impatiently the light of day is looked for. Gradually is discovered the "Maryland," but with no ensign flying to tell whether she brings friends or foes. Then is hoisted the time-honored Stars and Stripes from the battery and the ship, and at last, floating in the morning-sheen, the "Maryland" shows forth the Old Flag—and we are saved. Communication is at once established, and soon the steamer is alongside the ship, and we learn the history of the troops on board of her. Called from their homes at a moment's notice, they by no means presented the appearance of veteran soldiers; covered with coal dust, they looked very little like fighting men; but the Massachusetts Eighth has proved its qualities on many a hard fought field—and of those who first entered it as three months' men, scarce one but now wears shoulder straps earned by valor.

General Butler, with that energy so characteristic of the man, announces his intention of landing his troops there, and proceeding to Washington. But first, it is necessary to remove "old Ironsides" from danger; and in a very few moments, two companies are at work, removing the guns from the "Constitution" to the "Maryland," for the good old ship draws too much water to pass over the bar. The midshipmen are all sent on shore, with the exception of a few retained to assist the officers; and at length the anchors are up, and the ship ready to move. A strong flood-tide is running, and the "Maryland" does not make any headway. An investigation of the fire-room, discovers the fact that the firemen are not doing their duty, but a very judicious application of revolver restores them to their senses, and soon there is steam enough. Slowly the ship moves along, and at last the bar is reached; and just as all think that she is going over safely, she strikes, and is hard aground. Her progress is watched with anxiety from the shore, and as soon as she is seen to be aground, a boat is sent off to see if more help be needed. The "Maryland" makes a vigorous effort to haul the ship off, but she herself gets aground, and then there is more trouble. All this time, the soldiers on board of both vessels are without food, for their rations were used up on the previous night. A boat is despatched from the "Constitution," containing bread, pork and beef, and the famishing men are relieved. The tired officers and men at length rest, and wait for morning and high water to get off. But during the night, there is another alarm, and all work hard to kedge the good ship out of danger; but to no purpose, for a squall comes up, and their efforts can avail nothing. On shore the night is passed in the same anxious state of expectancy as before, for the soldiers are aground, and there is still fear lest an attack be made. With the dawn of morning, comes a tug from Baltimore, bringing a bearer of despatches, who is sent to the Academy in a small boat, while the tug is used to get the Constitution to a safe anchorage. Soon comes in sight another steamer, and she is found to be the "Boston," with the New York

Seventh on board. She proceeds to the assistance of the "Maryland," and soon both go up to the Academy wharf, and the first troops are landed. Then one after another pour in vessels of all descriptions, each one bearing men rushing to the defence of their country. The beautiful grounds of the Academy become one vast camp, and the Academy buildings one huge barrack. The midshipmen are relieved from guard duty, and saunter about in parties looking on the changeful yet picturesque scene. Back of the Academy a Pennsylvania Regiment is endeavoring to drill; on the walks, under the trees, on the grass, lie scattered soldiers, guns, and all the paraphernalia of warfare. The howitzers belonging to the Academy cover the gates, and all entrance is forbidden to the crowd without. Here are men writing home, there, a group of midshipmen who have resigned, and are waiting to go home; all round, the most inextricable confusion, while within the Recitation Hall, are gathered the officers of the regiments, discussing the state of affairs. And so the day passes, all uncertain as to the next step, but yet prepared for whatever may come. During the night the usual guards are kept, and when all others are buried in profound slumber, the sleepless sentinels see suddenly flashing out one, two, three, four, five rockets, in rapid succession, announcing the arrival of that number of vessels. Unfortunately, the signal is mistaken, and the long roll beaten, and in a very short time, the entire force of midshipmen and soldiers is under arms. After waiting for some time, an explanation is given, and all allowed once more to return to their dreams. At daylight, all are roused again, and the five vessels which had arrived during the night, come up to the wharf and discharge their cargoes of living freight. During the forenoon the Seventh New York is drilled, and in the afternoon the midshipmen go through their evolutions, much to the delight of the Seventh who applaud most vigorously their double quick; for that is what the corps of midshipmen always excel in. Another night of watching and waiting. In the early morning the Seventh New York and Eighth Massachusetts, set out for Washington. The lamented Theodore Winthrop has detailed that march, and it needs no recounting here. Meanwhile, despatches come from Washington. The midshipmen are to be transferred to the "Constitution," and to sail for New York, there to await further orders. The order is given, and the packing is commenced. Those who have resigned, go from one room to another to bid farewell to their classmates and friends. It is a gloomy scene. All are sad at leaving the sheltering walls of their Alma Mater. Finally, all is completed, the baggage is sent on board, the boat provided, and for the last time the Battalion is formed. Four abreast, the departing midshipmen march down the walk, lined on either side with spectators to the wharf. Then occurs the most affecting scene of all; realizing that they are leaving forever the place which had been home to them for so long; each one dares not look another in the face for fear that the unbidden tears will come. And when Captain Rodgers attempts to address them, he finds it impossible. His heart is too full for utterance; he can only say, pointing to the Stars and Stripes floating over his head, "Stand by the Flag, young gentlemen! Stand by the Flag!" And there is not a dry eye among those standing around; all are alike moved to tears. Then one by one the students go on board, and as the sun sinks in the west, all take a last look at the scene they have loved so well—and the Naval Academy at Annapolis, is no more.

Of those who then left, some have fallen in defence of their flag, and all are scattered throughout the various naval stations. Let us all hope that when peace shall come, the Academy may be restored to its original place, a fit monument of the patriotism of its founder, one of our country's noblest sons.

NATIONAL HYMN.

God save America!
God grant our standard may
    Where e'er it wave;
Follow the just and right,
Foremost be in the fight,
And glorious still in might
    Our own to save.
CHORUS.—Father Almighty!
        Humbly, we crave,
        Save thou America,
        Our country save!

God keep America!
Of nations great and free
    Man's noblest friend;
Still with the ocean bound
Our continent around,
Each State in place be found,
    Till time shall end.
CHORUS.—Father Almighty, etc.

God bless America!
As in our Father's day,
  So evermore.
God grant all discords cease,
Kind brotherhood's increase,
And truth and love breathe peace
  From shore to shore.
Chorus.—Father Almighty, etc.

O Washington! * to thee
Our country's Father, we
  Hallow this day;
Our gratitude we prove
Singing the song you love,
O join us from above!
  God save America!
Chorus.—Father Almighty, etc.

* Stanza to be added on Washington's birth-day.

TO WHAT PURPOSE IS THIS WASTE?

IN the material universe there is no waste. Nature hoards and uses over again the discarded portions of every organism, and the same particles in altered forms have been doing perpetual service from the beginning until now. No force is lost,—that which seems to spend itself is only transmuted, and under another name or aspect, still works on. In the world of resolves, deeds and activities, there is no waste of any thing good,—what seems lost is sown; what seems squandered is put at interest; what seems thrown away brings accumulating revenue. When Judas asked the question which we have taken for our motto, he not only wanted the money; but in his sordid soul he no doubt sincerely thought that the pouring of that precious unguent on the Saviour's head was a silly, senseless waste, and for once he was honest when he complained of it. But so far from being wasted, it is not spent yet. The odor of the ointment then only filled the house,—it now fills all Christendom. It is the divinely hallowed type and exemplar of all considerate kindness,—of the æsthetic element that forms an essential, and a large part in all real charity,—of the love which contents not itself with the bare supply of bodily wants, but ministers to the tastes, the sensibilities, the heart needs of its beneficiaries.

The lesson of this transaction is the one great lesson for our people now. Judas has, ever since the rebellion began, been repeating his old question, and he has induced not a few of the timid, anxious, desponding, yet loyal friends of the country to ask it with him. Let us answer it, if we can, so as to refute him and to encourage them.

"To what purpose is this waste?" If for nothing else, it has been essential, in order to prevent greater waste. Had the alternative at the outset been this long and disastrous conflict, or the mere division of the Union, we can conceive that a loyal patriotism might in sorrow have elected the latter as the least of the two evils. So thought and felt many who have never bated one jot of faith or hope in the common cause. But the alternative was the conflict or entire disintegration. The national bond was not strong enough to bear the fracture without being utterly dissolved. Not only between North and South, but between section and section, even in some cases between adjacent States, the dissilient exceeded the centralizing tendencies. Our General Government had made itself keenly felt in the faults and errors of its administrators, while its functions of defence and protection, its agencies for promoting the general prosperity, had been exerted so unobtrusively, and had so identified themselves with the natural course of civic life, that we were hardly aware that it did anything for us. Had it effected what it did with a showy array of instrumentalities and a heavy taxation, we should have recognized it as the best government upon earth; but because—still better—it worked almost unseen and unfelt, our recognition of it was faint, our attachment to it feeble;—while, the circle once broken, there were divergent sympathies and interests enough to have resolved us into half a score of nationalities, each too feeble to secure tranquility within or peace without, to establish protection for its industry or its commerce, or to maintain its rights, if so much as to be admitted to a voice in the forum of the nations. Our arms, even if they will not bring back, (as we doubt not they will,) the recreant States, have at least made a nation of those that remain. These States have now the sacred bond of common losses, sufferings, burdens and sorrows. Their citizens have stood and fallen in battle side by side. They have made like sacrifices for the cause of all. They have invested in the Union their treasure, their philanthropy, their honor, their best blood. It is a co-partnership from which, come what may, neither member has any longer the moral ability to withdraw.

Passing from this general view, let us consider for a moment the seeming waste of treasure in the war. We are aware that this has not been felt as was apprehended, that very many have been really and greatly enriched; nay, that the reputed aggregate wealth of many sections of the country was never so great as at the present moment. But this increased aggregate is apparent, not actual,—resulting, in part, from the fact that the credit of the Government has replaced the treasure spent by drafts on posterity, and in part from our reckoning our property and gains in a depreciated currency. It were well for us if the cost of the war bore on us with a more sensible pressure. Yet the pressure has been felt by not a few,—by some, in heavy personal losses due to this cause alone; by many, in a vague and fearful uncertainty as to the future of business and commerce; and by very many of moderate means, in free-will offerings beyond their easy ability for the comfort of the army and for the relief of the sick and wounded. But in all this, so far as we have felt it, we have gained, not lost. We have not thrown away our money, but have made the best possible investment of it in a revenue of conscious patriotism which could not have been ours without sacrifice,—in a love for liberal institutions and the cause of universal freedom, which is well worth the heaviest price we can pay, in the blessing of those ready to perish, and of their God and ours. David, on a memorable occasion, insisted on buying the threshing-floor of Araunah, the Jebusite, as a place of sacrifice, saying, "Neither will I offer burnt offerings to the Lord of that which doth cost me nothing." Cost is not only the measure of value,— it creates value. The greater the price we pay, the more dearly cherished, the more sacredly guarded will be the liberty and the peace we win; and in the debt we shall bequeath to our children and our children's children, we are pledging in advance their loyalty, their vigilance and fidelity as citizens, their enduring attachment to the institutions which we shall transmit to their keeping.

Like considerations, and others of a kindred nature, apply to the untold expenditure of time, and patient toil bestowed on the country's cause by the women of our land, and even by children of tender years. This is no waste, but an unspeakable gain. It has deepened the fountains of fervent patriotism in the hearts whence flow the earliest and most enduring sentiments that shape the character. The country which, wives, mothers, and sisters have so largely aided in saving, is henceforward associated in their religion with the most sacred names and themes. Loyal maxims will blend with the lessons of domestic piety. Our homes will be nurseries of patriotic feeling, and the guardians of their purity; the priestesses at their sacred altars, will keep watch and ward over the republic, and transmit in peaceful years the pure love of country kindled in strife and violence. Then too, can we over-estimate the self-denial, the habit of continuous industry, the wise forethought, the administrative ability developed in thousands whose destiny had seemed that not of ministering, but of being ministered unto; and who, but for times like these, would never have known the blessing of a weighty charge, the wealth of power and faculty, sympathy and love, that grows from generous toil and sacrifice?

But what shall we say of the fearful loss of life,— signal, even less for the number of victims than for the unprecedented proportion of those eminent for genius, excellence and promise. In numerous instances, the fatal lot has fallen on the confessedly noblest inheritor of a distinguished name, on the prime hope and joy of a large circle of kindred, on the very youth who seemed the born and designated exemplars and leaders in all that is beautiful in character, graceful in attainment, and honorable in deed. Yet, with a profound sense of all that the living and the dead have suffered, with the most tender sympathy with those whose choicest treasures have been laid on the sacrificial pile, we would say emphatically, this is not our loss, so much as our gain. To be sure, in individual affection, the void places will still remain void; in the nearer circle of home-love, none can stand where the departed stood; to our fond admiration, no new luminaries can reflect the specific light-beams of our own bright, particular stars. Yet we are experiencing the multiform fulfilment of those typical words, "Except a corn of wheat fall into the ground and die, it abideth alone; but if it die, it bringeth forth much fruit." The virtues and graces which, living, might have been rejoiced in, yet not copied, which, perhaps, because they inspired so much confidence, might have weakened in some minds the sense of their own kindred mission and equal responsibility, by death are quickened into a diffusive life. The martyr-blood has become the seed of patriotism, and of civic and social virtue. The faithful that have fallen have bequeathed their charge and trust to those who would not have shared it with them living. A higher tone of manhood, a more strenuous purpose, a nobler aim, a loftier moral sentiment has been breathed largely into our young men. The elements of national greatness, which reside wholly in individual character, have been stimulated through the swift ministers of death, into rapid yet healthy growth; and, with the multitudes that have fallen, there are at this moment more than ever before of those in opening manhood, or in the prime of their maturity, who are fitted to be the strong pillars of the state, who are reproducing all that was noblest and best in the Fathers of our Country, and whose loyalty has been sealed and pledged in the solemn sacrament by which they have entered into the places of the dying, and have taken from their lips the parting charge that the republic receive no detriment.

THE THREE ERAS OF THE UNITED STATES.

AS IT WAS.

Born to grow up rich and free,
   Suffering neither stint nor care,
Standing at their mother's knee,
   — Who so happy as these are?

AS IT IS.

Did you never chance to see
   One young flushed and angry brother,
("Cause he wouldn't let me be,")
   Pitching hot into the other?

AS IT SHALL BE.

Every trace of childish passion
   From their brows, the mother wipes;
As she smooths, in nightly fashion,
   Their coverlet of Stars and Stripes.

A WRECKER AMONG THE SEMINOLES;

AN EPISODE OF THE FLORIDA WAR.

The Florida War, as a conflict with savages in which but little glory was to be gained while great hardships were to be endured, was admirably calculated to bring out the daring characteristics of our countrymen. It is a large field of unwritten romance.

About the time when Dade's massacre gave the first token of sanguinary warfare, I visited St. Augustine with a sick friend, and passed from that balmy region to Key West with the hope of prolonging a cherished life which was flickering in the socket. I had hardly reached the island, so renowned in the annals of marine disaster, when the news of the fearful murder of our officers and soldiers was rapidly followed by accounts of the ravages committed by the indians throughout the peninsula, where solitary settlers had begun the task of redeeming the wilderness. One of the most tragic of these affairs, was the massacre of the Keeper of the Cape Florida Light House. It was appalling, not only on account of the sad fate of the keeper and his family, but because it extinguished a beacon whose absence might betray many a coaster that drifted, during the night, along the perilous breakers. Indeed, no greater danger is known to our seamen than the sudden or unexpected absence of one of those great watch-fires which the government has established for the protection of our commerce.

It would be hard to imagine or describe a more desolate spot than Cape Florida, nor were its ordinary loneliness and hazards diminished by the savage war which surrounded it landward, while the sea, surging and howling over its coral reefs, hemmed it in toward the east. The Light House of Cape Florida, and in fact, the Cape itself, are not situated on the main but on an island, in Biscayne Bay. Indeed, it was not until quite recently, that our surveyors ascertained accurately what was island, swamp, flat, key, shoal or reef, on the borders of that debateable land which is now known as "the everglades" of Florida. It is extremely difficult to define outlines in such a mesh of coral and mangroves. The coast between Cape Florida and Cape Sable is better marked by its steep and continuous bluffs, while the intervening shoals are studded with islands, which, at times, form an uninterrupted chain, and at others break into archipelagos of innumerable islets, so closely interwoven as to be almost impenetrable in their labyrithine folds. From the

Tortugas in the Gulf, the Keys bend in a crescent till they converge towards the mainland at Cape Florida, in the Atlantic, so that the light on this point becomes the warder of the mariner as he approaches those perilous fangs of the Mexican Gulf, which are always gnashing and foaming for their prey.

Key West was, of course, soon alive with interest when it became rumored that the keeper of so important a point was, in all likelihood, no longer among the living. It is probable, that many a wrecker's heart beat high with hope, as he dreamed of the harvest he might shortly reap from the bristling reef. Yet, there were honest men, also, on the island; and, among them, there happened to be a distinguished naval commander, who had looked into Key West, to get tidings from the imperiled main.

This officer no sooner heard of the keeper's fate, than he began to cast about among the "forlorn hopes" of the island for some resolute person, who, for a suitable recompense, would venture to rekindle the extinguished light

For several days, no one responded to the summons. At last a volunteer appeared on the quarter deck of the cruiser, and accepted the service, provided he might be allowed a favorite negro as companion in the enterprise. The stranger was an old and well known wrecker on the

Key, whose exploits in company with his sable comrade, had won for him a reputation of extraordinary hardihood. The black was his property, and perhaps, the only possession with which he was encumbered in the way of worldly goods.

It may readily be imagined that not the slightest objection was made to the wrecker's demand. The captain was glad to secure any one who would venture to the Cape. A reward was promised to the negro as well as to the white man, and in a very short time the vessel's launch was fitted out for the expedition, in charge of a midshipman with a well armed crew.

MITCHELL, the Key West wrecker, was a compact, slim, wiry, man,—case-hardened by long exposure to his dangerous work. His head was one of those gnarled knobs, whose red and yellow skin, like wrinkled parchment, was a map of his weather-beaten life. In every way, he was just such a person as one would naturally picture a regular "Key-Wester," whose flesh and sinews had been tanned and tempered for thirty years by the surf and sun of the Florida Reef. Except in complexion, the negro, in every respect, formed a counterpart of his master, and was remarkable for a blended companionship and obedience, which really made him a sort of additional member of Mitchell's body.

10*

The reef was soon coasted by the boatmen and Cape Florida reached. The story that alarmed and aroused the people of Key West proved true. The keeper and his family were indeed destroyed! Their dwelling was a wreck, and every vestige of its inmates and property gone As fate would have it, however, the Light House itself was still unharmed, and its burners, reflectors, and even the oil, were entirely adequate for all requirements. A reconnoissance was quickly made of all the hiding places wherein the enemy might lurk, and it was soon agreed that the savages, after satiating their passion, had, in all likelihood, departed for the main. Accordingly, Mitchell and his companion at once proceeded to their quarters, and judging that the light-house would unquestionably prove their stoutest fortress in case of assault, they resolved not to occupy the desolate dwelling but to ensconce themselves within the tower. An abundant supply of balls, powder, weapons, water and provisions was given to the adventurers, who, for their greater safety, not only barricaded the doors of the light-house within, but caused the entrance to be as effectually walled up as the materials at hand from the dwelling would allow. This accomplished, the naval escort went away and left the wrecker and his slave to their fate.

For some days, all went well with the solitary adventurers on their lonely island. But it was not long before the savages on the main perceived the rekindled beacon flaming out its luminous message over the sea. One day, Mitchell observed a canoe stealing across the bay, with a single indian, in the direction of his island. That night, as usual, he lighted the lamps and kept a wary watch, more however, with his ears than his eyes:—it would have been imprudent to risk the exposure of his person with but two to guard the post.

The night and the following day passed without assault. On the succeeding evening, however, as he kindled his watch-fires in the lantern, a ball shivered a pane of glass at his back, and, whistling by his ear, destroyed one of the lamps. Mitchell dipped instantly below the screen of the parapet wall, and reaching a torch aloft, completed his duty in spite of the warning.

There was now no longer any doubt that the spy who had been seen coming from the mainland in his canoe had borne back the news after reconnoitering the tower, and that, still uncertain how many whites were shut up within it, the savages were resolved to pick them off in detail after dark, as they attempted to kindle the light. It will surely be believed that Mitchell and Dick did not take turns in mounting guard that night. Indeed, Mitchell knew perfectly well that it would be worse than useless to entrust his slave with a prolonged watch in an hour of such imminent peril, for the habitual drowsiness of his race would have lulled him to sleep even if a battle were raging.

But there was no night attack, nor was there a vestige on the following day,—until the afternoon,—of a human being, either about the bushes, on the bay, or among the ruins of the house. During the morning, Mitchell and the black slept for a couple of hours, lying down within the base of the tower, directly in front of the door, so that if any attempt at breaking in should be made, they would be instantly aroused. Such was the toughness of their nerves or their exhaustion from previous vigils, that they slept as soundly as if they were rocked in a wrecking-clipper "laying to" snugly during a gale.

But things changed in the afternoon. Mitchell and his slave had not exposed their persons on the top of the tower, or, indeed, in any way, since the ball whistled by the old man's ear; yet they took advantage of one of the narrow slits or embrasures in the wall, designed to light the spiral wooden staircase, to reconnoiter the surrounding country. It was from this place that the wrecker, about one o'clock, detected a couple of red-skins peering cautiously above the sill of a window in the neighboring dwelling-house. The weather was extremely bad. A stiff north eastern gale was blowing from the sea, and as the frequent squalls of rain increased, Mitchell observed that the two indians became more careless and remained longer exposed at the windows. He could not, however, determine whether they had companions concealed within, or whether they were only scouts for a body that might be hard by in ambush.

,,Well, Dick," said Mitchell, "these devils seem as fixed as hulks in the sand! I wonder if they're hatchin' turtle-eggs? How would it do, old nigger, if you popped at one while I tried 't'other."

"Dat's percisely what I was gwyne for to think myself, massa Johnny!" replied the darkey, with a chuckle.

"Of course, you eternal swamp, you're always sure to have thought of what I've been thinkin, and 'termined to do what I've 'termined to do. Never mind boy, let's try;—but avast there a bit, till the devils make their next dive, so that when they come up agin we'll be sartin to have another settin' match of five minutes;—then's our time to let drive at 'em. Look out for the starboard ing'n, Dick, and I'll take care of the port one. Keep your muzzle well inside the winder. Es your hand aint half es steddy es mine, lay your muskit on the sill, while I hold my rifle at the top. Down, Dick, down, I tell ye;—quick!—there they come!"

There was a moment of breathless silence, broken only by the howl of a fresh squall from the sea, during which the two savages looked about quite unconcernedly.

"Now's your sorts, Dick; now's your sorts, old fellow! Look sharp and steddy at the starboard devil, and git your aim!"

"Yes, massa!"

"Hev' you got him?"

"Sure and sartin', Massa!"

"But don't fire till I whistle,—then blaze away like thunder."

There was another interval of silence, till Mitchell's soft whistle was succeeded by a simultaneous flash of musket and rifle, and in a moment the two savages sprang into the air with a yell, and fell dead in their tracks!

"Them's done for eney how!" exclaimed the old wrecker; "and now let's see who'll come to the berryin'!"

"Dive, Dick, dive, you sarpint, and load like a shark, while I watch 'em!"

Hardly were the words uttered, when half a dozen stalwart red-skins rushed from within the house to the bodies of their slaughtered comrades, and dragged them from the window.

"Quick, boy,—are you loaded?"

"God a'mighty, massa, what you think I made of?"

"Hurry up, hurry up, you infernal nigger!" shouted Mitchell, restless with impatience, and in a jiffy he was again in possession of his rifle.

"Mark your ingin, Dick;—crack when I tell ye! Now then,—go it!"

Whiz went the balls, with as sure an aim as in the first instance, killing one of the reinforcement and wounding another.

But, with this discharge, Mitchell judged that as the smoke from the embrasure must disclose the spot whence the fatal missiles issued, it would be best not to repeat the fire.

Accordingly, with the negro in his grasp, he leaped from the slit as soon as he saw the result. And well was it that he did so, for hardly were they safe, when a ball and an arrow fell within the tower through the aperture, while a couple of shots might have been heard spending their ineffectual balls on the splintered sides of the embrasure.

It may be said that Mitchell was unwise in his attack on the savages, and that he would have acted more discreetly by awaiting an assault from them. Be that as it may, the wrecker had two objects in view, and he gained them both. He was anxious to know the absolute force of his enemy, and at the same time, he wished to weaken or cripple the foe. The war party had evidently consisted of eight, four of whom were "done for." Had the force been more numerous or overwhelming, the wrecker's fate was evident, but with four only to contend against, his spirits quickly rallied.

The besieged remained for a considerable time, not only motionless but silent, when Mitchell finding that shots at the slit were not repeated, crept up the stairs to the embrasure with five additional muskets which he had loaded in the interval, and, cocking all, laid them as close as he could, with their muzzles to the edge of the external wall, and yet within the screen of the sill. He then leaned downward over the top of the slit, and by diving his head rapidly below it, took glimpses of the field of action. This manoeuvre he repeated several times before he descried any evidence of life within the house. At last an unmistakeable sound, heard so often in Florida, within the next three years, broke from the ruined dwelling,—it was the war-whoop!

"To your gun, Dick, and mind what I tell ye!" With this, rifle in hand, he commenced a series of dives beneath the embrasure's lintel;—but, for a while, no indians appeared. Five minutes, however, did not elapse before some jets of flame spirted from an unnoticed crack in the wall of the house, followed by several balls in the embrasure; and instantly, with a whoop, the remaining savages, stripped to their skins, and armed with guns and tomahawks, rushed towards the barricaded door.

"At'em, Dick,"—shouted the wrecker,—at'em as they run;—and blaze away with all seven barrels at the devils!"

Yet, rapid and careful as Mitchell had been throughout his earlier movements, all the shots on this occasion were unavailing against the indians, who, bounding like deer across the space between the house and tower, were soon beneath its walls, and of course entirely screened by them from the risk of bullets from the embrasures above. Neither Mitchell nor his slave dared ascend the lighthouse and shoot from the parapet; so that the volley from the windows only served to deceive the savages as to the number who might be hidden within the walls. But it was not long before the sound of blows at the door gave token of the indians' design and progress. All that could now be done for the preservation of life was to meet the savages, singly if possible, as they edged their way up the spiral staircase, and to be in advance of them either in firing or with the knife. Accordingly, Mitchell loaded all the weapons carefully, and ordered Dick to carry them, with an axe, a bag of balls, and a keg of powder, to the highest interior platform of the stairway.

It was an anxious time. For men who were not as familiar with life's risks on the surf of the Florida reef—a surf and reef that are as perilous as the savages whose land they guarded,—the half hour would have been insupportable before the blows ceased and the voices of the savages were heard rising through the tube of the tower. The indians were evidently in anxious and even angry deliberation. After awhile, all was still again. There were neither blows nor talk. What did it mean? What where they about? Why did they not come with a yell and a rush? Were they stealing, cat like, up the stairs? Should he descend to meet them? Could he safely revisit the embrasure and survey the field?

"No,"—said patience;—"wait!"

By this time the sun was sinking. Nearly an hour must have elapsed since the first cessation of noise, yet no sign of life or motion was discernible at the base of the tower or its neighborhood. Mitchell was quite as still as the enemy, while Dick, propped against the wall, sat with his lips pouting, and his eyes slowly opening and shutting, till, at last, the stolid negro fairly nodded with sleep!

Ever and anon the wrecker put his ear to the planks to listen if they conveyed the least creak of a footstep. At length a low grunt and a rapid sniffling of his nostrils aroused the sleeper, as Mitchell scented the odor of smoke.

The stratagem instantly flashed across his mind — Doubtful of the white man's numbers and of the success with which a winding stair might be ascended against an unknown and dangerous foe, the indians had fired the frame-work of the wooden steps!

"And now, Dick," whispered the weather-beaten sailor, "the worst's come to the worst at last. They're afeared to fight us, nigger, and we'er to be burnt alive! Do ye hear that?"

"Well, massa, what mus' we do to help it?"

"Nothing, Dick, nothin'; least-ways, that is to say, Dick, you aint to do nothin'. They aint a goin' to come up here, anyhow; that's sartin'; and another thing's just es sartin, which is, that I aint a goin' down stairs to them! Now, let's wait and see what'll turn up next. When you don't know what to do, Dick, never do nothin'—that's always my rule, and its a fool that don't foller it! Hold your tongue and go sleep agin."

And so, for quite a quarter of an hour, the imprisoned twain sat like statues, till the smoke began to pour up so densely that respiration became almost impossible. There was no escape for the vapor through the lantern. But this was quickly remedied; for, keeping his head within the screening summit of the tower, with a single circular sweep of his axe, Mitchell shivered the glasses and gave vent to the smoke. At the same time, he thrust the weapons and keg of powder on the external promenade gallery or balcony, which was guarded by an iron rail and a very thick oaken washboard at its base.

The want of sufficient draft for the smoke had hitherto prevented the fire from burning with the rapidity that might have been expected; but as soon as the lantern was gone, the crackling timbers below gave token that the fire was under full headway and the light-house converted into a chimney!

"And now I must *meet it;*" said Mitchell sharply, as he arose; "but do you set still, Dick, where you are, while I cut away the steps below for fifteen feet or so, and we'll have the platform above to lie down on, and be es safe es on a raft when the hull's foundered!"

A couple of leaps took the wrecker to his post below, and instantly his sturdy strokes with the axe were heard upon the splintering timbers. Standing above, he cut away step after step beneath him as he retreated upwards, pitching the untouched planks in the fire, and thus establishing a vacuum between the summit and the blazing mass in the base. It did not require much time for him to clear eight or ten feet of the tower, but unfortunately, the increased fire augmented the heat and smoke to such a degree, that he could no longer continue his work or remain within the tower. Indeed, our hero had already fought the element longer than he ought to have done. As he reached the platform, leaving four or five of the last steps still unhewn, he sank exhausted on the base of the screened balcony, but, luckily, as he fell to windward, the torrent of vapor that rushed up the tower was drifted away from him by the gale, leaving nothing but the pure sea wind for his refreshment. To this spot, the negro had already preceded him, and, stretched flat on his back, was invisible from the outside.

Yet hardly had Mitchell revived from his exhaustion, when he perceived that their danger was no longer from suffocation, but that the intense heat from the fuel below had kindled the dry fragments of the upper steps which he had been unable to cut away, and that the fiery tongues were already beginning to lick the edges of the boards. The flame was within eight feet of him, while by his side was the keg of powder!

"It's awful bad, boy, any way you look at it!" said the wrecker.

"Mighty awful, massa," echoed the negro.

"Hold on where you are, Dick, and don't show your black muzzle over the parapet."

"But what are you gwyne to do wid de powder, massa, when the fire gits up here, right 'long side ob us?"

"God knows, Dick, God knows! Pitch it over to the red-skins, perhaps—but not till the last moment;—never give powder to an ingin' till you can't help it."

11*

Meanwhile, the fiery serpent wound his spiral way up the remaining stairs, and began to lay its blazing head upon the platform.

"Now den, massa, pitch him over, pitch him over," said the slave with quick, anxious, nervous utterance,—pointing to the keg,—"pitch him over to the injins,—for God-a-mighty's sake."

"Hush, man, I tell ye! Lay still, don't stir for your life!" as he saw the flames begin to crawl and crackle in the direction of the powder. "Lay still, Dick, I say, like a man, till the last moment. One way or 'tother, 'twill soon be over,—for we've nothing to do but to leap over the wall, break our necks and be scalped,—or tumble into the tower and be burnt alive! Lay still, Dick, I say again, and take it like a man!"

But Dick, who had always obeyed his master implicitly in every emergency by sea and land, had never before encountered the double perils of fire and gunpowder. Although he remained quiet as long as ordinary flesh and blood would allow in such a trial, yet, at last, the nervousness of frail humanity began to get the mastery, till drawing himself up into the smallest possible space, and crawling to the remotest possible distance from the keg, he suddenly sprang to his feet on the edge of the parapet, clinging with a convulsive hysterical grasp to the iron rail of the guard.

He could not have been half a minute in this exposed posture before a ball through the head tumbled his corpse on the balcony!

"What's the use of it—what's the use of it;" muttered Mitchell, through his teeth, as he saw his slave fall. "Why, in the name of all the devils, didn't you lay still as I told ye?"

"Over with ye!" shouted the wrecker, at the top of his voice, as with a wild, sudden impulse—half passion half despair—he pushed the keg from him *towards the centre of the burning aperture,* and with closed eyes, grating teeth and clenched hands, held on to the bottom of the balcony, as he heard the heavy mass plunging downward through the tower, till with a mashing sound, it fell within the base.

He heard no more. He heard no explosion; he felt no concussion. How long, after the deafening sound that rent the air, he continued utterly insensible, I do not know. It may have been a few hours, or it may have been a whole day. The recovery from this profound stupor was gradual. At first, he seemed to be half awake, conscious of an oppressive difficulty in breathing, and after lying in this semi-torpor for a considerable time, he at last became fully aware of his position, though his muscles were entirely incapable of motion. He was thoroughly drenched with rain and chilled with cold, while the bright moon was shining over him from the mild winter sky of Florida.

It was long before Mitchell could divest himself of the idea that he had become drowsy while tending his lamps at night, and, falling asleep on the balcony, had become the victim of a dream whose horrid incidents slowly recurred and rose up like a dreadful tragedy in his memory. He looked around, and every vestige of the lantern was gone, while a black gulf yawned beside him, disclosing the whole of the scorched and riven interior. The ledge of the upper balcony, on which he rested, was all that remained except the walls of the tower!

He remembered Dick, and, as the first effort over his regained muscular control, put forth a hand to feel for the negro and thus assure himself of the truth or fiction of the drama. He touched the body—it was cold. He strove to rouse it,—it was rigid as iron. He crawled to listen for breath or a beating heart,—the foulest odors saluted his nostrils. It was corruption! His trance must have lasted over twenty-four hours.

Strange as were the scenes through which he had passed, the doubt that next bewildered him arose from *the conviction that it was impossible for him to be alive* after the explosion of the powder in the tower, or that the tower itself could have resisted the effect of so tremendous a discharge.

Rude as was the wrecker's mind, all these thoughts pressed upon or passed athwart it. What miracle had preserved him? Were such things possible? Was he alive, or was this—*death?*

He bit his arm to assure himself of existence; and in a moment the whole current of his thought was changed. He became a prey to the most horrible pangs of hunger and freaks of fancy, until by degrees, the world was again a blank to him and the wrecker fainted.

Mitchell had no distinct recollection of anything that occurred during the delirium which no doubt supervened when he was seized by the pangs of hunger. When the fresh sea wind revived him from the swoon, he found himself lying on the body of his dead menial, and at once crept back to his former lair on the ledge of the parapet. All craving of the stomach for food was gone, but a low fever had followed the chill and hunger. As the night wore on, clouds drifted up again from the sea, and for more than an hour before daylight, it rained in hard squalls so as to drench him thoroughly and subdue his blood.

At sunrise there was but a single line of saffron light on the horizon, in which the orb rested a few moments like a ball of fire, and then disappeared behind the lid of leaden clouds that covered the blackened sea like a pall. Athwart that streak, relieved against the sky, appeared the masts of several vessels skirting the reef. The love of life and hope of succor sprang once more strongly in his heart, but even had prudence permitted him to disclose his person or hoist a signal, the strangers were too distant to be reached by his lonely beacon. He remembers that, at this time, he was revolving in his mind the propriety of looking over the screen of the balcony, when a sudden languor and drowsiness stole over him, the result perhaps of his ebbing fever,—and he fell into a profound sleep.

It was mid-day before he awoke. The storm, portended by the dawn, had been swept away by a smart nor'-wester, and the sun shone sharply from the zenith. When he awoke this time it was not with the feeble consciousness of his first restoration. He stirred as from refreshing sleep, and though the sun had dried his raiment and almost scorched his skin, the weather-beaten sailor was too familiar with Floridian skies to be harmed by the burning rays.

Once more, therefore, in thorough possession of his mind though not of his bodily strength, Mitchell saw that his fate must soon be terminated by some decided act of his own. He was doubtless, safe from attack in his solitary and concealed perch, but his physical powers must soon yield to utter exhaustion unless he obtained water and nourishment. After a cautious examination of the neighborhood by peering over the barrier, he might satisfy himself whether the enemy was still on the island. He concluded moreover, that no one,—not even a Florida indian,—would imagine that a human being could remain suspended in mid-air on the top of that tower and *alive*, at least, forty-eight hours after such an explosion as must have occurred at its base. Nevertheless, he remained perfectly still for some time hearkening anxiously to every sound from land and sea. Nothing was borne to him that gave the slightest indication of a savage. At length he ventured to lift up his head and look towards the dwelling. A glance assured him that it was deserted, for it had been burnt since the catastrophe, and the whole of its blackened exterior was visible from his elevation. He searched the surrounding sands which had been beaten by the recent rains, but he could not detect the track of a human foot. As he cast his eyes towards the strait, in the direction of the main, he descried a canoe containing at least three persons crawling slowly from under the lee of the island, and passing towards Florida. It bore unquestionably, the remnant of his red-skinned tormentors!

Nor was his seaward view less cheering. A couple of miles from the landing, within full sight, so that he could distinctly discern the people walking her deck, a trim little schooner, under full sail, was steering southward!

It was the work of a moment to bind together, with his braces, a couple of ramrods from the muskets that still rested on the ledge, and to attach to them the shirt of which he stripped himself.

He was seen! Sail was shortened on the schooner, till under easy canvass, she approached the land as near as practicable; when backing her mainsail, she "laid to," and sent her boat ashore.

The excitement of hope and present rescue quickly aroused the torpid blood and benumbed limbs of the weather-beaten prisoner. Yet Mitchell did not start from his ledge till he saw the skiff dash through the breakers and come within hail. Then with a vigor that nothing but the joy of escape could have imparted, he sprang to the lightning rod that still clung to the wall, and gliding down it to the ground, ran to the beach and fell swooning in the bottom of the savior boat.

THE MISSISSIPPI.

Monarch of rivers in the wide domain
Where Freedom writes her signature in stars,
And bids her eagle bear the cheering scroll
To usher in the reign of peace and love,
Thou mighty Mississippi!—may my song
Swell with thy power, and though an humble rill,
Roll, like thy current, through the sea of time;
Bearing thy name, as tribute from my soul
Of fervent gratitude and holy praise,
To Him who poured thy multitude of waves.

Shadowed beneath those awful piles of stone,
Where Liberty has found a Pisgah height,
O'erlooking all the land she loves to bless,—
The jagged rocks and icy towers her guard,
Whose splintered summits seize the warring clouds,
And roll them, broken, like a host o'erthrown,
Adown the mountains' side, scattering their wealth
Of powdered pearl and liquid diamond-drops,—
There is thy source,—great River of the West!

Slowly, like youthful Titan gathering strength
To war with heaven and win himself a name,
The stream moves onward through the dark ravines,
Rending the roots of overarching trees
To form its narrow channel, where the star
That fain would bathe its beauty in the wave,
With lover's glance steals, trembling, through the leaves
That veil the waters with a vestal's care:—
And few of human form have ventured there
Save the swart savage in his bark canoe.

But now it deepens, rushes, struggles on;
Like goaded warhorse, bounding o'er the foe,
It clears the rocks it may not spurn aside,
Leaping, as Curtius leaped, adown the gulf,—
And rising, like Antæus, from the fall,
Its course majestic through the land pursues,
And the broad river o'er the valley reigns!

It reigns alone. The tributary streams
Are humble vassals, yielding to the sway;
And when the wild Missouri fain would join
A rival in the race—as Jacob seized
On his red brother's birthright, even so
The swelling Mississippi grasps that wave,
And, re-baptizing, makes the waters one.

It reigns alone—and earth the sceptre feels:
Her ancient trees are bowed beneath the wave,
Or, rent like reeds before the whirlwind's swoop,
Toss on the bosom of the maddened flood
A floating forest, till the waters, calmed,
Like slumbering anaconda gorged with prey,
Open a haven to the moving mass
Or form an island in the vast abyss.

It reigns alone. Old Nile would ne'er bedew
The lands it blesses with its fertile tide.
Even sacred Ganges joined with Egypt's flood
Would shrink beside this wonder of the West!
Ay, gather Europe's royal rivers all—
The snow-swelled Neva, with an Empire's weight
On her broad breast, she yet may overwhelm;
Dark Danube, hurrying, as by foe pursued
Through shaggy forests and by palace walls
To hide its terrors in a sea of gloom;
The castled Rhine, whose vine-crowned waters flow
The fount of fable and the source of song;
The rushing Rhone, in whose cerulean depths
The loving sky seems wedded with the wave;
The yellow Tiber, choked with Roman spoils,
A dying miser shrinking 'neath his gold;
And Seine, where fashion glasses fairest forms;

And Thames, that bears the riches of the world:—
Gather their waters in one ocean mass,—
Our Mississippi, rolling proudly on,
Would sweep them from his path, or swallow up,
Like Aaron's rod, these streams of fame and song!

And thus the peoples, from the many lands,
Where these old streams are household memories,
Mingle beside our River, and are one;
And join to swell the strength of freedom's tide,
That from the fount of truth is flowing on
To sweep earth's thousand tyrannies away.

How wise, how wonderful the works of God!
And hallowed by His goodness, all are good.
The creeping glow-worm—the careering sun
Are kindled from the effluence of His light.
The ocean and the acorn-cup are filled
By gushings from the fountain of His love.
He poured the Mississippi's torrent forth
And heaved its tide above the trembling land—
Grand type, how freedom lifts the citizen
Above the *subject* masses of the world—
And marked the limits it may never pass.
Trust in His promises and bless His power
Ye dwellers on its banks, and be at peace!

And ye, whose way is on this warrior wave,
When the swollen waters heave with ocean's might,
And storms and darkness close the gate of heaven,
And the frail bark, fire-driven, bounds quivering on
As though it rent the iron shroud of night
And struggled with the demons of the flood—
Fear not—if Christ be with ye in the boat:
Lean on His pitying breast in faith and prayer
And rest,—His arm of love is strong to save.

Great source of being, beauty, light and love!
Creator, Lord: the waters worship thee!
Ere thy creative smile had sown the flowers,
Ere the glad hills leaped upward, or the earth,
With swelling bosom, waited for her child;
Before eternal Love had lit the sun
Or time had traced his dial-plate in stars,
The joyful anthem of the waters flowed;—
And Chaos like a frightened felon fled,
While on the deep the Holy Spirit moved.

And evermore the deep has worshipped God;
And bards and prophets tune their mystic lyres
While listening to the music of the floods.
Oh! could I catch the harmony of sounds,

As borne on dewy wings they float to heaven,
And blend their meaning with my closing strain!

Hark! as a reed-harp thrilled by whispering winds,
Or Naiad murmurs from a pearl-lipped shell
It comes,—the melody of many waves!
And loud, with freedom's world awakening note,
"Father of Waters,"—thine to lead the choir
And shout the triumphs of the toiling hand,
In reverent hope obeying God's behest—
"Subdue the earth—'tis man's dominion given:"
And now, what happy voices swell the strain!
The pure sweet fountain's chant of heaven's bliss;
The chorus of the rills is household love;
The rivers roll their songs of social joy;
And ocean's organ tones are sounding on
The holy anthem—peace and brotherhood
Among the nations—and "good will to men"—
When CHRIST shall rule the world in righteousness.

"Father of Waters,"—whose far-reaching arm
Binds West to East like brothers heart to heart,
And, through thy bounteous tributary streams,
Our Country's healthful arteries of life,
Dost send, on either hand, thy blessings free,
Alike to Southern gulf and Northern lake,

THE MISSISSIPPI.

Great river of America for all:—
Our Country lifts thy waters to her lip,
In reverent thankfulness and patriot hope,
As pledge of peace and bond of unity,—
And prays that God, who made our fathers free,
And crowned them with a diadem of stars,
One name encircling all—"OUR WASHINGTON;"—
Would pardon all our sins and keep us one;
In heart and name, in law and language one;
To worship Him and do His will as one,—
Till earth's great day of peace and rest shall come.

PHILADELPHIA, *January*, 1864.

WOMEN OF SEVENTY-SIX.

A MATRON of Philadelphia, writing in June, 1780, thus expresses the general sentiments of American women. "Our ambition is kindled by the fame of those heroines of antiquity, who have rendered their sex illustrious. I glory in all that which woman has done, great and commendable. I call to mind with enthusiasm and admiration, all those acts of courage, constancy and patriotism, which history has transmitted to us. The people, chosen of heaven—preserved from destruction by the virtue, zeal and resolution of Deborah, of Judith, and of Esther! The fortitude of the mother of the Maccabees, in giving up her sons to die before her eyes; Rome saved from the fury of a victorious enemy by the efforts of Volumnia and other Roman ladies; so many famous sieges, where the women have been seen, forgetting the weakness of their sex, building new walls, digging trenches with their feeble hands, furnishing arms to their defenders; they themselves darting the missile weapons on the enemy, resigning the ornaments of their apparel and their fortunes to fill the public treasury, and hasten the deliverance of their country; burying themselves under its ruins, throwing themselves into the flames, rather than submit to the disgrace of humiliation before a proud enemy.

"Born for liberty, we associate ourselves with the grandeur of those sovereigns, cherished and revered, who have held with so much dignity the sceptres of the greatest states: the Matildas, the Elizabeths, the Maries, the Catherines, who have extended the empire of liberty, and, contented to reign by sweetness and justice, have broken the chains of slavery forged by tyrants in times of ignorance and barbarity. The Spanish women—do they not make, at this moment, the most patriotic sacrifices to increase the means of victory in the hands of their sovereign. He is a friend to the French nation. They are our allies. We call to mind, doubly interested, that it was a French maid who kindled up among her fellow citizens the flame of patriotism, buried under long misfortunes; it was the maid of Orleans who drove from the kingdom of France the ancestors of those same British whose odious yoke we have just shaken off, and whom it is necessary that we drive from this continent."

A kindred spirit showed itself in two Southern women, Mrs. Barnett and her daughter—whose good deeds no history has recorded Susannah Barnett was born in Mecklenberg county, N. C. in 1761 She described the great gathering of the people of Charlotte in May, 1775, as "the day of the throwing up of hats." The battle of Lexington had taken place a month before, and the news had just come in hand-bills by express. *Then* there was no sectional feeling; the same sentiment pervaded the masses North and South. In 1780, when, after the fall of Charleston, South Carolina, as Gen. Greene said, was "cut off from the Union like the tail of a snake," Susannah and her family gave all possible help to the flying patriots, hastening to form their camp at Clem's Branch.

One day a dusty, travel-weary party of fugitives, arrived at the large, three story log-house, occupied by John Barnett, and craved hospitality. It was GENERAL SUMTER and his family. His wife, a cripple from infancy, was placed on a feather bed on horseback, with a negro woman behind to hold her on. She had fallen off several times, and her face was black with bruises. Her son Tom, a boy of sixteen, was with them; and a young woman, their housekeeper, named Nancy Davis. She told their kind hosts how the British and Tories had come to Sumter's house; how she had locked up every thing and flung the keys among the grass in the yard; but it availed nothing: the enemy fired the house, and all was soon a pile of ashes. General Sumter's family had escaped with difficulty. They were warmly welcomed, and remained at Barnett's more than a month.

After the slaughter of Buford's men at the Waxhaws, the wounded were brought to the house; and Susannah aided her mother in feeding six men who had but two arms among them. Her father and two brothers were at the battle of Hanging Rock. Mrs. Barnett went to Charlotte, to obtain tidings of their fate; and the wounded were brought to the place. On the morning of the 19th August, 1780, the road was full of soldiers and fugitives making their way thither. General Sumter, with one or two of his aids, rode up to Mr. Barnett's house, dismounted, and entered. "Mrs. Barnett," he said, "do let us have something to eat, if only a piece of johnny cake and a cup of milk." The matron answered, "General, I have fed more than fifty men this morning; but I'll try." Some provision had been laid by for the family: it was then produced and set out for General Sumter. While eating, he turned to Susannah, and said; "Miss Sukey, please to arrange my hair; but never mind combing it; it is so tangled." His hair was long, and rather light colored. The young lady, during his repast, clubbed it as well as she could, tangled as it was. In reply to Mrs. Barnett's enquiry, how it was that the American soldiers and patriots were all flying? Sumter said: "It was indeed a surprise; (alluding to the memorable surprise on Fishing Creek,) the enemy crossed the creek before we knew of it, and was in the midst of the camp. I was in the marquée, asleep at the time, and was carried out at the back part, and mounted a horse that stood ready. But it was soon shot down under me. I obtained the horse I now have, not a very good one to be sure, and the saddle rather the worse for wear. So I am here. You see I have lost my cocked hat and fine feathers; but this old hat, torn in the rim as it is, has sheltered my head from the burning sun: it was the gift of a noble soldier." With many thanks for his breakfast, and a hearty shaking of hands, the General then mounted his horse, and went on his way to Charlotte.

Another of the refugees sheltered in this hospitable home, was Walter Brown, father of the distinguished divine, Dr. John Brown. He and his family, after they had been plundered of every thing, were entertained some time at Barnett's. At length, came news that the British were advancing on Charlotte.

Mrs. Barnett, standing at her door and looking anxiously down the road, perceived some one approaching. "Sukey and Jenny Brown," she cried, addressing her own child, and the pretty daughter of her guest—"run out to the road and enquire the news."

The traveller was a lad on a sorely jaded horse; his face was very long and sunburnt. Susannah asked him whence he came.

"From the Waxhaws," was his reply.

"Do you know Major Crawford?"

"To be sure I do; he is my uncle."

"And who are you?"

"My name is ANDREW JACKSON."

"What is the news about the British?"

"They are on their way to Charlotte."

"What are you doing down there?"

"Why, we are popping them occasionally."

The long slender face of the stripling lighted up with a pleasant smile, and bowing with the ease and grace of a polished gentleman, he said: "Good morning, ladies," and passed on. As he went by the house, Mrs. Barnett had a full view of his sallow cheeks and lanthorn visage, and laughed heartily when she heard of his remark about "popping" the enemy.

"Little Andy," as young Jackson was called, was followed by an advance of some three hundred men under the command of Colonel Davie, who had a skirmish with the British by night at Wahab's, in the Waxhaw settlement. Jack Barnett, Susannah's brother, was of this party. The British carried their wounded to the house of Thomas Spratt, who, being wounded himself, was removed to his kitchen.

It was here that Major Frazer, of the British army, died; while Cornwallis and Rawdon both stood by his bed, and averred with lifted hands, that "he was one of the best officers who had crossed the ocean." A Scotch physician who was in attendance, afterwards went into the kitchen to examine Mr. Spratt.

"What is the matter with you maun?" he asked.

"I have a fever." The physician felt his pulse, and exclaimed —

"Why, maun, you are wounded!"

"And what if I am!" said the patient.

"Ah! I am fearfu' you have been fighting against your lawfu' sovereign, King George!"

"I have been fighting for my country, and if I was well, I would do it again," replied Spratt.

"Well, well, you are a brave soldier, and I'll dress your wounds for you," said the Scotchman; and he did so, attending upon him as long as the British troops occupied the house.

These unbidden guests took from Spratt, over a hundred head of cattle, hogs, &c.

Mr. Barnett's house was also plundered. When one of his horses was brought up and bridled for the use of a British soldier, Mrs. Barnett walked up and pulled off the bridle. Some of the men threatened to kill her. "You can do so," she answered: "I am in your power, but you will be punished for it." Seeing a crock of milk which the intruders had brought from her cellar, she passed near and pushed it over with her foot. The infuriated soldiers rushed at her, swearing they would cut her to pieces. "Do, if you dare!" said she, with an air of haughty defiance. "You will be shot at from every bush in the country." They did not molest her, but went away without the horse.

Susannah was married to George Smart, in 1795. She related anecdotes of two United States' Presidents; Andrew Jackson, and "little Jamie Polk" who used to run along the road, with his breeches rolled up to his knees. This worthy matron, when informed that a political meeting had been held in York District, South Carolina, to advocate the secession of South Carolina from the Union, said: "The North and South stood shoulder to shoulder in the times of '76. We should settle our family bickerings at all times by a compromise."

SONNET.

On the Field of Antietam,
Sept. 25, 1862.

As if with Autumn's leaves the failing year
   Too soon these wasted hills had covered o'er
   The soil is crimsoned: but, of human gore,
On nearer sight these deeper dyes appear!
Oh, what a dread Aceldama is here
   Of those the treach'rous steel that dared to draw,
   And those, asserting Right, avenging Law,
Who nobly fell in duty's high career!
As lustrous amber meaner things contains,
   So glory's field embosoms foes unjust
   Who found a brotherhood foresworn, in dust:
But the pure ichor from the patriot's veins,
   How hath it changed, in one triumphant day,
Antietam's name unnamed to Fame's proud word for aye.

DRUM HEAD NOTES

FROM THE CAMP AND FIELD.*

Four Locks on the Ches. and Ohio Canal,
October 31st, 1862.

It is now about day-break, half past five o'clock. The stars are still bright, though light from a superior source is beginning to be visible. The sun rises here on the Virginia side of the river. In Williamsport, the sun sets on the Virginia side. This is owing to the crooked course of the Potomac, which doubles upon itself at this point, and throws a narrow neck of Maryland soil forward into Virginia. Our present station is at a point on the Canal, where a store, a warehouse, a few scattered dwellings, and

---

* The fragments of correspondence published under the above title, taken from such private letters as have been preserved and could be hastily collected, are not in any sense to be understood as a narration of events. On the contrary, all details of important military movements with which the writer was connected, were expressly requested by him to be omitted. If this has not in all cases been carefully done, it is because he had no opportunity either of selection or of revision.

a distillery, are all generalized as the "Four Locks." The locks themselves, like almost everything else belonging to this Canal, are well built, and very creditable to the State. As an investment, it has never paid, although it cost the State upwards of fifteen millions. * * * * Our regiment is now guarding the fords of the river, and the culverts and draw-bridges of the canal, for a front of over five miles, from above McCoy's Ferry to below Dam No. 5. McCoy's Ferry is where Stuart crossed the Potomac, and then the Canal, through a culvert beneath it To see the precautions taken to prevent another similar raid through the same place, would remind one of the old saying, about "locking the stable door," etc. As I went up the Canal with the Adjutant, and a citizen named Hazlett, to visit McCoy's Ferry and the upper posts, the moon shone brightly upon the Canal with its graceful curves, the windings of the river, the steep heights on the Virginia side, and the gigantic rocks on this side at intervals smoothing off into scarped precipices like the palisades on the Hudson; there was a fascination too in the romantic border tales of Hazlett, who, like many of the citizens of this part of the State, had from the first taken a deep personal interest in the war, and no little actual share in it, as guide, scout, and sometimes as a bush-fighter. The excursion had just enough of danger in it to make it a little exciting. I was cautioned by

General Vinton, that the rebels would probably make a dash that night, to capture some of our pickets, as a reprisal for the capture of several of theirs a night or two before, by Fiery's Maryland cavalry. All was quiet, however, through the night.

Maryland Heights, *Dec.* 23*d*.

We marched on Sunday, (21st,) from Williamsport to Sharpsburg, twelve miles. Yesterday, from Sharpsburg here, about as many more. Sunday was a cold day, the streams were ice, the wind piercing. * * * * * * About four miles from Williamsport, we passed on our left, St. James' College, of which I had a fine view. The country in the vicinity, and in fact nearly along our entire march, in places, had been stripped of fencing, etc. by troops. On approaching the battle field of Antietam, we halted, made fires and coffee; and began to see balls, fragments of exploded shell, graves, etc. From this place to Sharpsburg, the turnpike crosses directly through the scene of some of the heaviest fighting, marks of which were apparent for almost every step of the two or three miles. The fences on each side, where they had been left standing, were riddled with balls, some striking fair and going through, others hitting obliquely and tearing off splinters. Trees were perforated, their branches cut and swinging down. Long trenches of dead, buried in ranks, appeared by the road side. Some single graves were upturned, showing that their inmates had been removed. Occasionally rude head boards showed in pencil marks the name, regiment and company. The horses had not been removed or even covered. Their attitude generally was as if they had stiffened in the act of struggling to get up. Near Sharpsburg, a little "Dunkard" church in the woods, had at least fifty cannon shot and shell through roof and wall; yet the church was standing, and capable of being repaired. All the houses along each side the road, had been pierced with shot or shell. The majority of the houses in Sharpsburg bore similar marks. Of the four churches in the town, Alexander's Battery occupied one, (when we arrived,) the Eighth Maryland Regiment another, our regiment filled the third with five companies, and I went with the balance of the regiment to the remaining one, the Episcopal church. On arriving there, I found every sash taken from the windows. Some of the men, without my knowledge, cut a hole in the floor to build a fire on the ground beneath, but the smoke was so uncomfortable that they soon put it out. I was about lying down on the platform under the pulpit, but before arranging my blankets, I thought I would examine the place with a light, having heard that the church had been occupied as a hospital for wounded rebels. A brief inspection satisfied me that it was really no place to sleep in, being littered with dirty rags, bloody bandages, old poultices, refuse lint, and all the offal of a hospital. I did not see any vermin, but was willing after what I did see, to take them on trust. I then made my head-quarters on the ground outside the church, had a rousing fire built, and slept two or three hours by snatches, getting up every once in a while to warm. The men, after grumbling a little at first, finally made themselves as jolly as possible, and the talk around the bivouac fires was highly amusing. Daylight next morning revealed to us, that we had spent the long, cold night of the 21st December in a grave-yard, peopled mainly by the Southern wounded from the field of Antietam. In some places, where too thin a covering of earth had been disturbed by dogs or hogs, a protruding foot, or hand, made a mournful monument above the nameless grave. With the levity and bad taste too common among soldiers, ghastly jokes were being made over this touching spectacle—I thought of my old school-mates, college friends, and of the hands which in better, happier days, I had pressed in cordial intimacy. I thought too of the quaint inscription which I read on the tomb of Shakespeare, at Stratford on Avon:

> "Good friend, for Jesus' sake forbeare
> To dig the dust encloased here;
> Blest be the man that spares my bones,
> And curs't be he that moves these stones."

I ordered these gloomy relics to be respectfully covered with the frozen clods. I was informed that the church had only been evacuted as a hospital some two weeks before.

Although the sky lowered before the sun went down, and snow fell during the night, the next day (Monday 22d) was clear, and by comparison mild. From Sharpsburg to the mouth of the Antietam, the havoc of battle continued visible along the road. Here we commenced ascending the mountain, the men began to sweat under their knapsacks, the artillery horses labored as if they thought the term "Light Battery," a misnomer, the wagon mules behind them in mute protest; the defile narrowed, precipices yawned, the road clung to the scarped mountain side; dense pine thickets vainly strove to hide awful gulfs; bursts of poetic scenery broke from mountain, valley, gorge and river, like a song of joy. I saw again the Simplon, the Rhine, the Simmering Alps, Mount Washington, all in miniature. In fact, as I rode along, sometimes ahead of the regiment, I became so absorbed in contemplation and retrospection, that I almost imagined myself a lonely traveller, a careless tourist among the tranquil scenes of nature. The sharp crack of a minie rifle from a picket on the river bank, many hundred feet below, broke into one of these reveries, and I then noticed the branches of pine and fir cut down and piled on the side of the road on the crest of the heights, as a mask for sharp-shooters, when pickets exchange shots across the river.

Maryland Heights, *Dec. 28th.*

The summit of this mountain, (a part of the Blue Ridge,) is 1200 feet above the river. Loudon Heights is the continuation across the river; that is, the Potomac cuts the mountain in two,—Maryland Heights on this side, Loudon on the other. The Shenandoah again divides Loudon from Bolivar Heights, and Bolivar looks across the Potomac at Maryland Heights. In the apex of the angle, made by the confluence, shudders the God-forsaken, man-destroyed village of Harpers Ferry. The ruins of the Government works, armories, etc. are a brickyard. Churches have become hospitals,—gardens and pleasure grounds, grave-yards,—private residences, barracks and stables. Most of the inhabitants have fled. Of the few old settlers who remain, some have a scared and anxious look. Only nature is as calm and magnificent as ever; the confronting Heights survey each other blandly, with arms folded in placid repose; the Potomac and Shenandoah have not yet heard of the dissolution of the Union, and swear by all their commingling waters that—they "don't see it neither." Just as I was about rounding off that last sentence rhetorically, I was interrupted by a mighty noise, laid down my pen, went out of my tent to see what was the matter, came back and wound up as above. Something less than forty mules and horses, hitched to a huge Columbiad, came scratching, puffing and digging up the mountain, cheered by the outcries of some hundred or two men, using prolongs or heavy ropes, now tugging up with might and main, now pulling back as she plunges down a descent in the road, passed directly in front of my tent, and were creaking, thundering, snorting, and shouting up to a naval battery of heavy Dahlgren guns, mounted in sand bag embrasures directly over our heads, some six hundred feet up.

It is about eleven o'clock at night. The Great Bear is standing rampant on the end of his tail. Orion glitters fiercely over Maryland Heights. The Pleiades have reached the zenith, and seem, as they look down upon the two rivers babbling innocently as they meet beneath, to be weeping, not so much for the lost sister above, as for the divided sisters below. Mars and a half moon are keeping company to-night; they have long since crossed the river, and got into the Southern Confederacy, glaring in the Southern sky, like a token of war and division. And there are still more striking omens of hostility below. The mountain upon whose side we are encamped, is rapidly becoming another Ehrenbrestein; the Potomac, is being made another Rhine.

"IN THE FIELD."
ROWLESBURG, PRESTON CO., VA.
April 30*th*, 1863.

From Altamont to Oakland, we proceeded through the "Glades," leaving the former place a little before daybreak. Part of the way, I walked ahead of the train, with the advance guard,—part of the way, I rode on the locomotive. Tracks of the rebels were discernible at intervals, one or two small bridges burned and repaired; telegraph wires cut, etc. Just before sunrise, I noticed a landscape which seemed the very original of Rosa Bonheur's "Morning in the Highlands." A group of small, shaggy, short-horned mountain cattle was just in the act of making up its mind that day was breaking, some had arisen and commenced to graze—others were still lying as they had reposed all night, the dew glistening on their hair. Arriving at Oakland, about six A. M., we were met by some citizens, full of what the rebels had been doing in their hitherto "unknown to fame" locality. * * * * * We left Oakland in a rain storm, in the very lightest marching order, all our knapsacks being left behind. Two or three miles out, we came to a stream, over which the rebels had burned a bridge the day before. The men walked over on a plank bridge which we built ourselves, the materials being at hand, as we crossed by a saw-mill. We unloaded our wagons containing hospital stores and surgical instruments, camp-kettles and mess-pans, forage and ammunition; and we, who were mounted, forded the stream, and a most difficult ford it was. The creek (named Youghiogheny) was swollen, and the banks steep and miry. The wagons had to be hauled through by the men. After this crossing, Colonel Webster threw out an advance guard, with the closest preparations against surprise on any side; some struck the line of the rail road, and marched along it ten miles to Cranberry Summit. The scenery was wild and interesting. The line between Maryland and Virginia, is marked by a small monument of limestone, having on one side the letter "M," and on the other the letter "V." We found the little town of Cranberry in a state of intense excitement. It had been visited the day previous by rebel cavalry. The citizens and a few soldiers had a skirmish with them. The rebels were too strong for them, and took the place—robbed the stores of their entire stock of goods, and stole all the available horses. Left Cranberry about seven, P. M , "in thunder, lightning, and in rain," and then made the most wearying, harrassing, forced march we have made yet; and thirteen miles further on, to "Number 72," a water station on the rail road. We did not follow the track, but took the "dirt-road," and it was certainly the dirtiest dirt-road ever travelled. Narrow, steep, out of repair, stony, muddy, slippery, full of sloughs, crossed and recrossed by creeks, such as Salt Lick, through which the men waded a dozen times, nearly waist deep, up and down mountain sides, along precipices, through gloomy gorges, from the very bottom of which gigantic hemlocks lifted up their solemn branches amid moss-covered piles of prostrate timber which had died and fallen in this primeval mountain forest,—centuries, perhaps, ago. Sometimes through the rain, a smothered moonlight would give us a glimpse of the rail road, passing through a monstrous cut, hundreds of feet below us It was in this way, that we crossed over Rodemar's Tunnel, ascending and descending the mountain, under which the rail road has burrowed.

May 1*st.*

General Kenly passed up the road this morning with several heavy trains and —— thousand men. As he started from this station, the brigade band struck up a tune, every note of which was reverberated from the mountains on either side of Cheat River. The effect was rapturously enchanting, as chord after chord came echoing back, the air for miles around seeming to swell and palpitate with mysterious, unearthly strains and harmonies, like those with which Ariel followed the wizard wand of Prospero. I cannot give the faintest approach to an appreciative idea of this Titanic concert.

I can only say that to hear once more the Alleghanies unite as they did this morning, their solemn voices, in a monster Union chorus, I would freely give six months service to my country, and consider myself rewarded. Perhaps the most peculiar effect was in the critical analysis, and discriminating musical taste, which the mountains evinced, showing that amidst the lore they had gathered in their "awful age," they have not neglected the cultivation of the fine arts. While one mountain, close at hand, would promptly repeat the air, another further off would chime in deliberately with the tenor; and others, miles away, with magnificent independence, ignored everything but the basso profundo, solemnly muttering, as if to themselves, long after every other mountain voice had ceased. Surely, I thought, such majestic music has never been heard since the stars shouted for joy in the morning of creation. * * * *

May 2d, 9 P. M.

I have seen three moon-rises to-night. I first saw a rising "large and slow" over the heights which form the eastern range of the mountain barrier that closely shuts us in upon every side. Two watch fires of our pickets were gleaming upon the summit of this height. Suddenly the trees between them were thrown into distinct outline, by the atmospheric illumination, which heralded the moon's approach, and then the "completed moon" herself gradually measured her diameter upon the trees, seeming to cover about half their height. This would make the *apparent* diameter of the moon about thirty feet. I was contemplating this spectacle in company with the Colonel and Major, and so interesting was it, that we caused the performance to be twice encored by approaching the mountain. On my way down, I noticed by the side of the path, a stain of blood upon a flat stone. Looking around, I saw bullet marks upon the trees. This was the spot where the rebels, who had dismounted and left their horses some distance back, received and returned the fire of the Union defenders of this place on last Sunday. Our people, (Sixth Virginia Volunteers,) were firing from behind the embankment of the rail road, just at the bridge, and with considerable effect. At the same time another demonstration was made by the rebels from the heights on the other side of the river. Both attempts, as I have said, were repulsed.

Bolivar Heights, *May 17th*, 1863.

From Rowlesburg to Amblersburg, or No. 72, we retraced our line of march on the rail road, going up the Salt Lick valley, and of course looking with interest upon the various objects which had attracted our attention before. From Oakland to Altamont, we passed again

14*

through the "Glades," the spacious heaths or moors which form the table-land at the crown of the Alleghanies. Here the streams are sluggish, winding through brakes, widening into ponds, or draining through morasses The shrill chorus of frogs pierced sharply through the din and rumble of our heavy trains. Here, on the ample crest of this continental plateau, might be concentrated into two vast, opposing camps, all the armed men now distributed throughout the whole theatre of war; and here a million of men might join battle, finding spacious plains for battalions to manœuvre, and for cavalry to charge in, finding commanding positions on the tops of gently sloping mounds for batteries to play from, and finding thickets, brakes and skirts of forest, for light infantry and riflemen to skirmish. The descent of the steep grade down the eastern slope of the Alleghanies from Altamont to Piedmont, rushing around sharp curves, clinging to the scarped sides of precipices where a pale star-light revealed black gulfs and chasms out of whose abysses rank after rank of gloomy hemlock rose in almost vertical ascent until the topmost boughs of the loftiest came nearly up to our level—was one of the most thrilling and exciting experiences of my life. I could not but feel a sense of awful peril, not so much on my own personal account, as on that of the entire regiment, distributed among three trains following each other in quick succession down the declivity. There was in fact greater actual danger on our ascent three weeks ago. The rebels had torn up the track at Altamont the day before. We were on the first train that went up, and part of the way I was riding with Colonel Webster on the engine, part of the way in an iron powder car next to the tender. Yet we scarcely felt at that time any other emotion than one of excitement at the prospect of meeting a supposed enemy. I must confess that I am much more afraid of the law of gravitation than I am of rebel bushwhackers.

Arriving safely at Piedmont, a curious sight it was to see the accumulation of tonnage trains, blowing off steam from their huge mammoth engines, drawn up abreast on twenty parallel side tracks, all waiting for us to come down, so that they might make the ascent. Here, our three trains were united into one enormous train of twenty-eight or nine cars. As we backed and filled, by the light of lanterns, amid all this complication of tracks to accomplish this result, it seemed a mystery how we we were to be got out. Once fairly started, I bid the scenery (which by the way had gone fairly to bed, and was invisible) good night, and slept to New Creek. By the time we reached the beautiful country about the South Branch of the Potomac, it was broad daylight. From where we first struck the head-waters of the Potomac, we had seen this pretty mountain stream gradually widen, as each successive tributary poured in its waters. And when it was swollen by the greater volume of the South Branch, it began to assume something of the character of a national river, worthy to divide *States*, but not *Empires*. Crossing the rail road bridge over the South Branch, a rich view of the meadows and green bottom lands of this beautiful Hampshire valley opened up a vista on our right. The greater forwardness of vegetation made our descent the more apparent. Soon after, we crossed the bridge over "Little Capon," and then for miles our huge train writhing and twisting its tortuous course, as the track followed the constantly recurring horse shoe bends and curves of the river; the roofs of the cars tiled with men whose bright arms flashed in the morning sun; suggested the fancy of some huge Python of antique myth, glittering with burnished scales, its flaming crest threateningly erect, swiftly coiling its way along, with "many a fold voluminous and vast." The arts of peace and the art of war, have made some progress since such fables were sung by poets, and taught by priests. The great captains and conquerors of ancient times were respectable enough in their day; but here, I thought, is a little regiment which could get off of these cars with its Springfield rifles, form line of battle in two ranks against any Macedonian phalanx with its hedge-hog formation of sixteen deep. with levelled spears sixteen feet long, and before it had used six out of its sixty rounds of cartridges, could put to flight the army with which Alexander the Great conquered the world, and speedily dry that hero's tears, at having no more worlds to conquer. But neither Macedonian phalanx, nor Roman legion, nor Carthagenian cuneus, appeared in force to contest our progress, except in imagination. It is "when Greek meets Greek, then comes the tug of war." Our arms are to be used against men having similar arms, as expert in their use, as determined to conquer, perhaps as confident of their cause, as ourselves.

* * * * * *

Instead of wondering at the reverses which our army in Eastern Virginia has met since the beginning of this war, the surprise with me is, that they have not been greater. Had the seat of war been in Massachusetts or Vermont,—had Lee and Stonewall Jackson been in command of an invading army of rebels there, I am satisfied that they would have been worse whipped than Banks or Pope was. Genius, courage, and discipline avail much in war, but timely and correct information is indispensable to success. To obtain this, a General, of course, makes every effort—spies, prisoners, deserters, signals, reconnoisances—no means known to the art of war is unemployed; and yet, a friendly population is worth all the rest put together. This advantage, the rebels in

Eastern Virginia have had from the start, and still have over us, but in a constantly decreasing degree.

Still, our Eastern Virginia campaigns have not been unsuccessful. They have resulted in putting *hors du combat*, many thousands of armed rebels. True, we have lost as many men, but we can better spare them. As to military operations elsewhere, I think it may be affirmed without fear of successful contradiction, that the scale of success largely preponderates towards the Union side. In the West, we have never met with a single conspicuous reverse, nor one humiliating disaster. We have on the contrary, gained naval and military successes in that theatre, eclipsing in brilliancy the most famous exploits of ancient or modern heroism. And if our cause is encouraging at home, it is daily gaining ground abroad, and fast becoming recognized everywhere as the cause of civilization and progress.

May 25th, (Monday in Whitsun Week.)

The weather for a few days past has been sultry, murky, hazy; sun setting copper-red, behind a brazen bank of mist—horned moon glaring awhile and then swallowed up in the thick air—no breeze stirring even on high points—extraordinary, portentous—boding earthquakes, wars, and rumors of wars. Last night high wind from south-east—moist wind from ocean—a Whitsuntide "mighty rushing wind," with real tongues of flame visible across the river, the woods on Maryland Heights being on fire, throwing a broad flash across the Potomac, now at its lowest, complaining audibly at night to its rock and grass islands, of its poverty of waters. Whitsuntide wind smiting our camp till its canvas shivers like an agitated conscience — Pentecostal flames illuminating it meanwhile.

May 29*th*.

Lo! from the top of Loudon Heights, that guerilla-infested, rocky promontory, that shoulders against the Potomac, on Wednesday morning, I looked down and saw a bustle of men over the site of the old encampment of the 1st Maryland on Bolivar. Thank heaven, Kenly has come back from Western Virginia with the rest of the Brigade. Like Balaam, the son of Peor, I could have exclaimed—"From the top of the rocks I see him, and from the hills I behold him. How blessed are thy tents, O Israel! and thy tabernacles, O Jacob!" Although, Israel's tents were not then up, nor indeed as yet visible at all, not having been brought up from the depot The tabernacle of Jacob, however, could be seen just beginning to go up, on the camp of the 8th Maryland Regiment.

MARYLAND HEIGHTS, *June* 14*th*.

The evening is calm and starlight, constellations walk their round, mountains sit in state, the two rivers roar at each other, frogs croak, and whippoorwills pipe, much as they used to do in the olden time when these ruined arsenals were vocal with the hum of human industry, and when gentlemen who have been firing guns at each other to-day within sight of our camp, sipped fraternal juleps together on summer balconies. The air which for several days past has been heavy and thick with rumor; to-day, crystallized with unmistakeable cannonading, which from our elevated position, we could both hear and see—"Night" here, as often before, "separated the combatants." If reports which reach us as to the result of to-day's business be true, it is not unlikely that the eloquent speakers in the batteries on Maryland Heights will have the floor to-morrow. These are the batteries, and these are the Heights, which it is our business here to support and defend. For my own part, I regard myself as fortunate in being so placed as to participate in the defence of my own soil. * * * * * *

CAMP OF FIRST ARMY CORPS, NEAR
PETERSVILLE, MD., *July* 17*th*.

The campaign may be said to have ended with the retreat of the rebel army across the Potomac. After a brief interval which is being employed in resting men and animals, re-clothing and re-fitting generally, a new campaign will doubtless open on the other side of the river. Ever since the defeat of Milroy, at Winchester, on the 13th June, we have either been drawn up in line of battle, or making forced marches, most of them within sound of cannon, or sleeping on our arms, ready to march, or fight at tap of drum. * * * * During these few weeks, events have succeeded each other so rapidly, and the scene has changed so often, that I find it almost impossible to retrace all my steps, or recall my varied experiences. My impressions have been somewhat like those of a tourist, who enjoys, admires, is astonished, is disgusted, and then forgets. Minor discomforts and privations, and petty disgusts, make up a large part of this personal experience; but it is a blessing that these are so soon forgotten. * * * * * Our great successes at Gettysburg, Vicksburg and Port Hudson, are indeed matters of congratulation, but the triumph and elation of the North will be alloyed with humiliation at the disgraceful anti-draft riot in New York city. This is as it should be. The finger of Providence, to my mind discernible in this civil war from its commencement, is no where more plainly visible than in this untoward catastrophe. *Pride*, the sin of Egypt, the sin of Babylon, the sin of Israel and Judah, has been and still is, the sin of America, the cause of our domestic troubles, the root of this war. Southern pride would have domineered over the country, pampered itself with new slave territory, and fed upon the slave trade. Behold it now! New York arrogance and conceit was about to strut in triumph "to the Gulf," when Ellsworth's Fire Zouaves marched down Broadway. They came back from Bull Run, and New York had to sit down in sackcloth. Baltimore was to be "wiped out" after the 19th April, and New York gloated over the vision of streets "ploughed with cannon balls and sown with gunpowder." New York has now on the 13th of July, received a lesson which it will not soon forget. Pennsylvania Congressmen have sneered at "Border State Loyalty," and insolently declared that *fear* only held Maryland in the Union. We have lived to see Pennsylvania cities hastening to meet a rebel invasion with contributions of flour, pork, sugar, coffee and Treasury notes, and to hear from the great rebel Chieftain himself, that he met a much more formidable and determined opposition from the loyalty of Western Maryland, than from the Pennsylvanians of the Cumberland Valley.

. CAMP NEAR WARRENTON,
FAUQUIER CO., VA., *July 24th.*

We left White Plains early yesterday morning, and arrived here about two P. M. The region through which we have marched for the last few days, is one of desolation. At Middleburg, not a young man was to be seen, save two or three who had lost a leg or an arm. Just as we were breaking our camp at that place, an old man, and about half a dozen boys came on the ground to pick up such things as are always to be found in a deserted camp. I said to the eldest and smartest looking of the boys, "I suppose you boys are all good rebels." "We all try to be. You would'nt expect anything else in Virginia, would you." I replied: "There was a time, when the same thing used to be said in Maryland, but to-day you see a Brigade of Marylanders in this camp, as part of the 1st Corps of the Yankee army." The old man remarked: "We have been grossly deceived with respect to Maryland, I was always opposed to going off of our own ground, any how."

Fine mansions are yet to be seen along the road, but the fences are down, the outbuildings a wreck, and the fields "gone to grass." Scarcely a wheat or corn field have we seen for the last three or four days. In some fields, the wheat is still left in shocks where it was cut last year or the year before. The only cultivation is a vegetable patch around the houses. The fields are overgrown with bramble bushes, or resigned to the pestilent Canada thistle. The pasture is yet good in many places, and it is fortunate for our horses, and mules and beef-cattle, that they almost always succeed in finding plenty of good timothy, blue-grass, red-top or herd-grass and clover.

About four miles from Warrenton, we came upon a Division of Cavalry (I believe Buford's,) encamped with their trains parked. They had their scouts out feeling the woods for rebels, as we approached. This side of their camp, our progress was cautious, and our advance flanked by skirmishers. Things began to look interesting as we approached the town. The artillery was hurried to the front and unlimbered, and the movements of our skirmishers indicated the presence of the enemy in their front. There was no opposition however to our entrance, and as we marched through Warrenton, our Brigade Band played the National Airs for the benefit of the few old men, women, children, and darkies that showed themselves. Of course, there was a marked expression of dislike on the part of the inhabitants, but none of that haughty scorn which some of the dames in Middleburg exhibited. It was rather a deeply sorrowful and heart-broken look which most of them, particularly the more intelligent and better dressed ladies, wore, and which made many of us, for once in our lives, southern sympathizers.

CAMP AT BEALETON, ORANGE & ALEX. R. R.

FAUQUIER CO., VA., *July 28th.*

There is no pasture about here, the fields have a semblance of verdure, but it is only sedge and swamp-grass, and poverty-grass with worthless weeds. From the universal and frightful barrenness, it would seem as if some blight from heaven had fallen upon this country to make it thrice accursed. That slavery has been that blight, no man can fail to see. Free labor filling this region with a self-relying, industrious population, and dividing it into farms of manageable size, will doubtless, ere another generation shall have been gathered to the grave, make this hideous desert blossom as the rose. I shall not live to see it, but the time will come when this desolate and destitute region of Eastern Virginia, will rival Massachusetts or Belgium, in population and wealth.

Within the last year, the Confederate States army must have been diminished by battle, disease, desertion and capitulation, to the extent of two hundred thousand men. Where can they find recruits? Their thinned army as it stands, is the net result of an exhausting conscription, stringently enforced. Another year's maturity may give them an excuse for forcing into the ranks a few more children, whose unripe age will probably, in the majority of cases, sink under the hardships of the march before they reach the battle-field. In the meantime, we are just

15*

beginning to make our first draft upon those vast resources which we have been holding in reserve. Heretofore, we have been fighting conscripts with volunteers. We shall soon commence to fight conscripts with conscripts. This opens the last act in the drama, and the swiftly following catastrophe will be the overthrow of the Southern Confederacy, the eternal downfall of secession, and the destruction of slavery as an institution. * * * *

CAMP BETWEEN STEVENSBURG AND CULPEPER C. H.
Sept. 16*th.*

Made an early start this morning, marched ten or twelve miles, and pitched tents as above. Passed through Brandy Station and Stevensburg. Saw some fences along the road, and one or two corn fields; but the general aspect of this old Virginia, is that of a dreary, abandoned, curse-smitten country, given up to wild-carrot, polk-weed and poverty-grass. After passing Brandy Station, heard cannonading in front, which ceased for awhile, and then became quite brisk again when we reached this place, about five P. M. Saw along the route many dead and crippled horses. Our tents are pitched in a field, which at a little distance appeared clad with verdure, but when our horses made a closer inspection, they were disgusted at finding it covered with a rank growth of rag-weed, which had risen in insurrection against a dense and tangled mat of dewberry vines, and was flaunting in all the green glory of vegetable aristocratic uselessness. Here and there are an ambitious family of jimson, or an impudent clique of polk stalks has risen into notice, and has been admitted into the circle of first families, basing their claims to distinction upon the efficiency with which they have contributed to the suppression of clover, bluegrass and timothy; those vulgar, plebeian and hard working grasses which have been generally banished from this section of the Old Dominion, together with other vestiges of Federal oppression.

BRISTOW STATION, *Oct. 25th.*

We left Thoroughfare Gap yesterday at day-light, in a cold, blustering north-easter. The rain of the night before, and that which fell during the day, made of the road, at no time the best, a slough of despond, through which the men dragged heavily, and in which teams sunk to their axle-trees. About midnight the weather cleared off cold, with a piercing north-wester. Unable to be quiet myself, I arose with the morning star. As I looked around upon the miry soil on which thousands of wet, muddy, human beings were sleeping off the fatigue of the day's march, without shelter, without fires other than an occasional smoky attempt at one with green pine, I felt inclined to moralize. Why was this poor, perishing human race of ours so constituted by its Creator, as that from the earliest times, men have taken every trouble, exposed themselves to every danger, and deprived themselves of every comfort, to segregate themselves together into inconvenient masses, which they call armies; and in this shape to enact scenes of wholesale slaughter and mutilation, as the grand aim and end of all this self-inflicted misery! It is easy to say, that it is for the purpose of developing self-denial, self-sacrifice,—in short, the heroic element of man's nature, which, with uninterrupted peace and self-indulgence, would soon degenerate into swinish sensuality and sloth. But then the question recurs, why was man so constituted as to require this severe discipline to keep his humanity up to this classic standard? At this point, I dismissed the speculation, as of the same unprofitable class as the discussion about the origin of evil; and day having broken, and my appetite having dawned about the same time, I turned my attention to the more practical question of hard crackers, pork and coffee. * * * * *

October 28th, 1863.

Two weeks ago to-day, one of the neatest and most complete little successes of the war for our side, was achieved on the spot where I am writing, by General Warren and the Second Army Corps. It was Wednesday, the 14th October. Our corps, which had bivouacked here the night before, marched that morning for Centreville. We reached Manassas Junction at 10 A. M., crossed Bull Run at Blackburn's Ford at 12 M., and gained the heights of Centreville at 12½ P. M., just half an hour ahead of the rebels. As we marched over the old Bull Run battle ground, the sound of cannonading from Bristow Station in our rear, and from the neighborhood of Thoroughfare Gap, on our left front, caused one of the most singular atmospheric effects I ever observed. There seemed to be a throbbing, palpitating noise, pervading space, and causing the solid earth to quake and shudder, as if the buried dead of two battles were strugling to unearth themselves for a general resurrection of carnage. * * * * * *

RAPPAHANNOCK STATION, *Nov. 26th.*

I thought I had seen *mud* about Harper's Ferry, and on Maryland Heights, but our march here from Bristow the other day has taught me a lesson in that respect. I refer more particularly to the last stage of it, between Bealeton and this place. The corduroy in many places actually *floats*—an unlucky horse who gets his foot in where a log has hopped out of place, instantly sinks to the shoulders. If, disgusted with the corduroy, and tempted by the firm looking ground on either side, untrodden, and covered with short gray moss, you think to pick your own way over it, down you go, befloundered and bemired. I should like some of those people who think it "stuff" to talk of an army's progress being seriously impeded by "a little mud," to come down and see the reserve artillery train, consisting of over five hundred wheeled carriages, with siege guns, forges, and caissons loaded with shot and shell, ploughing its way through these quagmires and quicksands. * * * *

December 16th.

Tattoo is now beating and blowing throughout all the camps of our corps—distant, feeble strains from the drum and bugles of other corps, more remote, leaking in now and then through an interval in the nearer din. Reveille, Retreat and Tattoo divide the soldier's day into three unequal periods, by a roll call and gush of martial music. Retreat is the least notable of the three in a musical point of view, being short, and usually merged with the Dress Parade, as part of that sun-down ceremony. It is at Reveille and Tattoo that drums, fifes and bugles delight to emulate each other, and surpass themselves. On the march, the hours for these calls are uniform. In camp, each regiment or brigade fixes its own time. In the former case, the soldier's dreams are abruptly drowned in a sudden and overwhelming torrent of tenor drums, brass drums, bass drums, cavalry bugles, artillery trumpets, and ear-piercing fifes, coming up from all quarters, under the morning star and the pale waning moon, in a very Niagara of noise. Simultaneously as it breaks out, so it ceases. With its last note begins the hurried call of the roll by the Orderly Sergeant, from memory,—the company lines already formed—an unwashed company officer looking on apart—and then almost as suddenly as if by magic, hundreds of weird camp fires throw a ruddier glow into the face of the dawn, around each of which flit a dozen hungry forms, stooping over a tin cup of boiling coffee, or toasting a savory slice of fat pork on the end of a stick. Before many minutes, an orderly, sometimes a staff officer, gallops up to brigade head-quarters, from which immediately is heard the bugle call to "Fall in!" "Fall in," bawl the colonels, with mouths full of hard-tack. "Fall in," echo the captains in a fierce, bustling manner; and "fall in" it is, on all sides,—the lazy ones scalding their throats with a last gulp at the tin cup before it is hitched to the haversack, where, during a long laborious day's march it is to jingle and tinkle monotonously against the canteen. Knapsacks are slung with a convulsive movement of frame, which wrenches out some expression of a character offensive to ears polite. The line is formed, by the touch of the elbow only, if not yet light. If it is our good luck to be the advance regiment, we move off, directly after the brigade standard; otherwise we wait till the column moves by, to take our place in it. If still too dark to see, guided by the tramp, the hum, and the clink, so we march in the raw, frosty dawn; and sun-rise finds us five miles perhaps from where we heard the reveille.

But in a sedentary camp, as I said before, there is no uniform and precise moment fixed for these calls to begin; and so the strain is heard passing from regiment to regiment, and from camp to camp, any time during an hour. Now is the opportunity for individualities to be developed. Now is heard a fashionable drum-corps, performing scientifically in a modern, Frenchy, tasty style, after the most approved pattern. Walks in upon this performance, and virtually suppresses it, a ponderous, old-fashioned bass-drum affair, reminding one of fishing-club excursions or militia musters. Fifes are now pitted against each other in fiercest rivalry. Choicest morceaux from some favorite opera delight the ear for awhile, when suddenly their toes are trodden upon by "Villikins and his Dinah," or "Rory O'Moore," squeaked out from some neighboring camp, and then they plaintively subside into, "When this cruel war is over." Ever and anon is heard amid this conflict of melodies, some of the good old marching tunes which carried our fore-fathers, bare-footed, through the Revolution; some which cheered the soldiers of Marlborough, in

Flanders; some which did duty so long ago as the days of Gustavus Adolphus, the father of the art of war. It is when beating to such music, that drum-sticks oftenest forget themselves, and become enthusiastic, and even fanatical in their energy.

January 23d, 1864.

The Southern Confederacy may now be likened unto a mighty tree, with the sharp axes of the woodmen ringing away at its trunk. Grant having hewn out a huge gash, has come to the rigid heart, and rests on his axe, to blow a spell. Opposite him, Meade has cut in until he has turned his edge upon a tough knot, and is now busy at the grindstone. Gillmore keeps pecking away at the bark, mainly to test the tenacity of the remaining fibres, and assist gravitation when chips enough have been cut out. A few withered leaves are all now left of its once green and luxuriant foliage. The rest have fallen in the shape of Confederate notes, sapless in consequence of the girdle of the blockade. And already a steady, sharp observation of the top-most branches will discover the commencement of that long expected, inevitable downward movement, which only seen at first at the extremity of the radius, where a slender net-work of twigs slowly moves across the clouds, will soon culminate in the crackle, the roar, and the thundering crash.

THE
BLUE COAT OF THE SOLDIER.

You asked me, little one, why I bowed,
    Though never I passed the man before?
Because my heart was full and proud,
    When I saw the old blue coat he wore:
        The blue great coat, the sky blue coat,
        The old blue coat the soldier wore.

I knew not, I, what weapon he chose,
    What chief he followed, what badge he bore;
Enough that in the front of foes,
    His country's blue great coat he wore:
        The blue great coat, etc.

Perhaps he was born in a forest hut,
    Perhaps he had danced on a palace floor:
To want or wealth my eyes were shut,
    I only marked the coat he wore:
        The blue great coat, etc.

It mattered not much if he drew his line
  From Shem, or Ham, in the days of yore;
For surely he was a brother of mine,
  Who for my sake the war-coat wore:
    The blue great coat, etc.

He might have no skill to read or write,
  Or he might be rich in learned lore:
But I knew he could make his mark in fight,
  And nobler gown no scholar wore
    Than the blue great coat, etc.

It may be, he could plunder and prowl,
  And perhaps in his mood he scoffed and swore:
But I would not guess a spot so foul
  On the honored coat he bravely wore:
    The blue great coat, etc.

He had worn it long, and borne it far;
  And perhaps on the red Virginian shore,
From midnight chill till the morning star,
  That warm great coat the sentry wore:
    The blue great coat, etc.

When hardy Butler reined his steed,
  Through the streets of proud, proud Baltimore,
Perhaps behind him, at his need,
  Marched he who yonder blue coat wore:
    The blue great coat, etc.

Perhaps it was seen in Burnside's ranks
  When Rappahannock ran dark with gore;
Perhaps on the mountain side with Banks,
  In the burning sun no more he wore
    The blue great coat, etc.

Perhaps in the swamps 'twas a bed for his form,
  From the seven days battling and marching sore;
Or with Kearney and Pope, 'mid the steely storm,
  As the night closed in, that coat he wore:
    The blue great coat, etc.

Or when right over as Jackson dashed,
  That collar or cape some bullet tore;
Or when far ahead Antietam flashed,
  He flung to the ground the coat that he wore:
    The blue great coat, etc.

Or stood at Gettysburg, when the graves,
  Rang deep to Howard's cannon roar:
Or saw with Grant the unchained waves
  Where conquering hosts the blue coat wore:
    The blue great coat, etc.

That garb of honor tells enough,
  Though I its story guess no more:
The heart it covers is made of such stuff,
  That the coat is mail which that soldier wore:
    The blue great coat, etc.

He may hang it up when the peace shall come
 And the moths may find it behind the door:
But his children will point, when they hear a drum,
 To the proud old coat their father wore:
  The blue great coat, etc.

And so, my child, will you and I,
 For whose fair home their blood they pour,
Still bow the head, as one goes by,
 Who wears the coat that soldier wore:
  The blue great coat, the sky blue coat,
  The old blue coat the soldier wore.

ON THE NAME AMERICA.

Our Country—What is the first thing about it? Its name of course. That is America. Though, as European statesmen long since found out that "the safety of Europe required the division of America," it has cost us some care and contention to keep it; and there is an importance in the fact that we have kept it bearing on the unity of our nation, past, present and to come.

It has been maintained by some of our literati, that since "United States" was no proper name, our country had none; and several were proposed. Of these Alleghania found most favor: English writers, in the mean time, were careful to so express themselves as to deny us any proper name. In the title of her History, "The Republic of America" therefore, the writer assumed for the nation, the name America; and defended her position in the following note now out of print.

'We use the term "Republic of America," in the same manner as we would that of the Republic of Columbia. We conceive that America is as much a distinctive appellation of the one country, as Columbia is of the other. Yet the fact is not universally, perhaps not generally acknowledged, except tacitly.

'But in fact, the style assumed, at the Declaration of Independence, is not the United States merely, but the "United States of America," and it may be fairly presumed that the term America is used in the same manner as in the expression, "the United States of Holland," or "the United States of Mexico," and that we may, except in formal state papers, abbreviate, and use only the last word. There are, it is true, inconveniences in bearing particularly the same name which is given to the whole continent generally; but nothing, by any means, new or absurd. The City of New York, in the State of New York, is not absurd, nor does any material inconvenience result from this use of words, as it is well understood; but if, while this was the *real usage*, it was not the *avowed* and *acknowledged* usage, there might be difficulties, and authors would fall into inconsistencies. To avoid such in the use of the term America, we have avowed what we consider its established, and therefore its proper use.

'This name was assumed, at least as early as the commencement of our disputes with Great Britain. In the British Parliament and in our own Congress, our country, whether abused or defended, was called America; and that in a way to preclude the possibility of the term being used in its extensive sense as applying to the continent. "Whereas," say the first Congress, in the preamble to the Bill of Rights, "the British Parliament claims the right to bind the people of America in all cases," &c. The same style is used in all the other public documents of the time. The historian styles our armies, the American troops; and our ministers, the American negotiators. The poet invokes the genius of our country under the name America. Our officers have led our troops to battle, under the impulse of addresses made to Americans; nor did the soldiers suspect these addresses to be made to their Canadian or Indian foes, as well as to themselves. Our orators call on Americans to defend the rights, bought with the blood of their fathers, nor do their hearers once imagine that they mean to include the inhabitants of European colonies, or of monarchical Brazil. No, the name America comes to our hearts with a nearer and dearer import. America is to us the only name which can conjure up the spell of patriotism, and by this token we know that it is, and is to be the name of our country. And it is a noble name; dignified in prose—harmonious in poetry; and marching as we are in the van of the nations which are forming within the precincts of the new world, why should not our country have the distinguishing honor to bear the same name as the continent?'

That most honored patriarch of American history—Abiel Holmes, D. D., in kindly looking over the work for criticism, was attracted by this note, and the title-page of his celebrated work being yet under revision (for a new edition,) he changed it from "American Annals," to "Annals of America." He said the Union was the palladium of our strength; and disunion, most to be feared of all political calamities; that to have a name common to all, was a bond of union more difficult to break than any other; and if ever it should be temporarily broken, nothing would so powerfully tend to re-unite the severed parts. What this learned patriot of the Washington school saw in vision, we devoutly hope, may ere long, become a reality.

In 1828, the following article was inserted in the Troy Post: "Having seen, in an English periodical, the 'Christian Observer,' what a spirit is manifested in regard to a name for our country, I felt that we, on this side of the Atlantic, should stand up for ourselves; and I therefore send you what I was provoked to write, by reading the expressions in the English Observer referred to, which are as follows: '*We suggest to all writers and speakers, never to call the United States, America. Some vain American Unionists affect that title, but it is not for us to yield it.*' I began to put down my cogitations on this unpalatable interdiction, in a ballad form, but only produced these two stanzas:

> To Jonathan said big John Bull—
> Of lordly pride his heart was full—
> Your farm was mine, and now I say
> It sha'nt be called America.
>
> Out spake bold Brother Jonathan,
> 'Mind yours, and let *my* farm alone,
> For since you interfere, I say,
> It shall be called America."'

The remaining part of the article showed that America was already our name, and advised that we should not allow ourselves to be deprived of it. I had found, even in the little printed sheet before me, "The Troy Post," abundant means of fully proving my case, particularly in the advertisement of a then recent work, by the learned German historian, the Baron Von Reamer, entitled "America, and the American People:" and also, in an old Bay-State Thanksgiving Proclamation, which was taken from the Boston Almanac of 1776, where the name America was repeatedly used. Thus in its very birth-year, while its existence was yet numbered by months, the Fathers of the nation, standing by its cradle, called the thrifty nursling "America."

Is there any writer, on either side of the Atlantic, whose authority on this subject would be regarded as more decisive than that of Daniel Webster? "I am an American," he says,* "I am against agitators, North and South! I know no country but America, and no locality in America that is not my country!" What a glorious day will that be when these words shall be uttered with acclaim, by every voice from the Atlantic to the Pacific!

* In the Senate, June 17th, 1850.

"THEY'RE COMING GRANDAD."

A TALE OF EAST TENNESSEE.*

'NEATH the ruins of a rustic porch pavilioned o'er with vines,
Through which the sunshine slanting down, made strange, grotesque designs,
Made dancing shadows on the floor, and like spirit-hands caressed
The hoary locks of an aged man, who sat him there to rest.
From the open door there came no sound, of song or pattering feet,
No tender, murmuring tones of home, his weary soul to greet;
Under the eaves the swallows chirped, the bees droned on their way,
But for him, that aged man, his house was desolate that day.

* Copy-right secured by the Author.

The household cat that used to fawn and doze upon his
   knee,
The refuge she was wont to seek from the children's
   stormy glee,
Stole past him now with furtive tread, and crept into her
   lair,
While the sunshine creeping through the vines caressed
   his snowy hair.
Silent he sat, and motionless, supreme amidst the wreck,
Where blackened rafters told of flame; of blood, each
   crimson fleck,
Where the grain, down trodden in the field, told of the
   brutal hoofs
Of rebel troopers' wild foray; and of shells, the splintered
   roofs.

But of all the ruin there was nought, that crushed the old
   man lone,—
Of all the dear lives blotted out, the dear hopes over-
   thrown;
Of all the loss in gold and goods, and his weary, woesome
   age—
As did the blow that traitor hands, struck Freedom, in
   their rage.
Through his thin and tattered garments, his wasted limbs
   appeared,

And the quivering of his hungry lips, shook his white
and tangled beard,
His blood-stained feet, his shoulders bowed, betokened
misery—
But an untamed spirit flashed like fire, from his dark and
sunken eye.

"God reigneth!" thus he mused, "and it's His mysterious
way,
That the darkest, blackest hour of night, comes just
before the day;
Now is the gall and bitterness, the passion of our pain;
Lord! strike the fetters from our limbs, avenge our loved
ones slain."
Fierce was the gleam that lit his face, while the sunshine
on his head,
Made him like a hoary prophet there, just risen from the
dead:
When lo! swift footsteps echo near, in clasping arms he's
pressed,
And a young wan-face is hiding, with wild sobs upon his
breast.

"Is the dawn near?" he murmured low, as in a long
embrace
He held the ragged urchin close, and gently smoothed his
his face;

"Are they coming boy, the serried hosts, the legions of
 the Free,
To hunt the traitors from the soil, of our dear Tennessee?"
"They're coming Grandad!" sobbed the boy, my father
 with them, too;
My mother sent me from the cave, to bring this news to
 you;
They set the blood-hounds on his track, not knowing of
 his flight,
But they tore my little sister's throat, and oh! she died
 last night!

"Oh Grandad! I was sore afraid! Their eyes were fierce
 and wild,
And a red froth glistened on their fangs, when they tore
 down the child;
Her face was like to frozen snow, and she screamed in
 sad affright;
The rebels then called off their hounds—too late—she
 died last night."
The old man gasped, a shuddering sob, shook him from
 head to heel,
He spoke no word, but his soul cried out to God in strong
 appeal—
"Then," said the boy, of "dog-wood flowers, and leaves
 we made her bed,

And I came, and left my mother in the cave beside her
   dead;"

For Grandad, some one brought the news, that at the
   dawn of day,
Full fifty thousand Union troops were marching down
   this way:
Oh Grandad! when I hear their drums, and see against
   the sky
The old flag waving in the wind, I think of joy I'll die!
"Lord! Thou hast smote Thy servant, with afflictions
   burning seal,
With fire, and sword, and martyrdom, my faith Thou
   doest anneal"—
The old man slowly murmured, "Now I only ask of Thee,
To live to see the 'Stars and Stripes,' wave o'er fair
   Tennessee!

Boy in the cushion of my chair, is the old State House
   Flag,
That I stole off the night before, the rebels raised their
   rag
That shadowed all the air around, with its flaunting rebel
   bars,
Where had floated like an angel's wing, the blessed
   Stripes and Stars.

If my heart breaks before they come, stand thou upon
  my grave,
And with the old flag in thy hand, above me, let it wave;
Speak out for me in loud huzzas, that our brave troops
  may know,
No traitor blood is in thy veins, no Judas sleeps below."

While the old man spake, the sound of hoofs, came
  tramping down the lane,
And three fierce rebel troopers soon drew up around the
  twain,
And swearing in their savage mood, as from their features
  grim,
They wiped away the sweat and dust, their leader ques-
  tioned him.

"Where are thy sons, old grey-beard? We're recruiting,
  dost thou heed?
For the South demands her stalwart men, in this, her
  hour of need."

"My sons!" quoth he, while a crimson spot flamed on
  each pallid cheek,
"One shot they down sir, like a dog, for the brave words
  he did speak;

Before his mother's frantic eyes, and his blazing home
    that day,
He fell, and his life-blood crimsoned deep, the sword on
    which he lay."

"Fit doom," the captain sneering said, "for a traitor to
    the South,
They should have smote him with their heels, upon his
    traitor mouth."

"My other son ——" "Aye what of him?" the rebel
    trooper said,
"It is the living one we want, you're welcome to the
    dead."

"He's been hiding in the mountain clefts, but now he'll
    soon be back,
If not, call out your blood-hounds, sir, and set them on
    his track;
I hear you have them of a breed, so savage and so wild,
That when they can't bring down a man, they'll tear to
    death a child."

Thus spake the old man's bitter wrath, as with out-flash-
    ing scorn,
His eye swept from the traitor's brow, adown his garments
    worn;

The taunt shot home, and while the trooper's swarthy
    visage glow'red
He sprang upon his aged foe, and smote him with his
    sword,
Smote him upon his hoary head, where the sunlight softly
    gleamed,
Where soon amidst the silver hair, a crimson fountain
    streamed;
The ragged urchin shrieked and fled, and then the
    troopers three,
Swore he should "take the rebel oath, or swing on yonder
    tree."

"Didst ever hear," he calmly said, "in ages long remote,
Of a Christian priest named Polycarp—nay do not grasp
    my throat—
Who when the proud pro-consul bade him 'to curse God,
    or die,'
He said: 'My Lord hath harmed me not, I will not him
    deny.'
I'll take no oath! I've loved my country, through her
    weal and woe,
I've fought beneath the 'Stars and Stripes,' from Maine
    to Mexico,
And now that dastard sons have pierced her, in her hands
    and side,

Shall I deny her, whom I worshipped in her days of
pride?"

"You'll have less breath for treason, when with hemp
your throat is drest,
But tell me first, old Dotard, why you gaze towards the
West?"

"The Jews, proud rebel, towards the East, watch for the
coming king;
I gaze towards the glowing West, for the succors it will
bring."

"Ho! ho! look not for succor there, 'tis the sunlight on
the pines,
And not the gleaming bayonets, of the serried Yankee
lines."

"Well! well!" the old man bravely said, "it may not be
to-day,
But with God's and Andy Johnson's help, they'll soon
march down this way."

"Come, comrades!" cried the swarthy chief, "one of you
gag his mouth,
And we'll hang him up—a warning—to the traitors of the
South;"

Then they dragged him from his old arm-chair, and
    bound him with a cord,
When there came a sound upon the wind, and he
    whispered, "Thank Thee, Lord."
'Tis not the wind among the pines, as the sound still
    nearer comes,
But the blaze of trumpets, and the deep fierce utterance
    of drums,
And the stately rhythm of a tramp, as of ten thousand
    feet,
And the thunderers tones of loud bassoons, and cymbals
    clashing sweet.

"They're coming Grandad!" screamed a voice, that from
    a tree top rang;
"The Yankees are upon us boys!" cried the rebels as
    they sprang
Into their saddles, and swept down the thickly wooded
    lane,
While the old man shouted wild huzzas, forgetful of his
    pain;
"They're coming Grandad," still he bawled—that urchin
    from his roost,
Then leaping o'er the furrowed field, his Grandad's arms
    unloosed;
And with a wild light in his eyes, and rapture on his
    face,

He hauled with glee the State House Flag. from its
quaint hiding place.

Up to the roof he swiftly sped, and to a rafter clung,
As out upon the golden light, the "Stars and Stripes,"
he flung,
And when the vet'rans caught its gleam, as they marched
down through the pines,
A shout from full ten thousand throats, rolled out along
the lines.
Then out upon the peaks, and cliffs, the hunted refugees,
Came from their caves with Union Flags, flung wildly to
the breeze,
Their cries of joy, the thundering shouts, while the music
madly roared,
Roused the eagles from their eyrie, fiercely shrieking as
they soared!

Then adown the purple hill sides, where the sun rays
lingered yet,
In long array of blue, and gold, and glistening bayonet,
With the Old Flag waving far and wide, the symbol of
the free,
Came BURNSIDE's legions sweeping down into East Ten-
nessee.
"Halt!" thundered down the weary lines, and the
General said: "Just there

Where that old man sits so silently with the sunshine on
    his hair;
Where that tattered urchin waves his flag from such a
    dizzy height;
We shall find right loyal welcome, and we'll rest us there
    to-night."

"That's my homestead," said a private, as he bared his
    heated brow:
Though nought is left of its old cheer—for 'tis a ruin
    now,—
You're welcome General, to its use, and my father waits
    to clasp
Your hand, sir, with a blessing, in his warm and loyal
    grasp."

But the old man's soul had passed away, his last exultant
    sigh
Had mingled with his country's strains, and the music of
    the sky,
Then they wrapped him grandly in his Flag, when they
    heard his story told,
And the General said: "a soldiers grave, we'll give this
    patriot bold."

    *   *   *   *   *

"They're coming Grandad," sobbed the boy, on the old
     man's silent breast;
"With little Minnie on a bier, with dogwood blossoms
     drest,
They're singing "Blessed are the dead," as from the
     mountain height
The sunshine's golden torrents roll to crown her head
     with light;—
In the Old Flag wrapped, she'll sleep with you, beneath
     the daisied sod;
Oh Grandad! blood like yours, and hers, like Abel's,
     cries to God!"
Said the General, as beside the dead, he sternly bowed
     his knee,
"Take heart my brave! such blood will bear rich fruits
     in Tennessee!"

Then ere the golden sun had swept morn's crimson blush
     away,
While the mocking bird among the vines still sang his
     roundelay,
They laid the old man, and the child, together on the
     bier,
Her brown curls stirring in the breeze, twined with his
     snowy hair,
Her fair white cheek lay close to his, her little dimpled
     hands

Folded together like a saint's, were bound with daisy bands—
With the Old Flag draped about them both, the martyred ones were borne
Unto their rest; while muffled drums, and the plaintive bugle horn,
The sound of women weeping, and the sterner sobs of men,
And the moaning of the pines above, made their sad requiem.

WASHINGTON, *Jan.* 14th.

WHAT OUR COUNTRY WANTS.

AMIDST the bounties and blessings which Providence has showered upon her, amidst the successes of her arms, and the assurance of a final triumph in her present struggle, our country wants one thing which is essential to the enjoyment of the one, and the maintenance of the other. And that is a *nationality*—her danger is in her very strength, in the vastness of her territory, the boundless resources of her wealth, and the multitude of her population.

The Revolution left the feeble colonies united by a common sympathy, and a sense of common danger. That feeling wrought out the frame work of a common government, in the day when patriots and statesmen had control in the policy of the nation. But, for the last fifty years, we have been growing strangers and aliens to each other, from the remoteness at which we dwell from one another, and the diversity of the channels of our business and intercourse. Portland, in Maine, is, geographically, farther removed from her neighboring city of Portland, in Oregon, than she is from Antwerp or Paris. And in business. they are separated by half the circuit of the globe.

The early generations that went out from the Atlantic States, to people the great West, have passed away, and, with them, the fond remembrances of early homes; while others, born upon the soil, and busy with their own affairs, ignore the tie that once served to bind together the widening regions of a common country.

But stronger in its influence even than this, is the crowd of distinct nationalities which have been attracted hither, by the cheapness of our soil and the freedom of our government, and now throng the rich regions of the West. Thousands upon thousands who share the protection of our government, and thrive upon the benefits which they derive from its institutions, cannot speak the language in which our Constitution is written, or its laws are published. The only things which they have in common with the native citizens, are the air they breathe, the soil they cultivate, the freedom they enjoy, and the rewards of a well protected industry which they share. There is no common chord of sympathy by which they can be moved; and the German and the Irish, the Norwegian and the Swede are slow to learn that a new nationality is yet to be formed, of which they are to be an element and a part.

Nor does the evil of this want of nationality stop with the mere weakening of the bond of union that binds the parts of our country together. It becomes, in the hand of designing men, an engine of positive mischief. It is made the source of sectional jealousies and local animosities, under the influence of which, the pride of country is sacrificed to that of the State; and the prosperity of one region becomes an object of jealousy and ill-will in another. This feeling is, moreover, cherished by the more immediate connexion there is between the citizen and his immediate State, in every thing that concerns him in his domestic interests, and the share he has in its government, than that which the people generally have with the administration of the Federal Government.

Mr. Calhoun had a field ready prepared at his hand, in which to cast the pestilent seed of State Rights, Nullification and Secession, under the guise of counteracting a tariff which other sections of a common country thought it for her interest to maintain, and under a still more palpable and sensitive pretence of guarding a cherished, local institution against the freedom of the press and the popular voice of more prosperous regions.

Add to all this the power which, in a country like ours, a few minds can practically exercise in controlling public opinion and feeling, and we can the more readily measure the importance of a sentiment of nationality which shall be to a people, what instinct and uneducated conscience is to the individual—which shall start up, unbidden, and prompt one to repel an attack upon the honor of his country, as he would upon the good name of the mother that bore him.

But from the want of this training, in the growing strength and expansion of our country, we shall grow weaker every day, if the parts of this mighty whole cannot be bound more strongly and intimately together. Rail roads, domestic commerce, a common press, and the intercourse of individuals may do much. But there is something beyond all these required, to give vitality to that sensitiveness which goes to make up a proper national pride. Nor can we regard the very war in which we are engaged as otherwise than doing, in this respect, for our country, what no minor agency could effect.

When the echo of the gun from Sumter was repeated— from every valley and hill-side in our land, it found the nationality of the people, asleep. But it was not dead. No shock, perhaps, less powerful would have aroused a nation of planters, and merchants, and mechanics, to the peril of seeing this great nationality crumbling and falling to pieces, and becoming the scorn of the old world, as the crippled members of a once mighty empire. Nor was this all. In the effort to restore the nation again to its integrity, the men of the loyal States forgot the lines that separated them in name. California and Minnesota, Maryland and New Hampshire followed the same flag into the battle, side by side, and shoulder to shoulder. And the men of Massachusetts and Illinois answered to the same watchword and countersign to the soldier from Ohio, as he stood sentry on the banks of the Mississippi, or among the wild fastnesses of Eastern Tennessee. It has been a nation's war, for a nation's glory, a nation's integrity, and a nation's independence. Europe has at last begun to measure with something of adequate estimate, the value of a nationality on this side the water, which, in her eagerness to see broken and dissevered, she had begun to despise, and looked forward to trample upon with impunity.

It is the great lesson of the day. Come what will, it should never be forgotten, that our country, united, nationalized, animated by a common will for a common cause, will stand as peerless in power as she has been prosperous and free.

The brain of the people should be taught, the heart of the people should be made to feel that the honor of the nation is in the charge of every freeman in the land. Let this lesson once be impressed upon the people of this country, and the world would learn to acknowledge that wherever her Starry Flag was floating, its folds sheltered whoever had a right to its protection. And that whenever her voice was heard, it was the language of a nation that was willing to be just and magnanimous, while it knew how to maintain its honor, and enforce its rights.

A VOICE.

A voice comes wailing o'er the wave,
  From the dear land afar;
Alas! my country, that such wails
  Should reach us here so far;
A trumpet note, a dread appeal,
  That shakes the throbbing world
Until the pulse of human hearts
  Stands still,—the banners furled!

There was a vase, a golden vase,
  Hid in that forest green,
Held by a chain, but cloud-wrought links,
  Now melted into rain;
The rain of human tears that fall,
  Because that vase is broken,
In fragments lie the shattered bits
  Mournful and sad a token.

A token of a Nation great,
  Of a great Nation's call,
O God! we cry to Thee too late,
  But deign to hear our call.

A VOICE.

Alas! the voice is wailing sad,
   O'er these blue fields of air;
Echoed in billows from the sea;
   From the dear land afar.
Alas! my country, broken links
   In that bright chain are riven;
We need the smile of God to cheer
   From these blue rents of Heaven.

Written at Rome, 1862.

BALTIMORE LONG AGO.

LIFE has a double expanse; one in the past, the other in the future: the present is but a dividing line—an isthmus, rather, between two oceans. Our retrospects widen every day; our prospects grow narrow.

I have come to that stage at which I live in the one as much as in the other;—puzzled to say whether I belong most to the antiques or the moderns. Why not confess it? To come smoothly and cheerfully up to the "great climacteric," is, of itself a glory,—being an honest victory over time, and always a good token of a tranquil future.

The past presents a mellow landscape to my vision, rich with the hues of distance, and softened by a sunny haze, that still retains that tint of the rose—now sobered a little into the neutral—with which youth and hope once set it aglow. The present is a foreground less inviting, with a growing predominance of sharp lines and garish colors wanting harmony. So, I follow the bent of my humor and, for a while, renounce the present, to indulge my affections in the dalliance of old memories. I detest these babblements of young America, and seek a refuge from its impertinent innovations in a genial remembrance of the older days of our city.

"Earth hath its bubbles as the water hath." Many break before our eyes, throwing into air their little volumes of cherished desires: many glide onwards upon the stream to meet that fate beyond our view, of which we too plainly see the certain token in the swelling of the brittle globe, and the jeopardy that grows with its increasing compass.

These bubbles have been my study.

It is my fortune, now and then, to encounter some long ripened and—I reproach myself for saying it—some long *forgotten*, object of my early passion, with whom, when every look had a mysterious sympathy that controlled the beat of my pulse, and every word a tone that found a musical echo in my heart, I was wont, in the old time, to dance quadrilles and country-dances. Waltz and redowa and polka had not then invaded the mannerly modest reserve of female toleration. How changed is this same toleration now! Time is a ruthless conqueror! Be on your guard, my good, ingenuous young friends. *Væ victis!*

That whilom neat little compend of wit and beauty which once inflamed my imagination by its vivacity and tenderness, its graceful outline, its aurora blush, its polished forehead, its jetty curls dipping to the round surface of an ivory shoulder—ah me, what has become of all these! Circe has touched that beautiful conglomerate with her wand. Who would believe in the identity of that past vision with this present domestic, motherly face, this superfluous double chin, this short, comfortable figure discreetly draped in supernumerary garments, and these four married daughters, respectable staid matrons, —the youngest of whom I sometimes meet in church with two boys draped like young Albanians! There is a remainder yet, I perceive, of that old roguish sparkle of the eye; and I think I discern the same lithe, well-turned figure, which I once followed with such devotion through the old ball rooms, in that grand daughter who is asking her mother my name,—as I perceive by her curious glance towards me. Not such ticklish ware, my old friend, I shrewdly guess, as in that triumphant day when you fancied you could banish me to the Desert of Arabia, by a frown! My palpitations are not so distinguishable now; and I would venture to remark that you have altogether a more charitable and generally benevolent human regard than when I first knew you.

I can affirm with a clear conscience, that I approach these old time idols without disconcertment, and even with an intrepid memory of the awful intensity of that passion which I have, more than once, known to endure without intermission for full six weeks. I am even hardy enough now—which, perhaps, is unbecoming my years and ought not to be encouraged—to venture on a comparison between the mother and the grand daughter, with an evident leaning toward a preference for the latter. It is one of the beneficent illusions of age, that we are apt to count ourselves *out* of that march in which the world is stepping along towards venerable eld; at least, to fancy that we go at less speed than others.

I make several epochs in the onward, or rather I should say backward, course of my recollections. One of my earliest landmarks is the epoch of the old Court House.

That was a famous building which, to my first cognizance, suggested the idea of a house, perched upon a great stool.

It was a large, dingy, square structure of brick, elevated upon a massive basement of stone, which was perforated by a broad arch. The buttresses on either side of the arch supplied space for a stairway that led to the Hall of Justice above, and straddled over a pillory, whipping post and stocks which were sheltered under the arch, as symbols of the power that was at work up stairs.

This magisterial edifice stood precisely where the Battle Monument now stands on Calvert Street. It has

19

a notable history, that old Court House. When it was first built it overlooked the town from the summit of the hill some fifty feet or more above the level of the present street, and stood upon a cliff which, northward, was washed at the base by Jones' Falls,—in that primitive day a pretty rural stream that meandered through meadows garnished with shrubbery and filled with browsing cattle, making a pleasant landscape from the Court House windows.

Of all the functions of municipal care, that which begins earliest and is the last to end in a thriving town, is the opening and grading of streets. Corporate vanity finds its great vent in this exercise. The egotism of the young city runs into streets. It is the only department of government that seems to be animated with an intense foresight for the wants of the future. Taxes get in arrear, schools are postponed, hospitals are put off, but the streets are always before hand.

The old Calvert street came handsomely up the hill, all the way from the wharves to the Court House, and the wayfarer, when he arrived at this point, found himself on the cliff looking northward over a beautiful valley watered by the roving stream which glided smoothly against the granite rocks that formed a selvage to the park belonging to that good and gallant old cavalier, Colonel Howard, and diverging from the foot of the park came, by a sweeping circuit, through the meadow under the steep and sandy hills that overhung it on the west.

The city fathers had grown tired of gazing over this scene of rural beauty, and had already begun to accuse the stream of an unbecoming departure from the true line of its duty. The circuit was an impertinence which called for correction. The surveyor's chain was already marking out a possible extension of Calvert street over the water course. The work was as good as done. Jones' Falls was whipped out of the meadow as an intruder, and consigned to a new channel cut along the cord of the circular segment which it had pursued before Columbus broke his egg, and the decree was sent forth for taking down twenty feet of the hill on which the Court House was perched.

And now the great question arose touching the fate of this majestical temple of the law. Was the street to give way to the Court House, or the Court House to the street? For a time that question convulsed the councils and the public.

A mighty man in masonry in that day—Leonard Harbaugh by name—stepped forward: a man born to still great commotions of state. He maturely perpended the problem and amazed the whole generation of puzzled quid nuncs, including Mayor and City Council, Judges, Sheriffs and Clerks, with the brave proposal, at his own risk and responsibility, to preserve the Court House safe and sound after twenty feet were dug away beneath its foundations. The town could not have been more incredulous if he had proposed to suspend the honored building by a magnet in the air. But he was a man of will and confident in his genius, and so went courageously to work.

All the old men, and all the boys, and all the idle negroes visited the work daily. Many shook their heads and watched to see the Court House tumble in ruins, and carefully "stood from under." But, day by day, Leonard adroitly knitted the masonry into buttress and arch, and, in good time, emerged that figure I have already described, of the old Court House quaintly seated upon its ponderous and solid bench of stone. Why is there no full length portrait of the doughty Leonard Harbaugh hanging in the City Hall? Alas, our true men of might find no place in the galleries consecrated to the encouragement of the growth of shams! Both Leonard and his work, the old Court House, have gone into dead oblivion.

The street commissioners came along once more, and decreed another reduction of hill. Another twenty feet or more were required. The Court House had grown mouldy and superannuated; stock, pillory and whipping post had gone out of fashion: Baltimore had become more ambitious Stately buildings began to engross the square.

The new Court House arose,—a model of architectural magnificence to the eye of that admiring generation, only second to the National Capitol—and the old one was carted away as the rubbish of a past age. Calvert street straggled onward to the granite hills. People wonder to hear that Jones' Falls ever rippled over a bed now laden with rows of comfortable dwellings, and that cows once browzed upon a meadow that now produces steam engines, soap and candles and lager beer.

Still dear to me is the memory of the old Court House. I have a sober faith that the people of the days of the old Court House and the old Court House days themselves had more spice in them, were more genial to the kindlier elements that make life worthy to be loved, than any days we have had since

The youth of a city, like the youth of a man, has a keener zest for enjoyment and finds more resource for it than mature age. Use begets a fastidious appetite and disgust for cheap pleasures, whilst youth lives in the delight of constant surprises and with quick appreciation and thankful reception of novelties.

Next after the old Court House, and in vivid associations far ahead of it, my most salient memory comes up from the old Play House. We had not got into the euphuism of calling it "the theatre" in those days, or, at least, that elegance was patronized only by the select few

19*

who in that generation, like the select few of the present, were apt to be caught by the fancy of a supposed refinement in the substitution of Greek for the Anglo-Saxon. The Spectator and Rambler and the Vicar of Wakefield supplied the vocabulary of that era, and I think Addison, Johnson and Goldsmith generally followed Ben Jonson and Shakespeare, and taught people to call it the Play House. I dare say the actors—especially the young ones who were proud of their calling and were inclined to strut in speech as well as on the boards—had, even then, begun to naturalize the new word. But there is such a perfume lingering about the old vernacular,—the aroma of flowers planted by it when all the world was fragrant to me—that I cannot give it up without risk of dulling the husbandry which yet keeps these fine odors alive.

"The theatre" would bring me to a later period, when the foot-lights were no longer fed with oil, when the glass diamonds and tinsel had lost their reality, and the stage had begun to reveal its tawdry secrets, to the disenchantment of that beautiful school-boy faith with which I plunged into this weird world of *féerie*.

This Play House stood in Holiday street just where the present "theatre" now stands. What a superb thing it was!—speaking now as my fancy imagined it then. It had something of the splendor of a great barn, weather-boarded, milk white, with many windows and, to my conception, looked with a hospitable, patronizing, tragi-comic greeting down upon the street. It never occurred to me to think of it as a piece of architecture. It was something above that—a huge, mystical Aladdin lamp that had a magic to repel criticism, and filled with wonderful histories. There Blue Beard strangled his wives and hung them on pegs in the Blue Chamber; and the glorious Valentine overcame his brother Orson, by the clever trick of showing him his own image in a wonderful shield of looking-glass, which, of course, we believed to be pure burnished silver; and there the Babes in the Wood went to sleep under the coverlet provided for them by the charitable robins that swung down upon wires,—which we thought was even superior to the ordinary manner of flying; and the ghost of Gaffer Thumb came up through the floor, as white as a dredge-box of flour could make him—much more natural than any common ghost we had seen. Alas, what has become of Orcobrand's Cave and the Wood Demon and the Castle Spectre, and all the rest of those delightful old horrors which used to make our hair stand on end in delicious ecstasy in those days? This reflection gives me rather a poor opinion of the modern drama, and so I do not look much after it. In fact, I suspect this age to be greatly behind ours in these terrible fascinations. Young America is evidently not so easily scared as old America was: it has a sad propensity towards fast trotters and to that wretched business of driving buggies, which has spoiled the whole generation of young gentlemen, and made a good cavalry officer, just now, an impossibility or, at least, a virtuous exception in one-half of the country. The age is too fast for the old illusions, and the theatre now deals in respectable swindlers, burglars and improper young ladies as more consonant with the public favor than our old devils, ghosts and assassins, which were always shown in their true colors, and were sure to be severely punished when they persecuted innocence.

The players were part and parcel of the play-house, and therefore shared in the juvenile admiration with which it was regarded. In fact, there was a misty confusing of the two, which destroyed the separate identity of either. The play-house was a compound idea of a house filled with mountains, old castles and cities and elderly gentlemen in wigs, brigands. fairies and demons, the whole making a little cosmos that was only connected with the world by certain rows of benches symmetrically arranged into boxes, pit and gallery, where mankind were drawn by certain irresistible affinities to laugh and weep and clap their hands, just as the magicians within should choose to have them do.

Of course, there was but one play-house and one company of actors. Two or more would have destroyed that impression of the super-natural, or rather the extra-natural, which gave to the show its indescribable charm. A cheap and common illusion soon grows stale. Christy's Minstrels may be repeated every night, and people will only get tired of the bad jokes and cease to laugh;—but Cinderella and her glass slipper would never endure it. The fairy bubbles would burst, and there would be no more sparkling of the eyes of the young folks with the delight of wonder. Even Lady Macbeth, I believe, would become an ordinary sort of person in "a run"—such as is common now. The players understood this, and, therefore, did not allow themselves to grow too familiar. One company served Baltimore and Philadelphia, and they had their appointed seasons—a few months or even weeks at a time,—and they played only three times a week. "The actors are coming hither, my lord," would seem to intimate that this was the condition of things at Elsinore—one company and a periodical visit. There was a universal gladness in this old Baltimore when the word was passed round—"the players are come." It instantly became every body's business to give them a good reception. They were strange creatures in our school-boy reckoning—quite out of the common order of humanity. We ran after them in the streets as something very notable to be looked at. It was odd to see them dressed like gentlemen and ladies: almost incongruous, we sometimes thought. as if we expected to see them in slashed doublet and hose, with embroidered mantles and a feather in their caps. "There goes *Old Francis*," was our phrase; not that he was *old*, for he was far from it, but because we loved him. It was a term of endearment. And as to Jefferson! Is there any body now who remembers that imp of ancient fame? I cannot even now think definitely of him as a man—except in one particular, that he had a prominent and rather arching nose. In regard to every thing else he was a Proteus—the nose always being the same. He played every thing that was comic and always made people laugh till tears came to their eyes. Laugh! Why, I don't believe he ever saw the world doing any thing else. Whomsoever he looked at laughed. Before he came through the side scenes when he was about to enter O. P. or P. S., he would pronounce the first words of his part to herald his appearance, and instantly the whole audience set up a shout It was only the sound of his voice. He had a patent right to shake the world's diaphragm which seemed to be infallible. No player comes to that perfection now. Actors are too cheap. and all the hallucination is gone.

When our players came. with their short seasons. their three nights in the week, and their single company. they were received as public benefactors, and their stay was a period of carnival. The boxes were engaged for every night. Families all went together, young and old. Smiles were on every face: the town was happy. The elders did not frown on the drama, the clergy levelled no cannon against it, the critics were amiable. The chief actors were invited into the best company, and I believe their personal merits entitled them to all the esteem that was felt for them. But, amongst the young folks the appreciation was far above all this. With them it was a kind of hero worship prompted by a conviction that the player was that manifold creature which every night assumed a new shape, and only accidentally fell into the category of a common mortal. And therefore, it seemed so interesting to us to catch one of them sauntering on the street looking like other people. That was his exceptional character, and we were curious to see how he behaved in it—and, indeed, thought him a little awkward and not quite at his ease in that guise. How could *old* Francis be expected to walk comfortably in Suwarow boots and a stove-pipe hat—he who had, last night, been pursuing Columbine in his light suit of triangular patch work, with his wooden sword, and who so deftly dodged the police by making a somerset through the face of a clock, and disappearing in a chest of drawers; or who, the night before that. was a French dancing master, and ran away with a pretty ward of a cross old gentleman, who wanted to marry her himself!

It has always struck me that the natural development of player life has something very grotesque in it. It amounts almost to transmigration. The public knows an actor only on the boards, and there he is so familiarly known as, in fact, to make that his only cognizable existence. We see him to-day in one stage of his progress, to-morrow in another. He is never continuously the same person— often totally a different and most opposite one—so different in quality, costume, deportment, that all identity has disappeared. It looks like metempsychosis. Francis began— or was transmuted into it, at some early epoch of his life— as Harlequin and he grew and grew, through successive states of existence, into a Turkish Bashaw, and finally developed into a fine Sir Peter Teazle, from which full blown perfection he vanished out of the sphere of mortal ken. What was the growth of the man Francis, few persons gave themselves the trouble to inquire, though I am quite sure he had a manhood as worthy of being esteemed as the most of us;—but the gradual evolution of that mythic being, whose nightly apparition before the foot-lights enchanted our merry world, through all the metamorphosis of dramatic development, was as notable and conspicuous, within its orbit, as the career of Daniel Webster. It was the only Francis ninety-nine out of a hundred knew any thing about; the only one, we of the younger and simpler sort conceived to be natural or even possible.

The growth of a City is a natural process which creates no surprise to those who grow with it, but it is very striking when we come to look back upon it and compare its aspect at different and distant eras. If I had been away during that long interval which separates the past, I have been describing, from the present, I doubt if I should now find one feature of the old countenance of the town left. Every thing is as much changed as if there was no consanguinity, or even acquaintance, between the old and the new.

In the days I speak of, Baltimore was fast emerging from its village state into a thriving commercial town. Lots were not yet sold by the foot, except, perhaps, in the denser marts of business;—rather by the acre. It was in the *rus-in-urbe* category. That fury for levelling had not yet possessed the souls of City Councils. We had our seven hills then, which have been rounded off since, and that locality, which is now described as lying between the two parallels of North Charles Street and Calvert Street, presented a steep and barren hill-side, broken by rugged cliffs and deep ravines washed out, by the storms of winter, into chasms which were threaded by paths of toilsome and difficult ascent. On the summit of one of these cliffs, stood the old Church of St. Paul's, some fifty paces or more to the eastward of the present church, and surrounded by a brick wall that bounded on the present lines of Charles and Lexington Streets. This old building, ample and stately, looked abroad over half the town. It had a belfry tower detached from the main structure, and keeping watch over a grave-yard full of tombstones, remarkable,—to the observation of the boys and girls, who were drawn to it by the irresistible charm of a popular belief that it was "haunted,"—for the quantity of cherubim that seemed to be continually crying above the death's heads and cross bones, at the doleful and comical epitaphs below them.

The rain-washed ravines from this height supplied an amusement to the boys, which seems to have been the origin of a sport that has now descended to their grandchildren in an improved and more practical form. These same hills are now cut down into streets of rapid descent, which in winter, when clothed in ice and snow, are filled with troops of noisy sledders who shoot, with the speed of arrows, down the slippery declivity. In my time, the same pranks were enacted on the sandy plains of the cliff, without the machinery of the sled, but on the unprotected breeching of corduroy,—much to the discontent of mothers who had to repair the ravage, and not always without the practice of fathers upon the same breeching, by way of putting a stop to this expensive diversion.

The little river—the Falls as it was always called—gurgled along with a flashing current at the foot of these hills, washing that grassy cantlet, which every body knew as "the meadow," over which Calvert Street now flings its brick and mortar, and where the rail road station usurps the old time pasture ground of the village cows. Hard by the margin of this stream, "the spring" gushed forth in primeval beauty, from the curtilage of a low-browed, rustic cottage, shaded by its aboriginal tree, which in time was rooted up, to be supplanted by the pillared dome which now lingers a forsaken relic, dependant upon the slow charity of the City fathers to save it from pick-axe and spade and the overwhelming masonry of modern improvement.

The stream, in its onward flight from this point, eddied under the high bank that supported the Court House, and, turning swiftly thence, foamed and dashed at the base of a precipice, on the top of which stood the Presbyterian Church,—only lately resolved into its original dust, to make room for the new Court-room, which Uncle Sam, quite regardless of the threat of Mr. Jefferson Davis to liberate Maryland, is fast rearing up to administer the laws of the "more perfect Union," which rebellion has been so savagely intent upon making more imperfect.

These are some of the more noteworthy changes which have crept over the physical aspect of the City. Those in its moral and social aspect are even more observable. As communities grow in density and aggregation, the individuality of men diminishes. People attend to their own concerns and look less to their neighbors. Society breaks into sects, cliques and circles, and these supersede individuals. In the old time, society had its leaders, its models and dictators. There is always the great man of the village;—seldom such a thing in the City. It was the fashion then to accord reverence and authority to age. That is all gone now. Young America has rather a small opinion of its elders, and does not patronise fathers and mothers. It knows too much to be advised, and gets, by intuition, what a more modest generation found it hard enough to get by experience. If we could trace this notion through all its lodgments, we should find that this want of reverence and contempt of obedience is the deepest root of this mad rebellion.

Baltimore had passed out of the village phase, but it had not got out of the village peculiarities. It had its heroes and its fine old gentlemen, and its accomplished lawyers, divines and physicians, and its liberal, public-spirited merchants Alas! more then than now. The people all knew them and treated them with amiable deference. How sadly we have retrograded in these perfections ever since!

Society had a more aristocratic air than now—not because the educated and wealthy assumed more, but because the community itself had a better appreciation of personal worth, and voluntarily gave it the healthful privilege of taking the lead in the direction of manners and in the conducting of public affairs. This was, perhaps, the lingering characteristic of colonial life, which the revolution had not effaced,—the, as yet, unextinguished traditional sentiment of a still older time—of which all traces have been obliterated by the defective discipline of succeeding generations.

The retrospect which carries me back to that jocund time, when I admired and loved that old society, is full of delight and sadness. I have a long score of pleasant recollections of the friendships, the popular renowns, the household charms, the *bonhommie*, the free confidences and the personal accomplishments of that day. My memory yet lingers with affectionate delay in the wake of past notabilities, male and female, who have finished their voyage and long ago, I trust, found a safe mooring in that happy haven, where we fondly expect to find them again when we ourselves shall have furled our sails and secured an anchorage on that blessed shore. Bating the ravages which time has made in the ranks of my compeers and comrades, it is a precious bit of the field of human life to contemplate. But those ravages! How few of the glories of that day remain. Some cord has snapped every year—even, as we advance, every month;—and, at each break, a dear friend, a familiar face, a genial form, upon which we were wont to hang our affections like garlands, has dropt out of sight and become a memory. A few sea-worn barks still sail on.

I grow too serious for the cheerful theme which my outset promised. Let me get back to my appointed task.

It was a treat to our ancestors to look upon this little Baltimore town springing forward with such elastic bound to be something of note in the Great Republic. They saw it just after the war of the Revolution, giving its first promise—a bustling, ambitious, I might say, rollicking young aspirant for municipal honors—growing rapidly, like a healthy boy, fat and frolicsome, and bursting incontinently out of his clothes in spite of all allowance of seam and selvage. Market Street (this has grown obsolete now—they call it Baltimore Street,) had shot like a snake out of a toy box, up as high as Congress Hall, (I forgot that Congress Hall, which stood between Sharp and Liberty, has also vanished,) with its variegated range of low-browed, hip-roofed wooden houses, standing forward and back, out of line, like an ill-dressed regiment,—as a military man would say. Some houses were painted blue, some yellow, some white, and, here and there, a more pretending mansion of brick, with windows after the pattern of a multiplication table, square and many-pained, and great wastes of wall between the stories; some with court-yards in front, and trees in whose shade truant boys and ragged negroes "skyed coppers" and played at marbles.

This avenue was enlivened with matrons and damsels; some with looped-up skirts, some in brocade luxuriantly displayed over hoops, with comely boddices supported by stays disclosing perilous waists, and with sleeves that clung to the arm as far as the elbow, where they were lost in ruffles that stood off like the feathers of a bantam. The whirligig of time has played its usual prank and brought these ghosts of the past back into the very same avenue. And then, such faces! so rosy, spirited and sharp;—with the hair drawn over a cushion—(they called it neither 'cat' nor 'rat,' my dear young lady, but simply by the name I give it)—tight enough to lift the eyebrows into a rounder curve, giving a pungent, supercilious expression to the countenance; and curls that fell in "cataracts" upon the shoulders, (much prettier, my pretty friend, than those netted 'beaver tails' you fancy.) Then, they stepped away in such a mincing gait, in shoes of many colors with formidable points at the toes and high tottering heels delicately cut in wood, and in towering peaked hats, garnished with feathers that swayed aristocratically backward and forward at each step, as if they took pride in the stately paces of the wearer.

In the train of these goodly groups came the gallants who upheld the chivalry of the age;—cavaliers of the old school, full of starch and powder: most of them the iron gentlemen of the Revolution, with leather faces—old campaigners, renowned for long stories,—not long enough from the camp to lose their military *brusquerie* and daredevil swagger; proper, roystering blades who had not long ago got out of harness and begun to affect the elegancies of civil life. Who but they!—jolly fellows, fiery and loud, with stern glance of the eye and brisk turn of the head, and swash-buckler strut of defiance, like game cocks, all in three cornered cocked-hats and powdered hair and cues, and light-colored coats with narrow capes and long backs, and pockets on each hip, small clothes and striped stockings, shoes with great buckles, and long steel watch chains suspending an agate seal, in the likeness to the old sounding boards hung above the pulpits. And they walked with such a stir, striking their canes upon the pavement till it rang again. I defy all modern coxcombry to produce any thing equal to it. There was such a relish of peace after the war, so visible in every movement. It was a sight worth seeing, when one of these weather-beaten gallants accosted a lady on the street. There was a bow which required the whole width of the pavement, a scrape of the foot and the cane thrust with a flourish under the left arm and projecting behind in a parallel line with the cue. And nothing could be more piquant then the lady's return of this salutation, in a curtsy that brought her, with bridled chin and a most winning glance, half way to the ground. And such a volume of dignity!

It was really a comfort to see a good housewifely matron of that merry time, trudging through town in bad weather, wrapped up in a great 'roquelaire,' her arms thrust into a huge muff, and a tippet wound about her neck and shoulders in as many folds as the serpent of Laocoon, a beaver hat close over her ears, and her feet shod in pattens that lifted her above all contact with mud and water, clanking on the sidewalks with the footfall of the spectre of the Bleeding Nun.

Even the seasons were on a scale of grandeur unknown to the present time. There were none of your soft Italian skies and puny affectation of April in December. But winter strutted in, like a peremptory bandit on the stage, as one who knew his power and wasn't to be trifled with, and took possession of sky and field and river in good earnest, flinging his snowy cloak upon the ground as a challenge to all comers, determined that it should lie there until he chose to take it up and continue his journey. And the nights seemed to be made on purpose for frolicks—they were so bright and crisp, and so inviting to the jovial spirits of the time who, crowded in sleighs, sped like laughing phantoms over every highway, echoing back the halloos of groups of boys that, at every street corner greeted them with vollies of snow-balls. And the horse-bells jangling the music of revelry from many a near and many a distant quarter, told of the universal mirth that followed upon the track of the old-fashioned winter.

Baltimore has altered since those merry days. It has grown up, since then, from a jovial, bustling little town into the dimensions of a fair city. The stages of that growth have been rapidly passed. Every year has witnessed a visible encroachment of the suburbs on the surrounding country, and every score of years the doubling of the number of the inhabitants. To my perception, the departure of each generation carried with it some precious remainder of the quality which made Baltimore an abode to be chosen by those who seek "to cast their lines in pleasant places."

It is no querulous temper nor predilection of age which prompts me to say that the later time has not repaired the losses of the old. I would not offend the present by comparison with the past: I simply note a fact in which, perhaps, some calm thinker may find a useful moral.

There was more public spirit in the young Baltimore than in the grown up City, and it was nursed by nobler men. There was a grander race of merchants in those days; —don't be offended, my worthy friends of the Exchange, there is a broad space below the top line of that old company, which may be occupied without disparagement to your respectability;—they were larger in their views, and larger in their hearts,—gave more time and money to public enterprise, were more elegant and more generous in their convivialities, more truly representative of a refined upper class, more open of hand and more kind to the world, than any society we have had since. I speak of society as an aggregate, because I desire to leave room for individual exceptions in which the old spirit survives. They were of the Venetian stamp, and belonged to the order of what the world calls merchant princes;—not so much in magnificence as in aim and intention. What a roll could I call of those departed spirits who made their names the favorite household memories of Maryland and famous in the history of commercial venture in every port of Europe, and down along the coasts of either continent "to utmost Indian isle."

And then, passing from the merchants to the old Bench and Bar—what a galaxy of talent and learning and eloquence was there! What grand, joyous, keen-witted, sparkling good fellows got together in that old

Court House and the new!—on such good brotherly terms with each other, so proud of each other; and in that little Academy of Themis, numbering not over some two or three score of barristers, judges, clerks, students and all, such an extraordinary proportion of notabilities, of renown throughout the nation—enough to give a reputation to half a dozen cities.

We had divines and physicians, too, who could face all the colleges of to-day and make them envious of the excellence which their most eager ambition would be satisfied to attain for themselves. Certainly, the City now fails in its emulation of that old time vigor of mental activity which made the former Baltimore so note-worthy in all its departments of municipal life. But this is casual and may be better by and by. Men of mould come in cycles, and we are in apogee just now. Wait awhile, and the wheel of time will bring better conditions around again. I prophecy something good from this great cataclysm of rebellion, which seems to be the travail of a healthful purification and the dawn of a new life for Baltimore. We are undergoing a very stern and solemn reformation which, if I mistake not, will evolve much new faculty with much prolific opportunity, in the future.

What is notable now is, that the City is care-worn and contentious. It is unpleasantly characterised by a struggle between generosity and selfishness:—many ready to give every thing and do every thing for the sake of the country in its need; many who will give and do nothing. It is cloven by faction, and it is more than the true men and women can do, by any persuasion or example, to keep it on decent terms of social toleration. There are sorrowful variances amongst us. Dissension has crept up to the verge of the altars, and invaded the firesides of the City, tainting both with an infection that good Christians are not accustomed to allow in such sanctuaries. Rebellion has vitiated the atmosphere of the market place, and flaunts its symbols on the street. Old friends keep apart, pass with unpleasant glances, or converse together without a topic and with a strange constraint. There was one point three years ago, upon which they had a difference of opinion—and this was a fountain of discord. What was it? Reducing the cause of quarrel to its simple element, as we sift it out of the protocols or counter-propositions which preluded the breaking out of this insane civil war, in the discussions of the opposing parties in Congress, it was neither more nor less than this:—Shall we have the privilege to plant Slavery in the bosom of the new communities which, in future time, are to inhabit that broad domain lying between the Lakes and the Rocky Mountains, and condemn that coming empire to endure the curse which, in old time, we complained against Great Britain for inflicting upon us?

The nation said no. And, thereupon, many in Baltimore thought there was sufficient reason for destroying our Great Republic! Marvellous, that any man or woman in Baltimore should even grow angry upon such a privation as this! Then, as the war goes on, things, of course, get worse; for rebellion is always creating new exasperations: it is, in its mildest type, a rough experiment, and not at all, as romantic young ladies think, sprinkled with rose-water. And so, we divide and become unhappy. Perhaps time will clear away the mist, and people, in Maryland at least, will see the folly of fighting for slavery in the Rocky Mountains and, in the end, the nation grow the stronger and the purer for this outbreak.

I perceive I am rambling towards a topic that might carry me into a long discourse. So I come to a halt, lest I should destroy the flavor of these kindly memories I would fain preserve for the pleasure of those who like to hear of Baltimore Long Ago.

THE FLOWER AND LEAF INTERPRETED.

"Once, to every man and nation, comes the moment to decide."
Lowell.

The Rose and Leaf, since Chaucer's hand
   Loosened our English rhymthic flow,
In poet's phrase, forever stand
   Types of true worth, or empty show.

Temptation's self, the brittle Rose
   Casts richest worship to the winds;
The Leaf's deep green unfading glows,
   Fast shrine of all adoring minds.

A poet's dream, of knightly times;
   A simple moral, sweetly told—
Chivalry's song, whose deep, rude chimes
   Teach every age, both new and old.

Ho! soul's broad table lands, among
   Whose gusty tops live master-minds,
Whose thunders roll through Milton's song,
   Where sense is dazed, and waking, finds

A starlit world, the clouds above
    Fantastic forests, fairy dells
Aglow with Una's face of love;—
    Hills, where the only Shakespeare dwells

Amid his "fair humanities."
    Ye but inspire; in vales of song
Below your trackless sceneries,
    Man's simple battle-hymns belong.

Again to-day with mailed hand
    Beck'ning the poet's pageant forth,
The age of Force cries through the land,
    "Choose 'twixt fair show and solid worth."

Inspired bequests of that rare age,
    When Force with Mind held equal sway,
Ye have no charm from sin to save—
    The Beautiful makes no man pray.

Interpret rather, cries the Voice,
    For this unhallowed age, such lay
As sharpest teaches only "choice;"—
    There self, here Christ's pure aye and nay.

A signal! The sword from its rusty niche dropping,
    Rings loud 'mid the revels of a nation's young pride;
A silence—suspicion from eye to eye glancing,
    Then true man and traitor for combat divide.

'Tis well—for Humanity needs crucifixion
  Of parchments, as all lighter loves of the heart;
From the blood of crushed manhood shall spring the
    new nation,
  With freedom's true motto graved on its fair chart.

Frail rose, lasting leaf, who wore each 'mid the fighting,
  The North or the South, be this history's text;
White armed peace shall wreathe both for the future's
    adorning;
  Man's frailty of this day, is God's strength for the next.

The passions, self-seeking, that dear human rights spurn,
  Faults fleeting as roses, with roses shall die;
Quick faith, slow sincerity, Northern or Southern,
  With the leaf in the wreath shall grow greener for aye.

Such seemeth the meaning of old Chaucer's vision,
  Two pageants, two colors, a worship diverse;
When crises of history confront a young nation,
  The Red and Green knights their homage rehearse.

Not a soul but must choose—God knoweth right choosing;
  Our discipline lies in the choice and the fight;
God grant us a conscience forever preferring
  To the roses' vain honors, the leaf's sober light.

THE TRUE BOND OF UNION.

In leaving the Old world our forefathers not only gave up what material inheritance might have fallen to them there, but cut off the entail to their descendants of the far more precious heir-looms of association and tradition which are there handed down from father to son, and which together with the great works of former generations connect the present with the past, reviving ancient memories, and kindling fresh imaginations. The emigrant from the old country to the new may bring his household gods with him, but he worships no longer at the familiar altars. There are things sacred in every land, which cannot be transferred to a new soil. The love of the native soil is in the texture of the soul, and there is a responsive sympathy between man and the earth on which he was born of a kind that can exist in no foreign land.

The aspects of nature are not the same for us as for our ancestors. The features of the land are changed; the sky is different; the trees have another growth; the birds have another plumage and another song. Our busy day is not waked by the lark. The nightingale does not make our thickets tuneful,—though she may indeed sing to our inward ear a song sweet and sorrowful as that which

> "Found a path
> Through the sad heart of Ruth, when sick for home
> She stood in tears amid the alien corn."

But these are not our heaviest losses, for nature has compensations, if not equivalents. It is the loss of the works of men which is the most grievous,—of the memorials of their lives, of the monuments of their faith, their love, their fears and hopes,—this is our irreparable loss, for by it our relations with our forefathers are cut off almost as if they had never been; our sympathies are narrowed, and our characters deprived of the refining and elevating influence which the force of associations with the works of the past exercises alike on the imagination and the affections.

Nor is this all. The absence of visible memorials of the past is a hindrance to our recognition of the relations of men through age to age, and our appreciation of the mutual dependence of the various races and generations of mankind. We are not free from relations to the past, even though the material evidences of those relations be all wanting. Our present is the product of the thought, the labors, the faith of the past. We cannot isolate ourselves. The larger element of our civilization is the traditional. The succession of generations, influenced by those that have gone before, and each influencing in turn those that are to come after, is never interrupted. The life of the individual ceases, the life of the race is continuous and unbroken. It is not one age, or one race, from which our civilization springs, but the whole past, and the whole human family are the source and reservoir of that stream of progress which, now and always, pours its continually deepening waters forward into the vast ocean of the future.

Thus are we members one of another; and if through the absence of memorials of the past, we fail fully to recognize the intimacy of our connection with preceding generations, there is the more need for us to quicken our apprehension of this truth by study and by thought, in order that we may fully understand it in its application to the present time, and our own present circumstances.

The doctrine of the moral unity of the human race not only affords such partial solution, as man may hope to attain, of the plan and purpose of human history, but lies at the very foundation of politics and of law. It is the doctrine of revealed religion, no less than a teaching slowly learned, and but imperfectly acquired by mankind from their own experience. "Thou shalt love thy neighbor as thyself," is the commandment in which it takes form; and it is expressed in the declaration, "He hath made of one blood all nations of men, for to dwell on all the face of the earth."

Hitherto, this doctrine has been so dimly recognised, so imperfectly understood, so frequently denied that it has been rarely applied to the affairs of the world. The ancients knew nothing of it. The idea of the unity of mankind would have been unintelligible to them, that of the brotherhood of men would have been alike ridiculous and offensive. The modern nations, notwitstanding the influence and authority of Christianity, have been slow to admit a brotherhood which should be real and not factitious; the strong should at least be the elder brothers and have the largest share of the goods; all men might by a figure of speech, be called the children of God, but it was plain that some of them were his favorites. We ourselves, here in America, went further than the world had before gone in the acknowledgment of the moral unity of the race, when we declared that all men are endowed by their Creator with certain inalienable rights; and we went further than the rest of the world in our practical denial of this doctrine in the violation of the inalienable rights of men of a different color from our own, and of other capacity.

But the time has come, when the contradiction between our Grand Declaration and our Institutions, is to be destroyed. Not, alas! as the result of our strong conviction of duty, not as the consequence of our natural shame at so flagrant an impiety, not as the consequence of our moral improvement. but as a "war measure," a "military necessity," a political expedient, a social change required by existing circumstances!

We may well rejoice that our practice is to be in some measure, at least, conformed to our principles even if it be only by force. But if we desire to see our country not what we have boasted that it was, and have hoped that it might become, but what it ought to be, we must admit no divorce between morals and politics; we must act upon the noblest truths that we profess to believe. If we acknowledge the moral unity of the race, it is the claim of patriotism no less than the command of religion, that we secure to all men under our institution their inalienable rights; that we make liberty universal, that we maintain the equality of man as the children of God. and made in his image. Thus shall our Union rest on the eternal foundation of Justice, and our people be knit together in bonds interwoven in the very nature of human existence.

THY WILL BE DONE.

"Thy will be done," our lips are trained to saying;
    My will be done our urgent hearts implore;
But while we look for gifts to crown such praying,
    God's *No* has crushed us—we will pray no more.

We're slow to learn that we have asked insanely;
    Misread the text; and so reversed the spell
Of benediction meant for all—not mainly
    That *I* and *mine* may in its affluence dwell.

That we must loose the idols we are holding,
    Ere we can rightly lift our hands in prayer,
Though life go with it, and our arms unfolding
    That dear embrace, drop nerveless with despair.

When, swooning downward, prone before God's altar
    Our eyes close blindly, and we think all's done,
An arm uplifts us; and our steps that falter
    Are guided forth—and lo! a day begun.

With morning brightness all the East is burning,
    Although but now we deemed the daylight dead ;
And, up the rugged steeps our way discerning,
    We ask for guidance, and for daily bread.

Not bread alone, but all good gifts bestowing,
    God's angel sends us strengthened on our way,
With sacrificial wine life's cup o'erflowing,
    And palms kept clean from idols, let us pray.

WOMEN OF THE TIMES.

IN anticipating the numerous and important revolutions the present national crisis is destined to effect, it may not be amiss to consider what will be its influence upon the development of female character and intellect.

It has long been the complaint of woman that the sphere in which she moved presented little stimulus to mental exertion; that her laudable ambitions found few sources of gratification, and no adequate rewards; that if she aspired to any thing beyond the labors of her nursery and household, she was met with sarcasm from one sex, and rebuffs from the other; while the scanty pittance reluctantly doled out to her for all kinds of labor, whenever necessity compelled her to rely upon her own exertions, has been a sharp criticism upon the chivalry of those claiming to be her natural protectors, but who have been the first to denounce her for the independence poverty compelled her to assume

While we believe a woman faithfully discharging her social and domestic duties is fulfilling the very highest mission it is in her power to compass, since it is the one her Maker evidently assigned her, still we cannot be unmindful of the external pressure of public events upon her destiny, or of the development, both moral and intellectual, they must necessarily accomplish. If ladies have murmured at the narrow limits of their home-influences, gentlemen have murmured quite as loudly at the insipidity of our conversation, and the circumscribed range of reflections in which our minds seem always to be revolving. Nor can we resist the conviction that this imputation is well founded, when we listen day after day to the small talk of our drawing rooms, and find ourselves enlightened upon nothing beyond the fashions, the misdeeds of domestics, and the sagacity of a French poodle. That this plebian mental condition is not the necessary result of woman's domestic position is the more certain, since the larger portion of our most gifted female authors and artistes have originated from those classes of society which are more or less accustomed to labor; and very many of the happiest inspirations of poesy have welled up spontaneously, while the hands mechanically performed their menial offices.

It is the misfortune of our country-women that society and parental influence encourage young persons to resign the healthy discipline of the school room, while they are yet mentally and physically unfitted for the onerous duties with which they are so early invested. In this precocious pressure lies the real germ of mediocrity; and it is only when parents become discreet, and society judicious, that youth will be impressed that something more is required for home happiness, than a beautiful face or a golden fleece.

Since the women of the revolution manufactured their linen, moulded bullets for their defenders, and braved death for their little ones, American ladies have experienced no hardships calculated to bring out the innate strength of female character. Their minds have become too morbid and imaginative, their hearts too sensitive and exacting, and the result of both has been a painful reaction upon the *physique*, making them hot house buds, where nature designed them for prairie roses. The evils of the present crisis will fall heavily upon our sex. Woman must exchange her dream-life for real sacrifices, hardships and sufferings. For almost every victim that falls upon the field of blood, a wife or mother is left to assume his responsibilities, together with the support of his daughters and sons. Her experiences will be new and bitter, but beneath all the supineness and helplessness of female character, there is concealed a power of endurance, a submission and adaptation to suffering, which seldom fails to buoy her up, amidst the deepest waters of affliction. These will avail her in her hour of need, and as emergencies arise, demanding new energies and greater efforts, she will be found equal to meet and overcome them.

Life is no longer a romance—woman must struggle for support and resources. That she cannot provide for the necessities of her family upon the small sums her labor now commands is evident, neither indeed with increased remuneration would the present avenues of industry suffice her. When children cry for bread, mothers must, and will, have labor. When, therefore, the ranks of clerkships are thinned by the demands of war, the ingenuity and tact of woman will teach her how to press forward and secure the vacancies. As saleswomen, daguerrians, librarians, artistes, accountants, book-keepers, amanuenses, teachers, physicians, and indeed in most of the occupations not dependent upon physical ability, females would not only prove equally desirable, but in many respects more acceptable. Nor will applications for these positions be confined to any one grade of society. The destinies of war and financial uncertainty will involve all classes, and while some will be content to eat the bread of charity, the energetic and more intelligent will struggle to advance their pecuniary interests. As woman sees this, she will realize that knowledge is not only power, but that it is also money. Her own mental resources will not only be aroused, but she will be interested in qualifying her children for practical life. The whole tendency, therefore, of this struggle will be to increase woman's intellectual strength, to give her self-reliance, and enable her to forget her bodily infirmities in the intensity of her pursuits.

The facility with which most American ladies become authors will also receive a healthy reaction. The ridicule cast upon female writers may not be unmerited, but the stimulus to authorship is not so well understood, nor so charitably regarded, as the evil deserves. While all allow that woman is especially imaginative, and that most of her attractions have their origin in this redundancy of fancy, they forget that like all other gifts, imagination must be gratified, or it becomes a curse to the possessor. When, therefore, her life is too real and barren to satisfy the requirements of her nature, what can be more natural than that she should manufacture manikins to order, and invest them with the witcheries which she would be glad, but fails, to find in her daily life? If these manikins are imperfect and open to criticism it is not her fault. She frames them to the best of her ability, and finds the amusement she sought in draping their uncouthness. The publisher is at liberty to reject them, and certainly the book must be quite as agreeable to the critic as his phillipic is to the writer. We have often thought when looking over these cutting "notices" that if the critic

22*

could but realize what feminine heart-aches those stupid love-scenes had magnetized, and what fairy palaces those feeble descriptions had built up in many an ungarnished room, he would use his pen with more leniency and allow the hapless dreamer to idealize her hard lot with imaginary possessions. For the realities that woman must now encounter, her imagination will become more practical, as well as creditable, while in this diversion from self, and the intense mental irritability which has hitherto found so little negative influence in the hacknied routine of her home duties, she will find a natural restorative for the physical debility which so often renders her life burdensome.

There will always be females as well as males to whom authorship will be a mental necessity. If the South has been less prolific in female writers, it has been because its women have not had the same inducements to mental exertion as have urged on their Northern sisters. With the fatal shock which has startled their hot blood aflame, will spring up an intellectual rivalry of which we may well beware; in the thrilling incidents of our civil war, both North and South will find material for romances over which unborn generations will shed tears of blood. It will no longer be said that America has no past to inspire the novelist; while poets and sculptors shall forget their day-dreams in the East to wreathe laurels for our heroes, and chisel the cypress and the willow upon the marble that records their valor.

Never again during our life can such opportunities for noble deeds present themselves to woman, as are now offering themselves to her acceptance. The woman who stands in her cottage door and waves her tearless adieu to her brave volunteer, is no less a hero than he; for does she not remain to suffer a thousand deaths through her affection and fears? The mother who blesses her son and consigns him to the sacrifice, is braver than her child; for a mother would give many lives for the lad who has but one to lose. The female who administers to the dying necessities of the soldier, is worthier of immortality than he from whose brow she wipes the death-damps, for does she not, through her sympathetic nature, expose herself to heart-wounds more cruel to be borne, than the sabre's gash or the fatal shell?

If, therefore, there are women sighing to distinguish themselves and seeking for ambitions worthy their abilities,—to-day they have abundant opportunity for both, and history is waiting to write out their meritorious record. Wherever the poor wife is left desolate with her group of little ones—wherever poverty flings its cold shadow over the hearth-stone—wherever the wreck of a true-hearted patriot, or a broken foe stretches itself out to die—*there is woman's mission!*

Who is to bind up these broken hearts? Who is to provide for the tender orphans whose naked feet have but taken their first steps in this weary life-journey? Where are the ladies whose noble instincts the rust of opulence and ennui have corroded, who will atone for past inertia, by lifting up these impressible little ones where the vices of the City, and the snares of the wicked cannot reach them? What halo can adorn us like that which rests upon the brow of benevolence? Where is the pearl half so lustrous as the tear of gratitude? Or the jewel to be won, so imperishable, as the soul we bear up in our supplicating palms?

Let then, each American woman meet cheerfully the demands which the present emergencies of our country require at her hands, and prepare herself as she best can, for the new and prolonged sacrifices that she must surely encounter. If she does this, the future will be found pregnant with good for all classes of our country-women, and the phenix of her salvation will rise exultant from the ashes of her dead.

THE APOTHEOSIS OF PAN.

A FABLE.

But half a man and half a brute
    A listless Satyr wandered,
And all the golden hours of June
    In idle rambles squandered.

While roaming thus, 'twas ages since,
    He found, one morning early,
A spot where man, new comer then
    On earth, was reaping barley.

The Satyr paused, and lounging sat
    To view the operation,
And, as he sat, played with the straws,
    For want of occupation.

But, blowing in the square cut ends,
    His listlessness soon vanished,
And busy plans of cunning work
    All thoughts of reaping banished.

Before the reapers left the field
    The Satyr had completed
His pipes, and with new melodies
    Their wondering ears had greeted.

They left their sickles in the field
    And gathered round to hear him;
His wondrous music forces them
    To reverence and fear him.

He seemed at will to swell their hearts
    With sorrow or with pleasure;
Their every passion rose and fell
    Responsive to his measure.

No idle rambler then was he,
    No lounging useless Satyr;
They deified him, called him Pan,
    A demi-god creator.

Thus has it proved a thousand times
    In all succeeding ages,
And seeming trifles still convert
    The seeming fools to sages.

For highest deeds of usefulness,
    When Providence so pleases,
The chance is still to each man sent,
    Which—happy he who seizes!

A VISIT TO THE BATTLE-FIELD OF GETTYSBURG.

THE FOUR RELICS.

[THE following fragment, though strictly and literally true as to all its facts and details, was originally composed in the form of an episode, intended to be inserted in a little work of imagination, in which, spirits and supernatural beings form the principal agents. This will at once account to the reader for some allusions near the beginning and end, which might otherwise appear incomprehensible, as also for much of the general tone and coloring of the whole sketch.]

*   *   *   The world of spirits, of angels, and of visions is, perhaps, nearer to the actual working and fighting world in which we live and breathe, than most of us are apt to imagine. The last words of the Spirit with the Sky-blue pinions had brought so vividly to my recollection some little incidents which had impressed themselves on my mind some months ago, and which, by subtle ties of thought are so closely united with the subject under consideration, that I willingly suspend my narrative for a few moments to relate them. The two things, I think, mutually reflect light on each other, even as the illumination of a fire at night has been known to extend its glow over large tracts of the heaven above it.

Of all awful and at the same time sublimely horrible sights to be witnessed on this globe, it is said that the spectacle of a battle-field and its environs some days after the slaughter has taken place, is the most soul-harrowing. Such scenes have again and again been described of late, by pens far more graphic than mine, or by eye-witnesses who either wrote on the spot, or immediately after leaving it, with all its images of terror and of agony fresh upon their recollection. Particularly the scenes which occur at such times in military hospitals, in which are huddled together the dying, the mortally wounded, and the agonized subjects for surgical operation, are spoken of as terrific beyond all conception or belief. It has never been my lot to witness any of these, and I fervently pray to heaven, that it never may. What I did see was altogether of a softer, and some might say, of a tamer character. Such as it was, I shall narrate it in words as few and as simple as possible.

I think it must have been about three weeks after the great battle was fought—a battle, which, after three days of desperate attack and defence, ended in a glorious victory, consummated on the Fourth of July by the flight of the enemy—a battle, too, which as well for the numbers engaged in it, the valor and generalship displayed on both sides, as for its inappreciably important results, throws in the shade almost every other engagement of which we have any mention in history—about three times, I say, the moon, since the event, had changed her varying phases, when the present writer, in company with a clergyman and a few ladies, visited the scene of conflict.

Although within that space of time, many horrors must naturally have been abated, many sorrowful sights removed or mellowed down, we felt as after a long hot day of summer's travel we approached the painfully attractive spot, as though we were entering the rueful abodes of the dead. Fields trodden down and trampled into desolation; fences and enclosures torn away or consumed by fire; hundreds of stakes still sticking in the ground where tents had been erected or horses tethered;—such were the objects which for miles around environed the great central gloominess. To right and left of the main road, some nearer, some more distant, could be seen beside a clump of trees or on the open fields, small tented encampments, where, beneath the national banner, wounded or dying men were being nursed and waited on by surgeons, by charitable women who had volunteered their services and many of whom had left their comfortable homes to remain night and day with the sick, and by their own companions who had escaped the dangers of the battle-field. From some of these tents came delicious strains of military music, the effect of which on the ear, mellowed and sweetened by the distance, was beyond measure pensive and pleasing. And as in the act of dying, the sense of sight almost invariably fails before that of hearing, "perhaps e'en now," I thought to myself, "some one, over whose eyes the death-film is gathering, may hear those pathetic strains, and even in his death-agonies, when he can no longer *see* the weeping forms of his friends around him, may be soothed by them."

This state of things continued for several miles, until we came upon a region of desolation, where half-decayed carcasses of mules and horses might be seen in every direction, so that the hot summer air was completely saturated with the sickening odor of putrefaction. This peculiar and overpowering impression on the sense of smell, as much as anything else, made us realize that we were travelling into a realm of death and ghastly gloom. More than once, through the open doors of wayside cottages and farm-houses, we, in passing, caught a glimpse of some dismal figure, usually a person in the first prime of opening manhood—but pale, pale—and very much like one already bandaged up and stiffened in a winding-sheet. Arriving in view of Cemetery Hill, we passed four men in soldiers' uniform, bearing on a litter, what at first sight we supposed to be a corpse, but which proved to be a man still alive, though whiter than the sheets which covered him.

On the southern side of the Hill itself were many grave-diggers and many new-made graves. We found the same melancholy work going on there the next morning. Wagon-loads of coffins were moving about from place to place, or piled up ready for use.

Such were the sights, sounds and smells which impressed the senses, and through the senses affected the fancy and the heart, about the time of sunset.

But the three relics?—We will come to them anon. The next morning, after visiting the Theological Seminary, then a hospital, (how calm and quiet and even cheerful most of those wounded men appeared, how ready they were to talk and even to smile, what noble countenances many of them had, how pleased they seemed with our sympathizing questions!) we passed out and viewed the rifle-pits close by, which had been used by rebel sharp-shooters, and from which they were wont to pick off any luckless wight they caught passing over the distant square of the town.

Walking next down a little street, we came to where a few men, with an officer directing them, were working around a huge heap of articles, which had been collected from different parts of the battle-field, at the same time assorting them and putting them away in separate lots in an adjoining building. During the short time we paused to converse with these men, we were particularly struck with three objects, two of which we obtained, whilst the third was not procurable either for love or money.

This last was a long and beautiful finished bowie-knife, which had belonged to one of the Louisiana Tigers. The blade was very bright and sharp, the handle rich and artistically executed, and the whole instrument such as any gentleman would like to own and keep as a parlor ornament, to be handed down to posterity as a memento of a civil war destined to be memorable through all coming time. But the man who had it, seemed to value it far above its weight in gold.

Of the other two, one was a simple soldier's button, which, at first sight, presented nothing note-worthy. But upon closer inspection we found impressed upon it, the following little Latin inscription—*"Animis opibusque parati."* Whether the soldier who had borne it, had understood the import of the words or not, who now living can tell? Many thousand similar buttons had no doubt been worn by his comrades. Some directing mind, however, must have originally selected the motto and regulated the fashion of them, and even if the poor fellow himself knew not a word of Latin, we may reasonably suppose some of his officers had translated it for him. Hearing its meaning, he had no doubt gloried in the sentiment, and felt his bosom all the warmer, both for the button and its inscription, when, during a cold night-watch or a stormy day, he, by its means, protected himself against the chilling blast. Such things may seem to many the merest trifles,—but they are trifles which *tell*. Whatever tends to keep up the sentiment, the enthusiasm of an army, adds that much to its dash and effectiveness. An appropriate motto, an exciting melody, a soul-stirring song, are none of them without their charm; and in these things, I think the enemy has been rather superior to us.

Had the next relic not proved more interesting than the two just mentioned, I should never have troubled the reader with an account of it. And yet at first sight it seemed simple and homely in the extreme. It was a small slip of coarse yellow paper, about three or four inches long and nearly as many wide. It was much soiled and weather-beaten, and had been found on the body of a Louisianian—a private, if I mistake not. I wish the reader could see it, because with all its coarseness and weather-stains, it told its own story much more forcibly than any poor words of mine can do. It was evidently a communication from a young wife to a young husband, then the father of two small children. It was simply folded once, the crease or fold forming a dividing line in the centre, thus forming two pages, on each of which were written words, which, of all others, must ever be the dearest to the eye of a youthful parent. And not words alone,—on each little page was a small lock of hair, carefully plaited in the form of a small wreath or circlet, and fastened to the paper with pink ribband, which, though much faded, had once been fresh, and still retained the tasteful appearance with which it had been arranged by the hands of the mother. Each wreath thus occupying one side of the dividing fold, and each being similarly fastened with its little rosette of ribband, it naturally followed that when the paper was folded together, the two circlets rested lovingly together, (they were brother and sister,) and thus in affectionate nearness, both might be borne on the heart of the common parent. What an amulet it must have been to preserve the wearer against temptations both from within and without.

The lady who made this little relic her prize, valued it so highly, that I in vain endeavored to persuade her to present it to me. Not being able to become its owner, I studied it with more than usual care, and even went to the trouble of making a rough copy of it.

To Mr. Richard H. Willeford

this is fanny's willeford's hair (hair)   (hair) this is Richard's H. willeford's hair

Your two little darlings

THE FOUR RELICS. 271

How infinitely stronger than all artificial rules of rhetoric, syntax and orthography, are the simple artless words of a mother's love. These last go straight to the heart, the former, though very needful and excellent in their way, often chill the very things they beautify. The one may be compared to living water, pulsing up fresh from its fountain, the other, to water frozen into icicles, and sparkling with prismatic radiance.

Reader! those few unlearned words, in their unusual but touching arrangement, are well worthy of being pondered over.

Observe, if you please, how instinctively in all languages, the terms of affection, particularly when applied to children, assume some appearance of endearing littleness. Every one who has the least acquaintance with European languages, knows how much affectionate *diminutives* abound in them all, particularly in German, French and Italian. The English, though comparatively meagre in them, is not a total exception. "Your two little *darlings*." This last word, I suppose, was in old English "dearling," but by changing the pronunciation how much it seems to gain in richness—the original diminutive deepening into a broader and fuller sound. How the father's eye, before he went upon the battle-field, must have moistened whilst resting upon that sweet word, written by (to him) the very dearest hand, except their own, that ever he had clasped, or *could* clasp, in all this world! Those *darlings*, she, in the devotedness of her young love, had, with pain and peril, borne to him; and even if he had loved her ever so devotedly *before* the wedding-ring had symbolized the enduringness of their affection, how much greater must have been his affection, when from their mutual love, had sprung two other human beings fashioned like themselves? Perhaps the boy most resembled the father, the girl the mother. For the girl, most likely *he* experienced rather the deeper devotion; for the boy, the mother. You may notice the diminutive, f, of fanny and the capital, R, of Richard. And when he imagined, or remembered, the *three* as composing one heart-captivating group, in which the Youthful-Motherly, the budding Masculine and the buding Feminine were beautifully combined, how his young father's and husband's heart must have melted within him!

Much as I dislike the minute technicalities of grammar at such a time, necessity compels me to descend to them in order to make myself understood. You will please, dear reader, to notice another minute peculiarity, viz: the *double possessive*, or in other words, "an apostrophe with the letter, S," applied both to the christian and the surname of each of the children. Perhaps she retains some faint recollection from her early school-days of those mysterious letters and symbols, which now did her "yeoman's service,"—and so the dear simple creature writes, "this is fanny's willeford's hair"—as much as to say—'both by the strong bonds of law, and the still stronger and holier sacramental bonds of baptism, the little thing is yours—yours, soul and body,—yours through the Church and through the State.'

No doubt the father felt all these little touches at a single glance—it required for him no labored analysis, no lengthy train of reasoning. To us they are interesting, as showing how rapidly and unerringly, Nature, by a few untaught half-sentences, a few artless syllables imperfectly scrawled and ungrammatically worded, can say more than we, with all our fancied erudition, could, after filling many long drawn pages

In another respect, this little relic had for me a strong source of interest,—just enough was known to excite the imagination, and not enough to blunt curiosity. What, before he entered the rebel army, could have been the avocation of the bearer of it? Had he been a believer in the sanctity of the *divine institution?* If so, how are we to reconcile the existence of those soft emotions with the desire to aid in keeping in perpetual bondage millions of his fellow-beings, composed of flesh and blood like himself, with the slight difference of a skin differently colored? Could he ever have been an overseer, think you, riding from field to field with a cow-hide in his hand? Had he been a boatmen or lumberer upon the Father of Waters? Or, had he once kept a little shop in one of the obscure streets of the Crescent City,—for beautiful human blossoms sometimes are met with in dark and dingy places? To most of these queries fancy was disposed to answer in the negative.—What, if he had been torn by a rude military conscription from his wife and little ones, and been forced to fight for a cause in which he felt little or no sympathy! In sooth, such things have been. Perhaps, he may have been in his time, a jolly herdsman on the flowery prairies of Attakapas or Opelousas, or near the waters of the Atchefelaya, mounted on a cantering mustang pony, with Spanish saddle and huge wooden stirrups, with a horn by his side and a lasso at his saddle-bow, galloping with a few companions attired like himself, after countless droves of branded cattle? Perhaps, he had often indulged in the poetical pastime of arrow-fishing which Mr. Thorpe so graphically describes. Perhaps, but a truce to conjecture. Of one thing I think we may be pretty certain, that when the death blow came, his last thoughts must have hovered around the images of these dear ones, a memento of whom he ever carried nearest his heart.

It only remains to add that the hair of the children was very beautiful. The boy's was something between flaxen and auburn; that of the girl nearly a full auburn, a little softened into brown; both very smooth and silken, and although taken from the battle-field, each had much of its virgin gloss about it, like the plumage of a humming-bird after a storm. Often I held them in heaven's sunbeams to watch the play of light on their woven glossiness, and often,—but here's a little poem which may express what more I have to say, better than prose.

> Ye mourners, come, with bosom swelling,
>   Wrap him in his winding-sheet,
>   Cross his arms and bind his feet,
>   And, with ceremonies meet,
> Bear him to his last cold dwelling.
>
> A three-fold chain, a rapture treble,
>   A boy, a girl, a loving wife,
>   Once bound his heart to sunny life,
>   His blood was spilt in traitor's strife;
> But still we mourn him, though a rebel.
>
> Week after week its old grief carries;
>   Northward they gaze at dawn of day,
>   Northward at sunset, far away,
>   And as they gaze, I hear them say,
> "He never comes! How long he tarries."

Oh, for the lov'd ones that outlive him,
For his life-blood bravely spilt,
For love's floweret doomed to wilt,
Gracious God! o'erlook his guilt,
For his loving heart, forgive him!

Of these three relics already contemplated, the first was calculated to lead us to the study of those savage and tiger-like passions which lurk in the dark corners of the human heart, since tiger-like, though the weapon had a gay and brilliant outside, it was fashioned for the very purpose of feasting on human blood; whilst the second served to draw aside a curtain and to give us a hasty peep into the little secret springs by which large masses of men are spirited to action. The powers of our nature which these two conducted us to meditate upon, may be called the *destructive,* rather than the constructive or reconstructive ones. The third bore us among those dear emotions and sanctities to which we owe our very life and most of the good that is found in that life; which may therefore be called *productive* in their nature, and with which war of all kinds, and particularly civil war, is ever at variance. The fourth and last, will, I hope, unlock for us a dark portal, through which we may wander into a shadowy realm, where volcanic mountains cast their illuminations over solemn midnight seas, where destruction prepares the way for reconstruction, and where amid a world of chaotic din and darkness and havoc, a fair angel of love may be seen smiling over billows of blood and fire.

But before proceeding to it, I must beg the indulgence of a few preliminary remarks. To many of us residing in this latitude, the name of Gettysburg has for many years been so familiar, that it is not without considerable effort, that we are able to disentangle that name from a mesh of common-place associations. This task, however, once accomplished, the great battle that was fought there, at once assumes its due prominence. Even the great victory of Tours, usually spoken of by historians, as the most important in its results of any that has yet taken place, inasmuch as it secured Europe against the tyranny of the Crescent, and fully established the power of the Cross, was not more note-worthy. On both occasions, there is reason to believe, that the good principle would eventually have vanquished the evil one. Christianity must have conquered Islamism in the one case, and Freedom must have trampled out Slavery in the other. But in either case, had that good principle been temporarily defeated, there would have been a painful season of dismay and retrogradation. Both battles have upon them some marks which to the open eye of faith, speak plainly of the Divine. That of Tours, lasted for *seven* days—of which sacred number, few persons are ignorant of the significance. That of Gettysburg, was consummated by the retreat of the enemy on that ever memorable day, for which, even in this skeptical age of scoffers and secessionists, many of us still continue to feel a profound reverence. Was it not upon that day that Lewis and Clarke, the first explorers, who by order of government, travelled from the Atlantic to the Pacific, heard the sound of strange artillery echoing from the bosom of the Rocky Mountains, as if those mountains, of their own accord, were celebrating the epoch of the Declaration? And though those mystic sounds have been heard by many a traveller and hunter since, and are still unaccounted for, was it not singular, that of all the three hundred and sixty-five days of the round year, they should have first been listened to by men of Anglo-Saxon descent on the glorious Fourth? And did not, on the same never-to-be-forgotten anniversary, three of our most distinguished Presidents, close their eyes on this mortal scene? And during the last eventful year, did not we, on that day, obtain three notable victories—one on the Atlantic Slope, one on the East bank of the Father of Waters, and one on the West? Can all these things, think ye, be the result of mere chance and hap-hazard? It would require a greater stretch of credulity to think so, than to believe them the results of a superintending Providence.

The subject is a vast one, and to me one of absorbing interest: as yet, like children peeping at the stars through the windows of a dark room, we have only had a glimpse of it. This much I think we may safely do—viz: look upon the memorable day above alluded to, as one which has been canonized by three national deaths, and signalized by three synchronous victories, which may well be regarded as prefigurative.

The fourth relic was found in a different locality, and possessed an interest of a different character. Passing again by Cemetery Hill, we struck off into the woods to take a view of the ground occupied by the right wing of the Federal Army, and where some desperate fighting had taken place during the night-attack of the 2d of July. Here we found the entrenchments still standing which our men had thrown up with such rapidity, and which seemed to extend for the space of more than a mile along the curving brow of the wooded ridge. Here the ground was thickly strewn with old clothes, cartridge-boxes, canteens, beef-bones and bullets. Here too the odor of decaying horses and mules was again overpowering. As we advanced, we came in sight of large numbers of those vast rocks and boulders, some of which, taller than the tallest housetop, towered aloft like the remains of weird Druidical temples, and carried back the imagination to the days beyond the Flood. Had those enormous masses been rolled or heaved there, for they did not appear originally to have belonged to their present site? Had they been removed by the agency of fire, or of water, or of both combined? What vast forces of disruption, dislocation, and transportation must have been united to effect a scene which reminded us of the fabled wars of the Titans against the Gods! Were those indeed fragmentary ruins arising from the disintegration of old *primordial* rocks and ending in the formation of *secondary* ones? Had the waves of the ocean once ebbed away from the sides of the mountains, and gradually retreating eastward, formed the present Atlantic coast, or had the mountain chain itself been upheaved by volcanic forces above the sinking waters?

Such were some of the questions and speculations which crowded upon the mind, and even had no battle been fought there, no thoughtful man could visit that wild spot, without brooding over the awful secrets belonging to primeval ages, without picturing to himself inconceivably grand concussions and convulsions of nature, which usually accompany the transition period from an old to a newer and better state of the world.

It is whilst visiting such scenes as this that a pleasing awe comes over the mind: old earth, sphinx-like, seems to propound certain questions to us, threatening, if we do not answer them, to devour us. Dreams of the wonders of the first creation are followed by speculations concerning floods, earthquakes, volcanic eruptions and *new birth*, until from what *has been*, the mind naturally leaps forwards to visions of what *will be*. "May there not," it naturally asks, "again be convulsions, to be followed by another and more glorious Regeneration?" The reader will please to bear this last word in mind; we shall have to return to it again.

And so we went forward musing, dreaming and observing, now climbing one of those gigantic rock-masses and seating ourselves upon its summit, now marking the bloodstains and broken armor on the earth, now picking up some memento of the battle and tossing it away with the hope of coming upon something still more noteworthy, (for the great War Eagle has in this spot dropt many, very many plumes and feathers,) until at last two objects, not more than twenty yards distant from each other, arrested our full attention. One was a pack of cards, and the other, the remains of a New Testament, as if the Evil and the Good Spirit, each furnished with an appropriate instrument, had been warring together in the same army.

The cards we looked upon, but did not touch. Of the Testament, a few leaves which had been severed from the volume to which they belonged, seemed to offer a portable and convenient memento, which might easily be carried away in one's pocket. Such is the history of the fourth relic.

On the first Sunday night after returning from my visit to the battle-field, in a lonely country house, during those quiet hours when all the inmates of the family were sunk in slumber, I drew from a drawer in which I had carefully laid it, the holy relic, and read the whole of it attentively from beginning to end. I read it by the light of a kerosene lamp,—in other words, by a lamp fed by oil procured from a substance which may have been a vegetable, centuries before the time of the flood,—a casual circumstance which I mention only on account of the associating ideas.

The fragment extended from the second chapter of the second Epistle of St. Peter to the end of the first chapter of the third Epistle of St. John, and in the form in which it was printed, composed exactly *twelve* (double-columned) pages. The whole was very much soiled and discolored— in fact, in some places, so thickly was it coated with adhesive clay as to be utterly illegible. But all the more interesting to me was it on that account.

Twelve battle-stained pages from the Holy Book of GOD!

THE FOUR RELICS. 283

Most of us can recollect certain solemn occasions, times perhaps of deep family bereavement or of national consternation, when in the overwhelming awe of the moment, we have opened at random that sacred volume, and have found words to soothe, to guide, or to edify. We may also call to mind other occasions, when after a great rescue, or a danger safely passed over, the same heaven-inspired book has spoken to us in words, unlike any other words either written or spoken, of which we have ever had any knowledge. Remembering all this, it can easily be imagined that it was with no common emotions, that I sat down that night to peruse a message from the battle-field.

And although another Bible above me, which had been clasped by sunbeams during the day, was now wide open with all its starry pages, from which the hoary Hierophant Time nightly preaches to us,—a Bible composed by the same Almighty Author, and in which were likewise images of a Virgin, a Dove, a Dragon, an infant Demi-god strangling a Serpent, Wise Men travelling onwards from the East, even as one star followeth another westward, and (more beautiful than all the rest) a glittering Astral Cross—still, too thick an earthly film, had dimmed my mortal eyes, to read those glories right.

So I sat me down in my silent chamber, by my coal-oil lamp, to read those twelve weather-beaten, war-stained pages.

I forgot to mention that at no great distance from the place where the fragment was picked up, we reached a spot, which, of all others, bore the most unmistakeable evidences of the fury of the recent contest. There in fact seemed to have taken place the main sweep and havoc of the fiery war-tempest. Gigantic trunks of trees prostrate or riven in twain, others whose stems and branches were shattered, peeled or riddled by innumerable balls, showed how thicker and closer than the stones of a hailstorm, must have been the desolating tornado. Perhaps to the brave hearts, engaged in conflict at the time, in the excitement of the occasion, the reality may not have appeared quite as terrible as the whole appeared to us witnessing the effects after it was all over;—but to me, loitering and musing on the spot itself, it seemed an utter mystery, how any human being stationed near that place during the thick of the battle, could ever have survived such a hurricane of shot and shell. The bare sight of the war-marks impressed on the surrounding trees, made me shudder.

This scene all came back to me that night whilst reading. I pictured to myself the owner of the little Testament, perusing its pages on the night of the battle, but *before* the night attack had commenced. I saw him pouring over it by the light of surrounding camp-fires, with the entrenchments formed of logs and earth before him, the weird and druidical rocks behind, and the moon (then two days past her *full*) with all the constellations overhead. Perhaps he may have once been a lumberer in the forests of Maine, perhaps he had been born beneath the granite peaks of New Hampshire, perhaps his home had been in distant Minnesota near gelid waters which flow towards the Arctic Sea, perhaps his soul had from boyhood been attuned to sublimity by listening to the voice of Niagara.—Perhaps he had been among those driven back by the rebels, during the first day's disastrous conflict. Very certainly, he must have expected to be again in the thick of the battle before the whole should be over.

And with these recollections and these expectations fresh upon him,—behold him open his Bible!

Most of us live, habitually, too far down in the lowlands of earthly life—too far down among the swamps and miasmatic marshes of mortal care and passion, to read aright the words of the hallowed volume. Those words appear to us as incomprehensible as do those mystic pictures, which here and there in our country, are seen impressed upon the faces of lofty rocks, but *so high up*, that fancy, in vain, wearies herself to conjecture how or when they ever came there. So seem to us for the most part, the words of Scripture. Only rare or unusual occasions of sorrow, or of rapture, tide us up to the height of their high import. And then we not only *see*, we begin for the first time to *feel* their meaning.—

So when the brave-hearted soldier opened the Holy Book that night, how different the words must have looked to him from what they had ever done before!— Tall billows of elevated emotion have lifted his eyes nearer to their own altitude. He opens, perhaps, at random, and his eye lights upon these words of St. Peter.

"But, beloved, be ye not ignorant of this one thing, that one day is with the Lord, as a thousand years, and a thousand years as one day. The day of the Lord will come as a thief in the night; in which the heavens shall pass away with a great noise, and the elements shall melt with fervent heat, the earth also, and the works that are therein shall be burnt up. Seeing then that all these things shall be dissolved, what manner of persons ought ye to be in all holy conversation and godliness,— looking for and hasting unto the coming of the day of God, wherein the heavens being on fire shall be dissolved, and the elements shall melt with fervent heat? Nevertheless, we, according to His promise, look for *new heavens* and a *new earth*, wherein dwelleth righteousness."

Or going a little further back in the same chapter, he may have read the following:—"And this they willingly are ignorant of, that by the Word of God, the heavens were of old, and the *earth standing out of the water and in the water:* whereby, the world that then was, being overflowed with water, perished:"

Behold, gentle reader, in the first quotation a reference to the distant *future*, and in the second, to the far distant *past*. This last was the very theme on which those rocks had been preaching to us before. Almost we were inclined to fancy them vast natural pulpits, on which invisible ministers were stationed to impart high thoughts to those whose hearts were in tune for their reception.

But perhaps he read those wonderful words at an earlier hour, say about the time of sunset, when the day-star was sinking in the west, and the full moon, now two days old, had not yet risen in the east. Perhaps at that magic hour, he may have closed the volume to meditate, out there in the heart of the forest, and not until the camp-fires were lighted and but a short time before the sudden attack, may we suppose him to have again opened the heavenly pages. And this time, let us imagine that his eyes rest upon the following sentences from the Apostle of Love.

"Beloved, let us love one another; for love is of God, and every one that loveth, is born of God, and knoweth

God. He that loveth not, knoweth not God; for God is love. * * * And this commandment have we from Him, that he who loveth God, love his brother also."

Let us imagine that he has scarcely finished his reading these sweet words, when, with fiendish yells and savage war-shouts, ten thousand of his *brother* countrymen, born in a sunnier clime than himself, come rushing up the steep wooded hill, firing Indian fashion from behind the trees, come furiously on with intent to destroy him and his other *brothers* of the North, and the volcano of battle surges up ever higher and higher with its molten lava-floods, and the war-demons shriek ever louder and fiercer, and groans and howls, and shouts and convulsive sobs are dismally intermingled,—let us imagine that in that dread moment, he himself, in obedience to the words of command, must load and fire;—we say, that if he has rightly understood the words of the Apostle, even in the act of levelling his musket, he may feel no hatred against his advancing foe—but instead of hate, the softest pity, the softest brotherly love—nay, even when wounded unto death, he sees the earth and the sky reeling around him, and knows that his heart's blood is gushing away, his last words might truthfully be, "Father, forgive them, for they know not what they do."

* * * Such are *some* of the reflections which this fragment has suggested. Even now as I write, it lies

beneath my eye with all its battle stains. Empedocles is fabled to have plunged in the crater of Mount Etna, and his sandals to have been thrown up by the volcano. Were this true, and I could get possession of one of those sandals, it would be a relic not as worthy of preservation— not nearly as suggestive, as those twelve little pages. That soldier was also probably swallowed up by a volcano; but what is a sandal, even though it may have belonged to one of the poet-philosophers of the antique world, compared to even a few words of the talismanic life-book, which that hero bore with him into battle?

A word or two more and I leave the sacred fragment to preach for itself. Many of us still remember the accurate and vivid descriptions which floated from the pens of our "ready writers" whilst the battle was going on, and immediately afterwards. Scarcely in fact had the boom of the cannon died away in our ears, before, on chariots of swiftness, those eloquent and graphic notices were wafted as if by magic beneath our eyes. Most of these are as truthful as they are glowing and poetic. It was wonderful. It seemed almost as though the great Battle were writing its own history as it was going on, even as the sun in passing the meridian at Paris, announces the fact to the inhabitants by firing off a cannon, or as the winds and rains may by machinery be made to record their quantities or velocities. If I am not mistaken, more than one of these narratives contained the suggestive word, *Regeneration.*

And what that spot suggested physically and cosmically, the time, the occasion, and all the accompaniments suggested politically and socially. This wonderful parallelism between the outer and the inner world is too striking to be altogether fanciful. These two kinds of regeneration and transfiguration seem clearly, by the memorable epoch of its occurrence, by the words of scripture, and by the local peculiarities of the field itself, to be prefigured.

What new forms of matter, what new crystallizations, may take place at the end of this our solar system, when solids are to be heated into fluidity, and all nature under the beams of a brighter and intenser Sun than ours, under the influence of that *primal light*, which was created before the planets, may be melted and transformed and ennobled, no earthly imagination can even conjecture. But that the particles now composing our bodies will, in some strange way, partake of the change, Holy Writ unmistakeably reveals to us. The philosophic Chladni found that by playing musical tunes with the bow of a violin along the smooth edges of vibratory plates, he could cause grains of sand and light substances to assume a variety of beautiful shapes and configurations. Who can tell what new forms the atoms of *our* bodies and of other material substances may assume at the last day, should the music of the spheres, now to us inaudible, make itself heard throughout creation.

And as to that *nearer* future, which many of us, I hope, may live to witness, and which is destined to change all our political and social organization into something nobler, grander and more perfect than anything we have yet enjoyed.—Oh! who can tell, after Slavery shall have been dissevered from its unnatural alliance with Liberty, what of glory and advancement, may belong to the hereafter of our history!

And that little golden link of Brotherly Love, some notice of which has come to us in the message from the battle-field,—does it not belong to a chain, which after binding together more than hundreds of millions of human hearts, may reach up to the empyrean, and unite them *all* to the heart of the All-merciful!

A BATTLE-EVE.

The camp is silent. Weary soldiers rest
Before to-morrow's work. The distant tents
So white, and still, they look like shadowy sails
Upon a far-off sea,—or Arab tents
In drowsy, desert lands. All types of peace
Would image this false-seeming, fatal peace!
The blind mole burrows on the battle plain;
The ants build tiny houses upon sand,
A lamb might pasture here to-day unscared.

The sun dies slowly in the passive West
Not redder than his wont;—predicting blood
In all his ebbing veins,—unwarned of blood,
All nature dreams. Not yet the time for signs
In sun, or moon, or stars. The highest hills
That grow to know the secrets of the clouds,
Are still no seers, that they tremble not
With sense of coming thunder. Nor the flowers
Are sybils even, to foretell this sorrow—

A BATTLE-EVE.

Weep dew to-night—weep blood to-morrow.
Fair flowers of the fated field! The bees
May starve to-morrow for these clover-blooms!
And all these slender, golden Southern moths,
Like yellow marriage-rings that circle round
The fingers of the locust fringes here—
May thirst to-morrow for the nectar spilt.

The gray oaks, century-wise, feel not one thrill
The more, through all their ever shuddering leaves,
Prescient of the dropping nests, the boughs
Uptorn,—still less of all the graves, so soon
To mark the spot; the mad mirth of the guns,
The life-blood in heroic veins, as full
And blue as grapes trod out in such a press;
The cannon's shriek that makes the stars vibrate.
The curses louder than the cannon's roar!
For curses, though they're whispered in a vault,
Will reach the sad, recording Angel's ears,
Above the thunder of exploding shells.

What eye hath vision for to-morrow's night?
The battle fought, and past   The air on fire
Left smouldering into blackness,—and the dread,
Wide silence settling down upon the breathing Death!
The fearful silence, that will not be dumb,

But keeps on shivering with the passing souls,
And breaking into dying moans! The Death
That will be Life still in the open eyes
Fixed, staring at immortal mysteries
Of other worlds,—unclosed in this:

       The brave
Young Patriot, with the poor white face upturned,
The blank blue eye, the red wound on the brow—
So let him lie, and symbolize in death,
His dear flag's colors,—red, and white, and blue.

REMINISCENCES OF THE HANCOCKS.

My position with Madam Hancock was such as to give me a fine opportunity to listen to her oft repeated stories of the Revolution and its results.

Many facts are stereotyped in my mind, and I feel myself more familiar with the events of the years connected with 1775, than with any period in my own history. I have been often urged to transfer my remembrances to paper, but have hitherto deferred doing it, so that the following will be an original statement.

Truth is most desirable in all history. I am happy to say that I never could detect any deviation in my aunt's narration of the same events, for a course of years. Madam Hancock, previous to her marriage, was Miss Dorothy Quincy, the daughter of Judge Edmund Quincy, of Boston, Massachusetts. Her youngest brother, Dr. Jacob Quincy, was my grandfather.

At her earnest request I resided with her, and was her daily companion for the last ten years of her life. Her death occurred in February, 1830, at the age of eighty-two years. She was married in 1775, to John Hancock, afterwards President of the First Congress, and then for a number of years Governor of Massachusetts.

The wedding was in Fairfield, Connecticut. Mr. Hancock had gone thither for safety, and was in concealment there, together with Samuel Adams, as a price had been put upon their heads by the King of England. It was therefore not deemed safe for Mr. H. to return to town that the marriage might take place in Boston.

Their food was privately conveyed to them, and all social intercourse with their friends was prevented, lest it should expose their valued lives.

After a time they were permitted to sit down again to the dinner table with the members of the family, in happy expectation of a comfortable repast after long abstinence. Before, however, they had realized the anticipated pleasure, a farmer from the neighborhood came in greatly excited, and requested the Rev. Mr. Clark (at whose house they were staying) to lend him his horse and chaise to go after his wife, as the British were coming, and he did not know but that she was in eternity now. This news scattered in a moment the whole party. Messrs. Adams and Hancock were hurried away to their hiding place, and aunt said it was always a matter of wonder to her what became of that dinner, for none of those who sat down to it ever tasted of it. The alarm was occasioned by a false report, but there was a time when the leaden balls of the enemy reached their residence.

On one occasion the aunt of Governor Hancock was catching a sight from an open window of the distant conflict, when a soldier begged her to take her head inside of the window as a ball had just passed her and lodged in the barn. In a fortnight after the birth of her first child, Madam Hancock was conveyed on a bed with her baby to her carriage, to journey from Boston in the cold of winter to Philadelphia, to accompany her husband, who was chosen President of the first Congress. She often spoke of the reluctance of her husband, arising from his natural modesty, to take the chair of office. When hesitating to take the President's chair, one of the members clasped him round the waist, lifted him from his feet and placed him in the Chair of State. While in Philadelphia, one evening, hearing the cry of murder, he ran into the house from which the cry proceeded, and found a man beating his wife. He attempted to release her from her perilous condition, but was surprised by a furious attack on himself from the liberated wife for interference in their family difficulties. Mr. H. remarked it was a lesson that would last him for life.

While Madam Hancock was in Philadelphia, her husband came to her room one day saying that he had a secret to communicate which must be faithfully kept. It was, that he had that day received a letter from home stating that it was thought it would be necessary to burn the town of Boston for the public good, and to prevent its falling into the hands of the enemy: and as his large wealth was centred there, he had been asked if he would be willing to sacrifice his whole estate to such an object. He immediately replied that they had his full consent to commit his property to the flames, if the good of the people demanded it. This, Madam H. replied, was rather a disagreeable secret. Her husband acknowledged that it would reduce them to beggary. But his purpose was fixed. He wished his property to be devoted to the best interests of his country.

She was at this time just preparing for her first attendance upon a Quaker meeting. Nor did this terrible announcement, or the thought of what might be the fearful result, overcome her even so much as to deter her from the proposed attendance upon the meeting.

I have heard her relate how the room was crowded when she arrived at the place, and how the painful secret weighed upon her as she sat in that over-heated room for three hours, waiting to hear what she supposed to be a forthcoming speech, that she hoped would relieve her mind for the time. But no relief came, for no utterance broke the silence before it was time for the "parting adieu."

On further consideration, the inhabitants of Boston deemed it unnecessary to burn the town.

At the time when the "Continental Money" was nearly worthless, Governor Hancock expressed his opinion in favor of the poor soldiers who were thus wronged by receiving their pay in this depreciated currency. His generosity had long been proverbial, and he gave them dollar for dollar in good money, and took in return their valueless paper, for which he received only one cent for a dollar when he came to dispose of it. He gave twenty-five hundred dollars in this Continental Scrip for a bell-metal skillet, the price of which was twenty-five dollars in good money. This skillet was in a perfect state of preservation in 1830, and is probably now in Boston or its vicinity. There were men in high position who bought of the poor sailors and soldiers the depreciated paper they had received for their severe labors, and kept it till its value was increased, and thus made fortunes in an operation that was little better than robbery of the poor and destitute.

It was not so with Governor Hancock; his sympathy for the wronged and injured men led him to continue taking the bad paper of those who presented it, until his friends saw that he would soon dispose of his whole fortune in this way.

They told his wife that "the *money trunk*" must be removed from the house, or she and her child would be penniless; and without consulting the Governor it was removed. The wisdom of this precaution could not be denied.

At that time he resided in the then magnificent mansion built by Thomas Hancock, and left at his death to his adopted nephew John Hancock. It was situated on Beacon street, opposite Boston Common, and was the finest residence in the town. In 1863, this house, built in 1737, and remaining more than one hundred years, was taken down. It had been held by the Hancock family, till the last year, when it was necessarily sold in accordance with the will of John Hancock, nephew to the Governor.

His Excellency, lived in style and luxury. He was noted for his hospitality; kept an open house and a sumptuous table for his friends.

General Lafayette accepted the Governor's invitation on his first visit to this country, to pass his time with him at his house. The General was a warm friend of Madam H., who was the first lady whom he honored with a call on his second visit to our country. It is probable, that few, if any, in his day, surpassed the Governor in his style of living. His equipage was a carriage and four horses. His coach was fitted up in good taste. It was noted for its brilliant plate glass and handsome ornaments; and was suitable both for parade and for travelling, being provided with pockets and various conveniences. It is now in possession of Hon. A. W. H. Clapp, of Portland, Maine, whose mother was niece to Madam H. Thirteen servants, and a goodly number of horses were attached to the service of the Governor's family. His wife had a fine pony, with a light drab colored saddle-cloth, very richly embroidered with silver thread. Her riding-whip was first owned and used by the Governor's aunt, who gave it to her, and she gave it to me. It is now in the possession of Miss Quincy, daughter of Hon. Josiah Quincy, of Boston, Mass.

The hospitality of his Excellency was acknowledged by all. He gave weekly, what was called "a salt-fish dinner," on Saturday. This was an elaborate affair, and duly prized in those days. At these dinners, there was always a place for his minister, Rev. Dr. Cooper. Prince Edward, while travelling in this country, called on Madam Hancock, and made himself very agreeable, telling her that he was said to resemble some noted personage, and asking what she thought of his "red whiskers." The friends of the Prince, regretted that

Madam H. did not give him an invitation to her "fish dinner," as it was Saturday when he made the call.

We may gather some idea of the Governor's style of living, by the fact that at a time when visiting a niece of his wife, in Portsmouth, N. H., they travelled with their coach and four, with two out-riders, a postillion, a coachman and a footman; seven horses, with servants in livery. The first day of their journey, they reached Marblehead, on the second they arrived in Portsmouth which was sixty miles from their home. At another time, they were a fortnight travelling from Boston to Philadelphia, in similar style

Once when journeying on this route, Madam H. found after stopping over night at a certain place, that her horses were so jaded that they could not proceed the next day. On inquiry, it was ascertained that they had been taken in the night and used on a pleasure excursion in honor of St. Patrick's day.

Governor H. was a great sufferer from that "aristocratic disease," the gout. At one time when he returned from public business, he was so ill, that, as his wife said, he was taken from his carriage in the arms of his servants, and laid upon the sofa, till the tailor who made him the new suit of clothes he had on, could cut them off, so that he could be carried with less pain to his sleeping room. At another time, when suffering in a similar way, he went as usual to the State House, which was, at that time, at the head of State street, to attend to his appointed duties. He was soon surrounded by an admiring multitude who, after he had entered his carriage in which his wife had come to meet him, commenced removing the four horses from the carriage, with the determined purpose of themselves drawing him to his home in Beacon street. Four hundred men were already forming in procession with this intent.

The Governor was exceedingly overcome by this demonstration of public respect, and being so ill that he could not speak for himself, he requested his wife (who was noted for her personal beauty) to address the crowd from the carriage window, and say to them that the Governor was overwhelmed by the honor they desired to confer upon him, that he gratefully acknowledged the kindness of the feelings that prompted the act, but he must beg them to permit him in his present weak state, to be taken by his horses as rapidly as possible to his home. His request was granted.

I have often heard Madam H. repeat the circumstances of his being severely afflicted with the gout, when General Washington was expected to make his first appearance in Boston. The General had accepted an invitation to dine that day with the Governor; but there was a suggestion made to the General, that etiquette demanded that the

Governor should be at the entrance of the town to welcome him. After some two hours delay about this question, the General, who was exposed in delicate health to a cold wind, asked if there was no other entrance to the town by which he could speedily reach his lodgings. Being answered in the negative, he ordered the cavalcade to move on at quick pace, and went directly to his place of lodging. The Governor, all this time, was delaying his dinner in constant expectation of the distinguished guest. The report was soon whispered about, *why* the General was not present.

The next day, the Governor ordered his carriage, and with limbs wrapped in red baize, he was put into it in order to call on the General. When he arrived at his lodgings, he was carried in the arms of his servants to the head of the stairs, and from thence he crawled on his hands and knees into the presence of the Commander-in-Chief. The General meeting him in this position, was moved to tears. All difficulties being soon removed, kindness and cordiality were reciprocated. Madam Washington and Madam Hancock were friends. Madam W. would say to Madam H., "there is a great difference in our situations. Your husband is in the Cabinet, but mine is on the battle-field." Persons of high position of his own and other countries, were often the favored guests in Governor Hancock's family. While the French fleet was in Boston harbor, Count D'Estaing and some other persons of rank were with their life guards visiting the Governor. Governor H. sent a note to the Admiral of the fleet, to take a breakfast with him and to bring with him thirty of his officers. The Admiral accepted the invitation, but sent a request to the Governor to permit him the pleasure of bringing all his officers, including the midshipmen. This request was granted, but not without some solicitude as to the possibility of accommodating three hundred officers and providing for their entertainment. In those days, there were not the facilities of confectioners and other resources of the present time. It was summer, and carts and wagons were pressed into the service to bring from the surrounding country the various fruits of the season.

It was found that milk sufficient for the demand could not be obtained even from the whole vicinity of Boston. Boston Common was at that time used as a place of pasturage for cows, and Madam Hancock in her dilemma, requested the life guards and the servants of the family to take pitchers, mugs and bowls, and to milk all the cows on the Common, and if any persons objected to send them to her, and she would explain the matter. This was a novel proceeding, and made a laughable exhibition to the public, but it was a success, and gave offence to no one.

Eleven o'clock was the hour for breakfast. The officers at the appointed time were seen entering the farthest end of the Common, in front of the Governor's house. I have often heard aunt describe that scene and the events of the day. She was naturally very calm and tranquil in her manner, but when speaking of that day, she always evinced great animation, and seemed to feel again the fire and excitement of the scene. She said the Eastern sun shed his full rays on the bright gold lace that covered in a most elaborate manner the persons of the French officers, and in their march to the house, the brilliancy and beauty of the display exceeded anything she ever before or afterward saw of military parade. The whole affair was well gotten up, and gave great satisfaction to all. The Admiral soon after returned the compliment by giving a grand dinner on board his ship to the Governor and his lady. Madam H. occupied the seat of honor, and at her right hand was a large rosette of ribbons that was attached to something under the table by a strong rope. This was a mystery to her, and gave her no small curiosity as to its design. At the moment when the toasts were to be given, the Admiral's Aide who sat next to her, requested that she would raise the ribbons. She obeyed, and in doing so she fired the signal-gun, and in an instant, it was replied to by every vessel in the fleet. This was a distinguished honor paid to Madam Hancock, for the attention shown to the Admiral and his officers, by the Governor and herself.

At the Annual Commencement of Harvard College it was the custom for the Governor and the "Boston Cadets" (his escort) to be present at the College exercises. It was the pleasure of the Governor that this Military Company should take their breakfast with him that morning. And as the services at Cambridge commenced at nine, A. M., a very early breakfast must be given, in order that the Governor and his lady with his escort, might be able to be in readiness for their place and duties at the appointed time. But his indomitable will carried out this plan for several years, in spite of its great inconvenience to his wife, who was compelled, in order to be present at the breakfast table, to summon her hair dresser at four o'clock in the morning. The day was always one of extreme fatigue to her.

Governor H. was a friend of the colored race, and they were in the habit of marching in procession annually on a certain day before his house, and having stopped in front of it, the Governor would address them from the balcony. He was in the habit of riding through the country in the summer, and if he came to an unfinished church, he would inquire the reason of its remaining in that state. If the reply was that they could not command the money to complete it, he would encourage them to go on, by saying, "I will pay for the glazing if you will go to work and have it finished." He did this many times.

He kept the yearly fast in spring on *fish*, but his dinner was always from off the first salmon of the season, for which he paid a guinea. He had a fine dinner-set of pewter ordered from England. It was the duty of his household to see that this pewter was kept at the highest point of brightness, and used every day to the exclusion of the valuable Indian-China set, which he also owned. He preferred to use the pewter instead of the china, because, as he said, the contents of the plates and dishes were not so apt to slide off; and also, that the use of them made no clatter in contact with knives and forks. He had a large quantity of silver, much of it bearing the tower stamp of England. He had four dozen silver forks matched with the same number of silver table spoons. Among his silver were many tankards of different sizes. One very large, holding a gallon or more, he devoted to hot punch exclusively; this he called "Solomon Townsend," in honor of a friend. He had also a large silver porter cup, holding two quarts or more, with two massive handles, intended, I presume, to be passed from guest to guest, that each might quaff in turn from the same cup. Much of his silver not only bore the "tower stamp," but had also his own coat of arms engraved upon it.

I remember among his silver, a wash bowl, silver salvers, asparagus tongs, four heavy silver chaffing dishes, four silver butter-boats, with various other odd articles; also six heavy silver candlesticks, and a silver snuffer and snuff dish. The snuff dish was bought at the family auction for me and is still in my possession. It has the Hancock coat of arms upon it. The Governor had a passion for the portraits of his distinguished guests, which were painted to his order for his hall of paintings. Red coats and other bright colors were worn by the gentlemen of his day. Governor H. had an epicurean taste, and all the delicacies of the season might be found upon his table. After his death his wife kept up his custom in these matters; she said to me one day: "The Governor's hobby was his dinner table, and I suppose it is mine." From early morning till eleven at night, Madam H's house was open for the reception of friends and strangers, as it had been while her husband was living. She was for years one of the "wonders of the age"—and as the widow of Governor H., she was visited till the close of her life by distinguished persons from foreign countries, as well as our own. She so long studied the epicurean tastes of her husband that she excelled in the rich viands that were known at her table. With the Hancock house are associated venison dinners and mince-pies, that vanished when that house was taken down, and cannot now be procured anywhere in the country in the state of perfection in which they were found at the mansion on Beacon street, in the palmy days of the Hancocks.

There are some few persons living who have the luxurious flavor of those feasts still lingering on their palates, and who do not cease to aim at their restoration. Not, however, for the reason that such feasting bears any importance in comparison with the ample and true supplying of the intellectual and spiritual wants of our higher nature, but rather for the associations that exist in the minds of those who mingled with the society that gathered around that generous board of delicious tastes and fragrant flavors.

Governor Hancock was the son of a clergyman, but adopted by his uncle, who left him a very large fortune for the period in which he lived. At the age of twenty-one he went to England, was admitted to Court, and kissed the hand of King George. He was a man of warm sympathies, as well as of a strong will. One morning, when entering the town in his phæton, at a very early hour, he saw a poor woman with a large bundle, trudging along the road. He ordered the horses to be stopped, and inquiring where she was going, was informed that she was a "washer-woman" on her way to the town. He had both herself and her bundle placed in the open carriage, and went with them to her stopping place. Such acts made him *king* in the *hearts* of *the people*.

His temper was sometimes so violent as to lead some to question his benevolence; for when suffering from a fit of the gout, he would almost outrage common sense.

Two or three circumstances, illustrating this, will also show what prompt and perfect obedience he required of his servants. Shut up in his sick room, he could not always be sure that his orders were carried out to his full requisition. He had repeatedly forbidden the use of the China table service, and directed that the pewter should, at all times, be used. The unreasonableness of this direction consisted in the difficulty of keeping a pewter set in constant fitness for use. He called Cato, his favorite colored servant, to his room on one occasion, and asked him if the China set had been used that day. Being answered in the affirmative, he said, "I thought so. Now go down stairs and bring up a pile of China dishes." The servant soon returned with the dishes in his hands. The Governor said, "now open the window and throw them out." Cato did as he was told, but took good care to open a window over a bank of soft turf, and to give them a gentle slide as he let them drop, so that none of them were injured. The Governer said, "I don't hear them *break*. Go down, Cato, and bring them up again." The dishes were a second time produced. "Now," said he, "open the window over the paved coach-yard, and throw them out." This order being obeyed, the dishes were destroyed. At another time he told Cato he wished to have the "gobbler" in the coach-yard killed for the next day's dinner. The house being already supplied with provisions, it was deemed inexpedient to kill it then.

After dinner next day the Governor called Cato to his bed-side to know if that turkey had been cooked as he had ordered. The servant had to acknowledge that it was not even killed. His master said, "Go out now and kill it, and give it to the cook. Tell her to put it on the spit without picking or drawing it, and roast it *four hours* just as you carry it to her." The fire places were large and open for the burning of wood, and the turkey was put on a spit that turned regularly round, dipping the feathers into the fire, then into the drippings in turn continually, till the house was filled with smoke and the odor of burnt feathers, of which the Governor's own room received a full share. When his severe malady was playing its pranks upon his sensitive nerves, he could not tolerate the slightest noise, and the merest jarring of his nerves was no slight offence. A young girl was sitting in the entry near the open door of his room and busying herself in curling her hair. The rattling of the paper disturbed him, and he called to her to know what that noise was. She, fearing his reproof, quickly answered, "the cat scratching, sir." He pardoned the untruth for the adroitness with which she evaded his displeasure.

Governor H. was one day riding with his wife in their carriage, when they met Samuel Adams walking with the sheriff beside him. He said to Mr. A., "what is the meaning of this." Mr. A. replied, "I am going to jail, as I cannot satisfy the sheriff's demands." The Governor said he would see to that and settle the demand, and bade the sheriff leave his prisoner. Many times was his purse opened for Mr. A's benefit, under similar circumstances.*

The Governor had a very large marquée made, which he wished to see displayed for once at least, on the ground now occupied by the present State House. His wish,

---

* Samuel Adams was one of the great men of the period of the Revolution. His neglect of his own interests often involved him in pecuniary embarrassments. In the Memoirs of Hancock, in the Encyclopædia Americana, we find the following remarks: "Hancock was a magnificent liver, lavishly bountiful, and splendidly hospitable; Samuel Adams had neither the means nor the inclination for pursuing a similar course. He was studiously simple and frugal, and was of an austere, unbending character. In fact, they differed so widely in their mode of living and general dispositions, that their concurrence in political measures may be considered one of the strongest proofs of their patriotism."

EDITOR.

however, could not be gratified. The time for its erection was to be on the day of the annual General Review of all the military companies in the month of October. He requested his wife to have a collation provided on that occasion for all the officers. He was at that time prostrated with his last fatal attack of the gout. He did not appear to apprehend that he was so near the close of his earthly career. She was informed by the physician that his death might occur at any hour. Madam H. could not therefore make the necessary preparations for such a public display. At her refusal to comply with this long cherished wish of his heart, her husband was much displeased; and she often said she could not feel satisfied that she had his full forgiveness for not carrying out his plans on that occasion. He became increasingly ill, and at ten o'clock on that very day, the occasion of the great military parade, it was announced that he was dying—the companies were ordered to leave the Common; and hushed were the drum and fife with all their military inspiration, while the Commander and chief of the State was passing into the immediate presence of the Great Judge of all men.

Governor H. left orders that he should be buried without public honors, and forbade the firing of a gun over his grave. The State Government chose to have the management of the whole affair, and told Madam H.

that the funeral and its expenses belonged to the State. She submitted reluctantly to the arrangement But she finally had to pay the bills of the obsequies, which amounted to eighteen hundred dollars. This was occasioned by a vote of the Legislature not to bury any more Governors. However, the law was changed before the death of another Governor, so that this case is the only one on record where the funeral expenses of a Governor have not been paid out of the State Treasury.

A will was found after the death of Governor Hancock without signature, in which he gave the most of his property to the State. His daughter died at the age of nine months, and his son at the age of ten years. His patriotism remained unquestionable to the last of his life. Madam Hancock died in her eighty-second year. For some time previous to her death she went but little into society, but whenever she appeared was received with great attention.*

---

* As this article has already exceeded the space allotted it, we are compelled to omit interesting quotations from Mrs. Ellet's "Women of the Revolution," and the "Atlantic Monthly," on the taking down of the old Hancock House in 1863.—EDITOR.

THE SPIRIT OF MARYLAND IN 1794.

[The following Song was composed for S. Hanson, Esq. of Alexandria, and sung by him as President, at a public dinner, July 4th, 1794, at which General Washington was present.— The following memorandum in the hand-writing of the author, Chancellor Kilty, accompanies the original copy:

"At the first verse, which is copied from the old English Song, the English merchants and tories were much pleased, and crowded to the head of the table, and General Washington showed some surprise—at the third verse they resumed their places."]*

WHEN Britain first at Heaven's command,
    Arose from out the azure main,
This was the charter of the land—
    And guardian Angels sung the strain;
"Rule Britannia, Britannia rule the waves,
For Britons never shall be slaves."

* This Song was presented by a niece of Chancellor Kilty, as not being known to exist in print;—it forms the only exception to articles from living authors offered expressly for this volume, except in the Introduction —EDITOR.

Twas thus, when rival nations strove,
  Ere Freedom's sacred name was known,
That, ardent with their country's love,
  And claiming Ocean as their own,
They sung "Britannia, Britannia rule the waves,
For Britons never shall be slaves."

But wherefore Britons rule the waves;
  Why grasp the wide extended sea;
Must all the world beside, be slaves,
  That only Britons may be free?
Hence, then Britannia no more shall rule the waves;
Nor see the Nations round her slaves.

On every coast, on every shore,
  The bounteous sea her treasure spreads;
To countless millions wafts her store,
  Nor tribute pays to crowned Heads;
Hence, then Britannia, no longer rule the waves,
Nor seek to make thy equals slaves.

For see! Columbia's sons arise;
  Firm, independent, bold and free;
They too shall seize the glorious prize,
  And share the Empire of the sea;
Hence, then, let freemen, let freemen rule the waves;
And those who yield them still be slaves.

This glorious day which still shall live
    Illustrious, in the book of fame;
This day revolving, still shall give
    A kindling spark of freedom's flame.
And we as freemen, we'll use, not rule the waves,
Nor own a power to make us slaves.

And still on this auspicious day,
    Like friends and brethren, let us join
In concert tune the festive lay,
    Sacred to Liberty, divine,
Which still will guard us in land and on the waves,
Determined never to be slaves.

Nor on this day let memory fail,
    To celebrate each Hero slain;
With Patriot tears their fate bewail;
    Who died our freedom to obtain.
Which may we cherish in land and on the waves,
Nor change from freemen to be slaves.

But chiefly him whose faithful toils
    Led us to Liberty and Peace,
On whom America still smiles
    With gratitude that ne'er shall cease;
Long may the Hero live, who still his Country saves,
Nor ever let him see us slaves.

FIELD LILIES.

OUT of the most terrible of all human calamities, a civil war, a mysterious Providence elicits greatness, freedom and progress for a nation; and from the depths of individual suffering are brought up some of the brightest and rarest gems of character. In the hearts of the bereaved, (and this expression includes almost every person, either directly or remotely,) there has yet been a consolation in the thought of the noble qualities that sought activity in a struggle for right and freedom, against misrule and barbarism; and the mourner has said through all her tears for the slain, that it was "sweet and becoming to die for one's country." Even through the mist of blood and darkness that has hung over the land for the last three years, we can see the effect of this fiery baptism on the character of our people. Especially is it seen in the class of young women; and we might naturally expect this to be the case. Our women do not go merely as nurses to soldiers,—they go to bind up the wounds of brother, cousin, lover. In the veins of this northern army, bivouacked on morasses, rushing up against cannon, or sleeping exhausted on weltering fields, runs the blood of our noblest and best families, and invisible cords bind every beating heart on the battle-field to the warm hearth-stone of home, and the loving looks of wife, sisters, and parents.

As there never was such an army before, of unbought patriotism and fervent enthusiasm for national honor, so there never was a more beautiful corresponding effect on the character of our women. The Spartan mothers said as they handed shields to their departing warriors, "Return with it, or on it!" The Roman and Grecian soldiers marched away to rapine or conquest, cheered by the wild songs of Bacchantes and inspired by dusky Delphic prophecies. Our youth go, calmly and resolutely, with the patience and set purpose of their pilgrim ancestors, to the defence of all that is best and noblest in national character. They go with eyes wide open to all the possible results of the conflict, but with hope and determination stronger than the fear of death. Their battle-flag is the sign not only of victory, but of all that makes victory worth having, and "God save the grand old Stripes and Stars" stirs every drop of heroic blood, and gives the world assurance of a man!

Such lovers, husbands and fathers leave women of a corresponding type behind them to encourage, to strengthen, and if necessary, to console. The time and the circumstances, have brought out the character. Noble traits, that might otherwise have slept, are wakened by the stir of lofty emotion to happy self-sacrifice. Our field-lilies that toiled not, nor span, were yet rivals of Solomon in the glory of their apparel, are converted into seed-grain, ripe for the sickle. Vanity is turned into nobleness, and prodigality into thrift.

To see young girls, whose white and slender fingers have been too dainty to do, in all their lives, one useful thing; who not only did not know how to do one useful thing, but who piqued themselves on this delightful ignorance, who lived the lives of butterflies and humming birds, and sang and danced till the day was done,—to see them now, going out of all that frivolity and entering a new life of industry and interest, is to feel that indeed good does come out of evil. It is beautiful to see the steady and constant industry of these busy bees. How untiring in their work of making garments for the sick and wounded, and how industriously they toil at every variety, however coarse, for the comfort of the common soldier. How far removed even, is their daily talk and thoughts from the petty interests that formerly occupied them; how deeply engaged they are in discussing subjects above and beyond their personal occupations, and which often involve high and extended contemplations. In looking at them we feel that souls are indeed ripening in these Northern skies, and that the regeneration of so many brave and noble young hearts pays the price of much suffering.

"As their day is, so shall their strength be." Let us hope that this probation of effort and endurance may produce all the needed results of fortitude and self-reliance. For this war is to make widows and orphans, sisters with no brothers to care for and shelter them, and mothers with no sons to uphold their age and infirmity. In many places, the whole face of society will be changed. From being cherished, women must uphold themselves; and the wind that erewhile was not suffered to blow on their tender cheeks, lest it touch them rudely, will be left to strike blastingly with the tempestuous force of poverty and desertion. Let them not be afraid to look these possible, nay probable, results of war squarely in the face.

It seems likely that, for a long future, it will be necessary for women to make active exertions for their own maintenance, merely from the fact of their sex being in excess of the other. They must change their relations to the public in some measure, and perhaps assume many employments heretofore exclusively occupied by men. There have been many kinds of labor very well suited to the strength and ability of women, but which have been connected with a publicity, that made them undesirable. The free discussion of topics connected with female labor has, however, so far familiarized the public mind with them, that no surprise is expressed or felt at women's occupying places formerly prohibited to them, or monopolized by men. Doctresses, postmistresses and saleswomen, are likely to have a remunerative profit for their labor, as well as a respectable social position. Many kinds of domestic labor will be necessary, and in some degree fashionable If it is fashionable now to listen at the lecture-room, while the busy fingers weave coarse yarn into soldiers' stockings,— if the belle receives her morning calls, with the drawing room strewn with hospital socks and blue shirts, much more will it be fashionable to continue to labor, for one's self or for others, when exertion is sanctified by high impulses, noble sacrifices, and sacred recollections It is well that our young girls should look forward to this state of things. Not despondently, not fearfully, but with hope and cheerfulness. Better, a thousand times, that you wear out with the sharp attrition of active exertion, than that you rust out in the inanity of a useless existence. If it be denied to you to be a cherished and petted wife, you may still be a helpful sister, a devoted daughter, or a soothing companion to a helpless or wounded husband.

We knew,—for even in the midst of the blind rush of our old delirious prosperity, there was virtue enough left in the country to say it,—we knew that we had drifted, as a people, far out of sight of the principles of our fathers, on which this country was settled, and this republic founded. We heard the voice of prophecy and denunciation—the "*Wo! unto this goodly land!*" We heard, but we folded our hands, and said, "*Après nous, le deluge.*" The deluge, however, has come upon us, and not on our innocent children. For them, a brighter path opens through suffering. No more of pampering luxury, no more dreary idleness, vapidness and dissatisfaction. Instead of these, let them take on the ancestral virtues of fortitude and labor with cheerfulness and christian dignity. And this is well for our young girls; so well, that even if they must give up during their whole lives, the pleasing task of decorating their persons and adorning their minds, they will still have gained immeasurably in mental elevation, and their whole plain of action and thought be habitually higher.

Through the changes necessitated by this war, a large class of single women will be thrown out of employment. There will not be schools enough for teachers, nor pianos enough for the instructors of music. Let us hope there will be more attention to domestic labor, and to all the employments which serve as oil on the hinges of daily life.

In the immediate future of our country, there will doubtless be a closer inweaving of all classes, through the intense and common interest for the general good. For the homes made desolate, there is a common and tearful sympathy; as for the triumphs of the field, the whole city and country has one heart-throb of gladness. The cause is that of brothers, and unites us in one great and strong bond. Not the less shall we feel it, if, in a happy future, we behold ourselves once more, both North and South, rallied under what our soldiers joyfully die for, "THE DEAR OLD FLAG!"

A NEEDED REFORM.

One beneficial effect of the present war, may be to elevate the general tone of female character, by supplying generous motives for action. The habit of working, too, for a benevolent purpose, will be formed in many whose time has hitherto been frittered away in trifling occupations. An observing person can hardly fail to notice the fresh impulse given to industry among a class of women placed above the necessity of labor, and the laudable perseverance with which they support patriotic enterprises. Better, still, would it be, if economy in personal expenditure would go hand in hand with industry; if the inordinate love of display which gives a cold, hollow, and artificial character to social life in our large cities, could be effectually checked.

Our progress in luxury—in the taste for splendor and extravagant outlay—is universally known. The West became oriental long ago, and is growing "more so" every day. The Persian graces may have given up their hair-binding nets of gold; silver battle-axes may have disappeared from the plains of Tartary; and Circassian maidens may no longer imitate the blush of morning; but our horizon brightens as the East grows dull. We attire ourselves with the sunset, and deck our walls with the ornaments of buried cities. Our gold is double gilded, and our lilies are painted beyond description. We are a violet-broidered, saffron-mantled, rose-crowned, golden-zoned, impearled, pink and azure people. Our shawls are from the gorgeous looms of the Indies. We have basquines and bretelles of pearl-embroidered lace and gems; dove-colored taffeta and Raphael boddices; mantles of cerulean and ruby, bordered with silk and silver, and lined with costly furs; embroideries like rivers of pearls, clustering bouquets of rubies, sapphires, and emeralds. Our head dresses are a cloud of gold and silver tissues, embracing glowing wreaths and rich pendants of flowers; while silver rainbows encircle our necks, and serpents with eyes of flashing gems, guard the diamonds on our wrists. African jewels and Assyrian drapery; why not the golden bells of Arabia, the mirrors of Barbary, and the coins of Faristan! In the Malayan, the same term is used for a woman and a flower; here the whole floral kingdom would not be her match.

When their taste is so improved, or their vanity so kept in check, that our women cease to emulate the Indian lady who imprisoned a thousand fire-flies in her gauze skirt, their real grace and refinement will appear. The confusion of decorations and finery has hitherto obscured those charming qualities. As our men become more martial in deportment, more stern in probity, and more truly patriotic in character, the fairer part of creation ought to cultivate the enduring virtues, casting off the dross which is all sparkle and gorgeousness. The needs of the country might be supplied by the treasures saved from the dress of its women; saved too, without the sacrifice of a single genuine charm. But who shall set the example in the reform so desirable? Who, but those who can best afford to do without the tinsel and mockery of foolish extravagance, because they possess attractions not dependent on sumptuous array.

AIMÉ DE MON CŒUR.

With a dauntless daring high
Blazing in thine eagle eye,
And thy true hand lightly pressed
On thy maiden sword in rest—
Blessings on thy noble head,
Scion of the warlike dead!
Tears may fall, but not allure
From thy patriot purpose pure—
To the battle hasten on!
Aimé de mon Cœur!

Thou hast heard thy country call—
Thou hast seen her brave sons fall
In the fratricidal strife
With rebellious passion rife;
Thou hast seen the hallowed graves
Of her consecrated braves,
Claimed by mocking lips impure!
To the rescue thou hast gone,
Aimé de mon Cœur!

Thou hast seen our banner gleam,
Like a glory through thy dream;
Counted every blazing star,
As it beckoned thee afar—
Sainted sires of old renown,
From its azure field looked down:
Noble names thy cause assure;
Patriot deeds thy rights secure;
Guard their sacred ensign well,
Aimé de mon Cœur!

But alas! Thy haughty foe!
Striving madly to o'erthrow
Fairest fabric ever wrought,
Wisdom's sagest master thought!
Like proud Absalom in ire,
Battling 'against his kingly sire,
Must a Joab's arrow sure
Penetrate through shades obscure,
Striking at a brother's heart?
Aimé de mon Cœur!

Ay! the silvered heads of age,
Bow in shame! their heritage—
Must their blood bedew the soil?
Must it be the rebel's spoil?

Nay, young braves will still lead on
Guarding what their fathers won,
Keep their stainless altars pure,
From ambition's treacherous lure,
Pray that God may shield the right
Aimé de mon Cœur!

But should victory crown thy brow,
Humbly 'neath her chaplet bow,
Put thou forth a friendly hand
To the vanquished of our land!
Yield thee back the broken sword
With its pristine sheen restored,
Though it ruthlessly hath slain
Sires and sons on battle plain—
To the prodigal assure
Pardon, if he thus adjure;
God will thus avenge *thy* cause,
Aimé de mon Cœur.

THE

MORAL STRENGTH OF OUR COUNTRY'S CAUSE.

GOVERNMENT is of God. Himself a King, and King of kings, when He commands that earthly kings should be honored, He means the Law of the State, in whatever legitimate form it may be embodied. God is love; peace is one of the ministers of that love, and, in such a world as this, the sword is another. Justice must march in even step with mercy. The welfare of man as urgently requires that wrongs should be set right by some "terror to evil-doers," as that there should be tranquil air and cheerful praise for them that do well. We find no habitable or tolerable dwelling-place anywhere without the solemn array of courts, penalties, magistrates and arms. Together, these constitute the venerable and divine character of Law; venerable, because she is from everlasting; divine, because her seat is the bosom of God. Her hands may be of iron, but her countenance is benignant, and her heart is tender. Providence has hedged her about from the beginning with sacred safe-guards and immunities, turning all history into a record of her benefits, binding up all public prosperity and domestic comfort in her arms, and making her "the gracious mother of our peace and joy."

In the light of this comprehensive and profound truth, we are able to see the moral strength of our national cause. One of the grand compensations we are to reap for its vast sufferings, is a new realization of this majestic supremacy and divine sanctity of Law, curbing the conceit of our rampant and conceited individualism, exploding the philosophic fallacy of a "social compact," and putting an effectual contradiction on the current notion of so many victims of crude European democratic oracles, that it is competent to a majority of the people anywhere, if they happen to choose, to vote Government out of existence! "The people" cannot do this till they can vote one of God's designs out of existence.

First of all, our cause is the cause of Government, which God ordains and loves, against reckless and selfish insurrection, which he denounces and hates. With our adversary, it is not a case of the last and desperate resort of the right of revolution; for that exists only under actual and intolerable abuses or oppressions; whereas in this rebellion, even the grievances alleged are only prospective and contingent, on confession of its abettors. In the principles indirectly involved, ours is also the cause of liberty against bondage, honor against treachery, constitutional protection against usurpation, lawful administration against public fraud, and equal rights against feudalism and caste. Now, God loves liberty, honor, order, and brotherly equality among his children. In the distinction often drawn between offensive and defensive war, we have the further moral advantage of being on the defensive; actual aggressions being begun on the other side.

In the second place, lending this confidence of right to the cause, the Christian view of the subject points out in what spirit, and by what principles, the war shall be carried on. If it is a righteous cause, it can be righteously prosecuted. Man can make war not only *in the name* of the Most High, but in the solemn and tender *spirit* of His religion. Anger, cruelty, personal revenge, and all the hateful brood of satanic passions, have no more *necessary* place in the camp and on the field, than they have on farms and in counting-houses. In a conflict so sacred as ours, there can be no reason why regiments shall not be enrolled, batteries planted, campaigns planned, strategy conducted, battles fought, and blood poured out, with all the energy of the bravest soldiership, and with all the skill of the most masterly generalship, yet with every trace of wrath extinguished Indeed, I observe no brighter sign in the horizon than the intelligent testimony of one of the eminent statesmen of the country, after extensive travels through its great seats of population, that something like this is already true. He says: "I have nowhere found any feeling of exasperation against the people of the South, but in every point, a solemn determination to uphold the Government, at the same time with a sadness and a depth of tenderness I will in vain endeavor to describe. Strong and brave men when speaking of the distractions which rend our country, have wept in my presence. This is not a war *upon the people of the South*, but a war undertaken for their defence and for their deliverance." I cannot see why men should not move to the defence of such a cause as ours, with all the intensest energies of muscle and will strung to the combat, yet with just as complete an absence of personal spite or ill-will, as in the judge who, under the august forms of law, sentences a single criminal to the scaffold, or as in the sheriff who executes the sentence. These civil magistrates discharge their duty, and fulfil their oath, as a high and awful act of Christian obligation. So it might be, and ought to be, with every soldier in every division of our army. We can conceive of his being quartered in a Christian camp. where not only temperance and purity and reverence keep the air clear, but where the voice of God's daily praise is heard. where an altar is erected in every tent, and a temple under every company's flag. We can conceive of his marching in the ranks to his terrible office, with judicial, with devout, nay, with almost sacramental solemnity. There is nothing in the mere taking of human life—the life of the body—that is opposite to the law of Christ. Many things are more sacred and more precious, as our daily use of life shows, than bodily blood and breath. We give these things away, and we may take them away, for right, for freedom, for honor, for government, for the people's good, for God's glory. Hence the possibility and the fact of Christian, nay, of saintly warriors. Terrible as the temptation is to arouse all the worst passions of our lower nature, yet, in another view, the legitimacy of the cause makes every soldier a magistrate, investing him with something of the august responsibility of an impartial and impersonal application of the law. It is familiar that not only in the wars of God's chosen people in Judea, but in the wars of the English Commonwealth, and of the American Revolution, and more lately in the East, the most determined and most effectual fighting was done by the godliest and gentlest men,—men who went straight from their closet to the charge, and from their knees to the storming and siege of strongholds, under the fiery hail, in trenches of spouting blood, and dying, when they fell, with their Bibles on their breasts, and the peaceful name of Jesus on their lips. This is Christian war. The sublimity of martyrdom and the glory of the cross surround it.

Again, and more specially, the kind of conflict that Christ allows is one that repudiate, with scrupulous integrity, every unrighteous practice,—everything that the commands of God disallow. National retribution is just as sure and searching as the judgment of single souls. If a war is waged in a spirit of national selfishness and under wicked rulers, with corrupt contracts and bargains, with fraudulent enlistments, by reckless and blaspheming generals, no matter what temporary achievements overwhelming numbers may display, the result will be a national disgrace. The general cause may be just; yet no single insult to the Almighty can escape its curse. If a battle is deliberately planned and needlessly offered, for some trifling occasion of audacity or levity, on the day that God has hallowed and commanded all men to keep, it will not be strange if there is a panic before night; for if the guilty parties are not afraid of the enemy, they should be affrighted at Heaven and tremble for themselves. If officers turn their head-quarters into a stye of sensuality, what wonder if when they go out against the foe one way, they flee before him seven ways? If military messages between the forces are worded in terms of profane vulgarity, why should not God above, who is jealous for His honor, take away the staff of bread or the stay of water, and finish the engagement with a surrender? If our military practices sink back to the brutalities of a barbarous age; if all the amenities, courtesies, and kindnesses of civilized warfare are disowned; if sentinels on outposts are shot down with no possible influence on the result, in miserable sport or savage malice, the Lord of pity, who healed the ear of a servant that was causelessly struck, will be offended. Every such breach of virtue contravenes our prayers. Our petitions ought to be, in Christ's name, first of all, that every department and operation of so grand a struggle may be purged of impiety and be conformed to the irreproachable standard of our religion.

Again, light is given us, in this line of thought, to see how it is,—and to see that it is just as faith ought to have expected,—that the high and mighty Ruler of the universe, who is the only giver of all victory, carefully keeps the issues in His own hands. His are the sicknesses that waste, the drought that famishes, the tempests that wreck, the winds that hinder or speed fleets, and the rains that swell rivers, and the frosts that chill in one place and destroy miasma in another; and He means to make it manifest, doubtless, before the eyes of mankind, that by Him nations are ruled, squadrons turned, and wars made to cease. Numbers, armaments, drills, revenues, experience, courage, strategy,—these are the instruments of war. But the Almighty must accept and bless them before they prosper. He blows upon them with His indignation, and they are like the chaff of the summer threshing-floor which the wind driveth away. May He grant that as defeat and loss school us into energy and order and humble dependence upon Him, so every success may lift hearty anthems to His praise!

Finally, the whole truth before us clears the way for our minds to combine a vigorous support of the government God has set over us,—so rich in blessings and so fraught with hope to humanity throughout the world,— with affectionate fidelity to Christ, and with a spirit of perfect charity to all men,—even to the men whom we ask God to discomfit, and whom we are giving treasure and tears and the noble blood of brothers, husbands, and sons, to overthrow. Even this high attainment of Christian magnanimity is possible; and we are never to be satisfied till we reach it. Our foes may be our fellow-countrymen, they may be "of our own household;" yet, in a conflict so terrible as this, and with a stake only second to the ark of God, we are to stand courageously against them, and turn them back from the Capital of our freedom. We learn, though not believing with the Arabian Prophet that the sword is the key to Heaven, that loyalty to our country, and love to its blind and mad assailants, are consistent with one another. And while the sentiment of liberty and sympathy for the oppressed animate our arms, can we not, in the name of the merciful Lord, take some anxious thought for those doers of the wrong, who, when their doomed institution shall fall, may stand in all the peril and dismay of a servile revenge? We are sure that except we are willing to take up this cross also, with all its pains and consequences, regardless of interest or power,—stagnant markets or suspended commerce, private affliction or distresses ten times deeper than any we have yet borne,— we are no more worthy to be Christ's disciples than to be citizens of the Republic.

We may well remember our encouragements at the mercy-seat. We remember how the life and liberty of our mother-country, threatened once by the "Invincible Armada," which bore to sea beneath its sails all the strength of the great empire of Philip II., was so clearly delivered by the prayers of faithful souls, that the British admiral exclaimed, "It is the finger of God," and even Queen Elizabeth bowed her pride to acknowledge, "God breathed on them, and they were scattered."

Remember the Providence that averted ruin, by foreign and civil hostility together, from the little Republic of Holland, when the splendid armies of Louis XIV., headed by generals whose very names were like victories, moved against her; when the connivance of Charles II., in a duplicity not unlike that which stripped *us* three years ago of half our defences, kept up an appearance of friendship till the English fleet filled the channel, and then joined the invader, when the resources of the government had been loosened and spent in a long period of security, and the commander-in-chief was a youth of but twenty-two years; when, to help the parallel, several of the United Dutch States *seceded*,—with treason in camp and council and border cities. Then, writes one of the historians, Holland waged her war against these odds *with daily meetings for prayer;* her believing and adoring people fled to the temples of God; it was for their nationality and for their faith they were to fight; and as they prayed, their heroic hearts grew stouter and stouter. A tide of remarkable ebb kept the French and English from landing, and then a tempest swept them seaward; the patriots, who added vigor and ammunition and gold to their prayers, prepared their force, and pursued, and routed them; infatuation was sent into the French king's brain; and while one of the brave Dutch commanders was saying, in his great faith, "The weaker we are, the surer am I of victory, for my confidence is not in man, but in Almighty God," lo! the Almighty God scattered his enemies, and, with less than a year's conflict, the Republic was safe.

Remember, once more, an example of answered prayer for a people, nearer home, and in the history of our own Fathers. In the year 1746, the people of Boston, alarmed at the prospect of an armed French invasion upon their colony by sea, in forty vessels from Nova Scotia, kept a day of fasting and prayer. When they were assembled in their places of worship, after a morning which had been "perfectly clear and calm," a sudden gust of wind arose, and shook the buildings. That storm wrecked the fleet on the coast of the eastern provinces; the principal commander, the Duke d'Anville, took his own life in mortification; thousands perished; and the expedition failed forever. "It shall come to pass," saith thy God, "that while they are yet speaking, I will hear."

Righteous as our cause is, we have not been a righteous people. Official bribery, corrupt legislation, partisan politics, a besotted lust for promotion, luxury, and display, irreverence towards God's Sabbaths and sanctuaries, and a headstrong self-will,—these are but parts of the black cloud of our transgressions provoking the just judgments that are abroad in the land. Would that the supplications of the prostrate nation might be as the prayer of one repenting heart, that the God of our fathers would return, and spare and forgive us; make men to be of one mind in this house of their inheritance;

and yet cause it to be Emmanuel's land, loyal to the Great King, with the law and liberty and love of Christ blessing its borders, with one faith, and one baptism, and with the glory of the Lord both risen and abiding upon it!

THE PRESIDENT'S HYMN.

For the National Thanksgiving, Nov. 26, 1863.

GIVE thanks, all ye people, give thanks to the Lord,
Alleluias of freedom, let Freemen accord;
Let the East, and the West, North and South roll along,
Sea, mountain and prairie, One thanksgiving song.

Chorus after each verse.
Give thanks, all ye people, give thanks to the LORD,
Alleluias of freedom, let Freemen accord.

For the sunshine and rainfall, enriching again
Our acres in myriads, with treasures of grain;
For the Earth still unloading her store-house of wealth,
For the Skies beaming vigor, the Winds breathing health:
      Give thanks—

For the Nation's wide table, o'erflowingly spread,
Where the many have feasted, and all men have been fed,
With no bondage, their God-given rights to enthral,
But Liberty guarded by Justice for all:
      Give thanks—

THE PRESIDENT'S HYMN.

In the realms of the Anvil, the Loom, and the Plow,
Whose the mines and the fields, to Him gratefully vow:
His the flocks and the herds, sing ye hill-sides and vales;
On His Ocean domains chant His Name with the gales.
      Give thanks—

Of commerce and traffic, ye princes, behold
Your riches from Him Whose the silver and gold:
Happier children of Labor, true lords of the soil,
Bless the Great Master-Workman, who blesseth your toil.
      Give thanks—

Brave men of our forces, Life-guard of our coasts,
To your Leader be loyal, Jehovah of Hosts:
Glow the Stripes and the Stars aye with victory bright,
Reflecting his glory,—He crowneth the Right.
      Give thanks—

Nor shall ye through our borders, ye stricken of heart,
Only wailing your dead, in the joy have no part:
God's solace be yours, and for you there shall flow
All that honor and sympathy's gifts can bestow.
      Give thanks—

The Domes of Messiah—there, ye worshipping throngs,
Solemn litanies mingle with jubilant songs;

The Ruler of Nations beseeching to spare,
And our Empire still keep the Elect of His care.
     Give thanks—

Our guilt and transgressions remember no more;
Peace, Lord! Righteous Peace, of Thy gift we implore;
And the Banner of Union, restored by Thy Hand,
Be the Banner of Freedom o'er All in the Land.
    And the Banner of Union, etc.
    Give thanks—

UNIVERSAL PEACE.

An attempt will here be made to shew, that, by the course of human events, as overruled by Divine Providence, the time approaches, when wars shall cease; the nations forming a Permanent Judicial Tribunal, to which by mutual consent, their disputes may be referred.

It is not material to the proof of the proposition, that at the age of thirty-three, (1820,) I drew out a sketch of the idea, now to be further elaborated; but it is, that forming this idea at that mature age, (not then daring however, to advance it, except as a work of imagination,) my mind has, through all the subsequent changes of a busy life, retained the same view.

It first came into my mind from reflections on the American Constitution and its operations, similar to those De Tocqueville has since so well drawn out and expressed, dwelling as he has done, on the perfection of the system as developed in New England, particularly in the smallest division as uniting to compose the families making the towns—the towns the counties — and the counties the states, etc. I found less perfection as I advanced in the series, and the last link that binds all which is perfect to the throne of God, was wholly wanting.*

Thus the subject presented itself to my mind in 1820.

Happy Columbia! blest and honored land!
Wise were thy sires, who first thy charter planned;
But wiser far and mightier is that mind,
Who made them means to work what He designed.
Mark how sublime extends the wise device,
Of his dread order's ever-growing rise.
First the small family, and then the town,
The county, state, then all the states in one!
But here we pause;—thus far hath time expressed,
Of God's vast plan, and must mature the rest.

---

* If the American statesmen will examine this subject for the purpose of finding theoretical perfection, as a guide to practical wisdom, will he not find that our system as it is now working, shews a defect? That our country having become so large, and our States so numerous, our plan of Union makes too great and sudden a spread, in embracing at once in one General Government, forty-two States and Territories, extending over half a world? Would it not be more perfect, if an intermediate organization were made, and our immense empire of America were arranged into divisions, each taking in a number of the States,

UNIVERSAL PEACE.

At the time of composing this, I was engaged in writing with Mr. Woodbridge, our works on Ancient and Modern Geography, and as one of the grounds of my belief in the approach (whether near or far) of Universal Peace, was the prophetic assertions of Holy Writ, that there should come such a time, and that Jerusalem should be the chosen place, I was careful to examine maps and globes in reference to the question.

In rectifying the terrestrial globe to find a place for the zenith, which shall leave above the rational horizon, the greatest quantity of arable land, and the greatest number of inhabitants, that place will be found in, or near, the region of the Holy Land, other geographical considerations appear in the following extract:

less or more, say from five to seven or eight, according to circumstances—so that there might be about five or six of these larger divisions which we might call nations, (or any other name that suited us better,) they together forming as now the one Grand Empire;—as might be represented by the root-system of a tree which has first the fibres, uniting to form the smallest roots, then these composing those of the next grade, and so on, the roots gradually increasing in size as they diminish in number, till finally, a few large ones converge, and growing together they unite unto one great body; and thus present their whole strength and vitality to resist all foreign influences?

What then remains, to work war's final fall?
ONE MIGHTY COUNCIL, FORMED TO WATCH O'ER ALL.
Of this vast rule, say where shall be the seat,
Where on earth's face, earth's delegates shall meet?
Is there a spot, o'er all her lands contain,
Where best can gather the congressive train?
Where lengthened seas far inland mildly stray,
Nor stormy capes obstruct the needful way?
Or is a spot, o'er all her precincts wide,
That God hath honored more than all beside?
Now, Zion's prophet—now we think on thee!
And Zion's hill that chosen spot must be.
Commodious most, honored o'er all beside,
Where God, the Saviour lived, and where He died!

And if, in 1820, it could be believed that a World's Council of Peace might assemble at Jerusalem, how much more credible is it in 1860? For, in no period of the world's history, has man so rapidly advanced his empire over physical nature, and in no circumstance of his condition has he more changed and improved, than in the increased rapidity of locomotion for his body by steam, unless it be in that of his mind, by electricity. In 1820, steam had been applied to locomotion by water on the rivers, yet ocean steamers did not exist till more than ten years afterwards, and the time of steam travelling by land, occurred soon after. Now it is no new thing for a world's convention to assemble Delegates to a Permanent Peace Council—to reside for a term of years at Jerusalem, they might easily be accompanied by their families; there those who had business with, might easily approach them, and the publications which would of course emanate from so high a court, would require but a short time to reach the Capitols of the Nations. Or if greater speed were necessary than steam could furnish, to carry forth some important decision, the wonderful invention of the telegraph is at hand.

Let us now examine this great subject in the lights of History. The will of the great Powers, such as England, France, America and Russia, might immediately inaugurate a Council of Peace, with a view to its permanency; and they, being the largest and most prosperous, would have the greatest interest in retaining their boundaries, and keeping things without, peacefully, in statu quo.

How infinitely would it have been to the advantage of America, had such a Council existed six years ago, to whom the South would have brought their complaints against our Government, before proceeding to war.

Besides this general reason, has not each of the great powers its own complications, calculated to make the present, a time especially favorable to the consideration of Universal Peace?

The policy of Russia, has heretofore looked to Universal Empire, and hence has been aggressive; but Russia has now on her hands a war to make her wish for Universal Peace—the war with Poland—that ancient nationality, pitied by the world—sung by its best poets—and beloved by Lafayette and others, of its purest patriots. The present Czar of Russia found Poland as it is, and hence is not to be blamed for its wrongs; and we fully believe he would now be glad to be honorably rid of this living trouble.

Russia's latest war before this, was rather to gain a port on the Mediteranean, than to extend its dominions. And why were England and France unwilling that Russia—so great a portion of Europe, should have what is so needful to her commerce? It was not that they were unwilling that the Russians should be prosperous, but, such had been the aggressive disposition of their rulers, that France and England dared not allow them to become too powerful; and thus JEALOUSY *of power* became as usual among nations, the cause of war; and while this exists, nations will injure and despoil, instead of seeking to aid each other. Were there a Peace Tribunal, first agreed on by the nations, and then chosen from their wisest and best men—those among them who most command the world's confidence, then as this new Tribunal began to do its work, it would be more and more depended on as an arbiter; and it would soon be seen by all, how much better were its decisions, than is the unreasoning—the mad arbitrament of war;—and then would this jealousy of power subside. Russia might then agree with her neighbors, and peaceably gain a port on the Mediterranean; and England and France at the same time acquire a profitable customer. Then the American Republic would no longer be feared, (because the Peace Council would not allow her to be aggressive,) then she would no longer be hated, and practiced against to divide her. Germany and Denmark might then have a dignified tribunal to appeal to,—whose judgment of right it would be honorable to accept.

The first operation of a rightly established Council of Peace being to take away national jealousy; each Government no longer fearing others, would have nothing to do but to manage its own interior concerns; and it might turn all its energies to improving the condition of its own people; and each nation might peacefully move on its own way. The English would no longer fear that a mad democracy might, at some future day, invade them to destroy the social order of their society, their grand permanent estates, and the beauty which these give to their garden-island—but while each nation is experimenting in peace, each might be examining the systems of the other, and making mutual improvements.

There is one sovereign in Europe who has lately shown himself the earnest advocate of Peace—Louis Napoleon. He has lately made strenuous efforts to assemble a Peace Congress; and why did he fail? For the same reason that England would have failed to get a Peace Congress to London, or Russia to St. Petersburg—because by inviting, on his own authority, the nations to come to Paris, there to hold a Congress, he assumes to make Paris, Europe's metropolis; and rival nations will not allow it. Much less would they allow any rival capital to become the seat of a permanent Tribunal of Peace. But would Louis Napoleon consent "to cast away ambition"— and perhaps he already has—and give himself to the service of God in the cause of man, he might make for himself a far higher place in the temple of humanity and of true fame than that filled by his uncle. For it would be as much greater, to be the means of inaugurating a Code of Peace Laws for the nations, than it was to produce *the Code Napoleonic* as the earth's surface is greater that that of France. But the seat of this council cannot be Paris, it must be Jerusalem. And here suppose for a moment that Louis Napoleon were really thinking whether or not he could carry out this plan, why, he would ask, must Jerusalem be the place? A believer in the Scripture would scarcely ask that, but God sometimes employs men who are not believers to carry out his predicted designs. Those who believe not the truth of Christianity must yet believe its existence; and they must believe the consequent veneration of its votaries for the Holy Places. And Louis Napoleon knows, that this reverence is no inoperative superstition, by what occurred so lately at the opening scenes of the Crimean War. And let him now regard with attention that great standing historic miracle;—the greatest of all time;—a nation without a place! The Jews stand waiting. Hasten to do the Lord's work, in preparing for them their promised abode. When the Gentile nations gather to Jerusalem to make it the seat of Universal Peace, then must they aid the Jews to return.

But Turkey owns the Holy Land. Yes, but to whom does Turkey owe her past and present existence? When the "man was sick," nigh unto death, England and France saved him. And now if these powers should see the expediency of the Jews possessing the Holy Land, and that it would be for a purpose greatly advantageous to Turkey, and that ample money might be paid for it, would there be any formidable opposition from that needy and feeble nation? But how is this ample money to be obtained? Now is a time, when the wealthiest family in the world—the Rothschilds—are Jews. And could there be any doubt that—Great Britain consenting—if Louis Napoleon should conduct a negotiation with the Rothschilds and they thus be assured, that there was to be a movement among the nations by which, as is foretold in their Scriptures, as well as in our own, the reign of Universal Peace was about to be established at Jerusalem, can there be any doubt that these wealthy Jews would joyfully set on foot the purchase of the Holy Land—the making of a rail road from Jerusalem to the coast, and doing whatever else was necessary; so that by the time the nations had chosen the honored members, and prepared the code of international laws under which they were to act, the Council of Peace would find Jerusalem ready for their reception.

Shout, Zion's friends! break forth, O earth, and sing!
The Lord again doth his redeemed bring!
Awake, O virgin daughter! quickly wake!
Thy neck unbind, thy dusty vestments shake!
Arise and shine, for lo, thy light is come!
And GATHERING NATIONS fondly bear thee home!
Nor war, nor waste, thy borders more shall see,
AND THE WHOLE EARTH THY HAPPY BORDERS BE!

TROY, N. Y, *Feb.* 23, 1864.

SYMPATHY.

My country weepeth sore
    Above her fallen brave,
By field, by grove, by stream they lie,
Their faces toward their native sky,
    And scarcely find a grave.

She listeneth to the wail
    That from a thousand homes
By town, by tower, by prairie bright,
At dawn, at noon, at dead of night,
    In wild discordance comes.

She at the threshold grieves,
    Where stretched on pallets lie
Beneath the surgeon's scalpel keen
The stalwart form, the noble mien,
    Convuls'd with agony.

She bendeth o'er the wave
   Where sank the patriot train,
Whose volleying guns a farewell sent
As downward with their ship they went
   To the unfathom'd main.

She listeneth as the Earth
   Surcharg'd with bloody rain,
Her many cherish'd sons demands;
Her bold, her beautiful, whose hands
   Made rich her harvest-wain.

She kneeleth at the Throne
   Of mercy, day and night;
She looketh o'er the war-cloud dim,
With an unwavering trust in Him
   Who doeth all things right.

HISTORICAL SKETCH.

THE ANCIENT WORLD.

Our Country in the Past! What see we there,
On History's page, as guided by its light,
We seek her midst the dynasties of old?
Chaldea with her astronomic lore,
Mother of nations, long since passed away;
Egypt and Babylon, Israel's martial hosts,
The Persian rule—republics of old Greece;
And Rome with her long Carthagenian wars,
Had come, and gone, e'er Bethlehem's star had yet
Guided the Magi in their earnest search,
To find the infant Saviour, the Divine.
The Christian era brought a change on earth—
Th' upheaving of the nations marked the time
Of the grand advent—soon the British isles,
And continental Europe act a part,
Transplanting science from her ancient seats;
And art soon followed whither science led.

DISCOVERY OF AMERICA.

But ages dark of superstitions lore,
And legends false, corrupting the true faith,
Gloomed sadly o'er the horoscope of man.
Yet in that day of intellect enchain'd,
Columbus' spirit with its giant grasp,
Seized on the far off continent which lay
Beyond th' untravell'd ocean's distant bounds;
Collecting facts, and then subjecting these
To analytic reasoning profound,
Conviction came, and followed action then.
Yet much Columbus suffered in the cause
Which moved his noble spirit, till at length
A woman's hand bestowed the needful aid;
Oh Isabella! may thy honored name,
E'er serve as talisman to nerve the hearts
Of those who would,—but feebly dare not do
The noble deeds prompted by motive high.
Her jewels rare, Queen Isabella gave
To gain the means to send Columbus forth
Upon that voyage, mysterious and strange,
With nought to guide him on his trackless way
But a slight needle, as it chanced to point.
"Chanced," did we say? No, in Columbus' hand
It was th'unerring finger from above,

Directing where the indicated land,
Which science promised, should by him be found.
Yet small the sacrifice to Castile's queen
Of costly jewels, which her lofty mind
Had little cared for;—but for years she bore
The sneers of courtiers, and the sharp rebukes
Of those who sought to subjugate her soul.
But God sustained her, that she faltered not—
The new world was discovered, after years
Of suffering to him who ventured forth,
Guided by science and by trust in God.
And how was he repaid? let the sad tale
Of what Columbus bore from envious foes
Speak to the Martyrs in a righteous cause,
And point the moral. "look not for reward
To earthly favor; raise thy thoughts above."

THE SPANIARDS IN AMERICA.

We pause not to portray the sad events
Which followed in the train of Spanish rule,
When Montezuma's halls were crimsoned o'er
With blood of princes who with trusting hearts
Had welcomed to their land the treacherous guests,
"Conquests in Mexico" by Cortez' bands
Are chronicled by one, who never more
Shall labor for his Country's literature,

But ever honored be our Prescott's name.
We bid adieu to Spanish hunt for gold
In Southern regions, following in the bark
Which rushes onward, to more Northern skies
To find another continent, beyond
That narrow isthmus, where the gulf looks out
On neighboring oceans, circling round the globe.

NORTH AMERICA FOUND.

From Spain th' infectious passion wide had spread
Of greed for gold—and mariners went forth
To seek for mines in undiscovered coasts.
Sea-loving Portuguese their sails unfurl,
And French and English navies are afloat—
"Ho, westward ho," the cry from gallant ships,
And History's page, now teeming with events,
Tells of the great discoveries which reward
The navigators for their weary toils.
The beautiful Acadia* is found,
And Prima Vista† by the French first seen,
While England's subjects plant their country's flag
On rock-bound Plymouth's weather-beaten coast.
Yet farther South, beneath more genial skies,
Potomac's broad expanse and fertile shores

* Nova Scotia. † Newfoundland.

Allured adventurers to make their home.
True, savage owners of the lands there were.
But sooth to say their rights had little weight.
The curious natives wondered as they gazed
On their strange visitors;—and said, "well-come,"
The value of their lands was nought to them.
And glad they were to barter these away
For worthless trinkets, beads and trifling toys,
And counting them as good equivalents
For their vast hunting grounds—a nation's site,
Which was to be, hereafter:—so they deemed,
Those early pilgrims to the Western wilds.

NORTH AND SOUTH VIRGINIA.

In honor of their Virgin Queen was named
The region vast—from Prima Vista's shores
To Carolina's swamps, Virginia, all—
Called North and South, but all Virginia.
It is not in our purpose now to dwell
Upon the fortunes of the settlements,
The wars with Indians—and the contest dire
With France, for England's sake, when Quebec fell.
And Washington went forth, a rustic youth,
To battle for our haughty mother's cause.
The Red Man's fate must ever darkly shade
Our Country's records—arguments to prove

That might makes right, may blind, but not convince.
There is some show of reason in the plea
That the full time had come to wrest this soil
From savage rule—amid the deserts wild,
To plant the rose, and Christian temples build,
Where heathen orgies from the wigwam rude
In hideous sounds arose upon the air—
The fiat of th' Almighty we may trace
In man's misdoing, working out His will.

Fast grew the infant Colonies—"Virginia's weed,"
When known in Europe, brought them good returns.
And when the lonely planters wanted wives
They offered willingly a goodly price,
For such commodity—and then there came
A living cargo, duly shipped, in change
For hogsheads of tobacco—So we read,
Though this we do not care to dwell upon;—
But let us all confess with humbled pride,
That in our ancestry there may be flaws.
Proud England's aristocracy may blush
For blazoned scutcheons—often stained with blood
Defaced with treachery or violence,
Or issuing from plebian origin.

BRITISH COLONIES—THE SLAVE SHIP.

Great Britain saw her colonies increase;—
E'en nobles sometimes came to grace the land,
Though *graceless* in their lives perchance they were
But see, on ocean's wave a far off ship!
A black spot in the distance she appears,
Yes, dark indeed! for freighted is the bark
With slaves from Afric's coast, to sell for gold.
And soon the slave-ships multiply amain,
Filling the country with a fatal curse.
In vain remonstrance from the New-World went
Against this traffic foul—'t'was heeded not,
For foreign traders found it made them rich;
Our mother country saw the trade was good
For profit to herself, and liked it well.
The Northern colonies had, too, their share
In slavery; but when they found, in truth,
The negro was not fitted to their use,
That children of the Sun could never thrive
In their cold climate;—then they saw, how bad
Was slavery—and, magnanimous, resolved
To rid themselves of such a crying sin;
They gave it up to wicked planters, who,
'Neath fervid suns and alligator swamps,
By sweat of slaves might dare t'enrich their soil.

Some said 't'was merciful to Afric's sons
To bring them from their wicked heathen homes;—
So Cortez and his ruffians argued, when
They seized upon the natives of Peru,
And taught them Christian mercy on the rack.
Man ever finds an argument for what
He wishes, most himself deceiving, when
Seeking to disguise his acts with reasons
Drawn from his interest, until he ends
In fancying he is serving God in deeds
Which terminate, as they begun—in self.
Oh! God of Mercy, who shall dare assume
That he is righteous! And our country too,
Was born and nursed in sin.
      Yet would we not
Dwell gloomily upon the past—for sure
Noble examples of a virtue rare
Illume the annals of our early days.

THE AMERICAN REVOLUTION.

So England's colonies waxed rich and strong,
And gave great revenues unto her king;
But often avarice, in her eager grasp,
Destroys the source of riches;—thus it was
That by oppressive acts the cord was snapped,
Which bound the offspring to the parent's side.

And so the colonies in time, threw off
Their subjugation, and held up their heads,
Snuffing the air of freedom, looking round
Upon an empire vast—and this, *their own.*
"*Our Country*" then it was—bought by the blood
Of patriot sires, freed from foreign rule,
And given us "to keep," as Eden was
To our first parents in their innocence.
"One empire, undivided, it must be,"
Was nature's voice, as looking far abroad
The close connection of the whole was seen;
Interlacing rivers connecting all
In one grand system, bound by oceans round.
Thus Washington beheld it; and so he
Of Monticello taught, with others wise,
As fearless they, their venerated names
With a firm hand to Freedom's chart subscribed ;
The chart of Independence, and no less
A bond for Union, than in after days,
The Constitution, made to fasten firm
The compact under which the colonies
Fought for their freedom from a foreign yoke.
This compact made, they threw it in the face
Of royalty, nerved as they were to meet
Th' events which were before them, if perchance
A failure should befal their bold attempt.

"In Union is our strength," the patriots said,
All hearts responded, and the work was done.

Our Country in the Past! how swells the heart
At thought of days when, side by side were seen
Heroes from North and South, united firm
In the great struggle which should make them free
From foreign powers. Oh, little thought they then
Of sons degenerate, who would ever crouch
To France and England, begging them to come
Against their brethren; spurning under foot
The legacy bought with their fathers' blood,
More precious far than monarchs ever left
To royal heirs,—a country great and free.

OUR COUNTRY AFTER THE REVOLUTION.

We gladly linger here awhile, to view
"*Unum et pluribus*," the clustering States,
Many yet *one*, guarding the central point,
Round which in their due orbits, all revolved,
Like sun amid the planets; thus was seen
The central power giving both light and heat
To all around—encircling in its span
E'en the most distant of revolving States.
In Union lay our strength—our fathers taught,
And from our infant days, we learned to hold

In reverential awe, this Union dear.
The nation's strength required a firmer bond
Than first was made, when colonies became
States sov'reign, yet subordinate to rule
Of central government —Years pass'd away
E'er yet our grand republic had acquired
The needed force to execute its laws—
For cautiously the Sovereign States did yield
The powers demanded at the central head
To keep all steady, guard 'gainst foreign foes,
To levy taxes, save from treason dark—
The currency to regulate, and to send
Ambassadors abroad with the full power,
Treaties to make; and to enforce them too
At home, where central law should be obeyed.
But years had passed before the seal was set
To the great compact, firmly binding States
T' yield up interests sectional, that good
Might come to all, and harmony prevail.

THE OPINIONS OF FOREIGNERS RESPECTING SLAVERY IN AMERICA.

Now Europe wondering, saw the countless throngs
Of travellers from America, who seemed
T' abound in wealth, and liberal in all
"*Inquiring* and *requiring*," "moved by steam,"

As sometimes the phlegmatic German said,
When wondering to see how fast they went.
What traveller from our land may not have seen
Th' averted look, and ill-concealed disgust,
When ought was said of *slavery* in our land?
But brethren, sworn to stand-by at all needs,
We falter out excuse as best we can—
"Entailed upon us in our infant state,
By Europeans in their love of gain.
Slaves are among us—not by fault of ours;
We treat them kindly, mean to set them free
When the fit time shall come for such a change."
But we lik'd not the questioning on this—
It was the plague spot which we fear'd would work
Destruction for our Country—well we knew
How jealous England watch'd to foster strife
T'wixt South and North; how zealously she strove
To circulate suspicion through our land;
How sweetly smiled upon the holders forth
On the dark sin of slavery, as if that
Were the sole evil which survived the Fall,
And all were saints but those who in their homes
Made homes for negroes, bore their idle ways
And gladly saw them happy and content.
Thus have we often seen the life as led
In Southern regions—yet too true it is,

The world is full of evils—each relation hath
Its dangers of abuse, and well we know
That slavery, its hideous aspects hath—
Pandora's box of evils, it hath proved
Our Country's desolation and, its scourge.

THE AMERICAN REPUBLIC.

We see a vast domain extend beyond
The Atlantic shores whither the sultry sun
Reflects its beams from Rocky Mountain pass,
To where Pacific's wave from India's coast
Rolls on in savage grandeur; half the globe
Encompassing within its circle vast.
What empire of the world can we compare
With our republic in its wide extent!
Spreading through parallels of various climes,
Where isothermal lines from every grade
Of regions, temperate, tropical or cold,
Yield products of all lands, and thus secure
Our independence of the outer world!
Thought flew on lightning wings from farthest lands;
Space was annihilate by power of steam;
Flourish'd mechanic arts; while learnings fanes
As seen on all sides, well bespoke the care
For education which pervaded all.
From days colonial the custom came

To send the Southern youth to Northern schools;
Not but that colleges of ancient worth,
Existed nearer home; but many thought
It well that Southern intellect should gain
From Northern perseverance, greater strength;
And that the youth would doubtless better learn
Habits of industry and self-control,
When from obsequious menials separate.
There was a prestige in the Southern name;
Each student boy at Harvard or at Yale—
From Dixie's land, was counted a young prince,
His home supposed a palace, and his wealth
Unbounded;—many a fair Northern lass
Indulged in visions of romantic bliss
When her young lover should return to claim
The hand so fondly plighted to a *"soph"*—
But college loves full well she learned to know
Were only meant t' enliven college days;—
But we descend to notice trivial things;
We only wish to give a picture true
Of life, as late existed in the land,
The prestige of the South in Northern schools,
And elsewhere too,—as ever might be found.
Within our country's Capitol, where throned
In power, the Southern statesmen held their court.

ADDITION OF NEW STATES TO THE UNION.

Some thirteen colonies in early days,
Had formed the nucleus of our Government;
But soon from territories wild and far,
Came trooping in to join the circle bright,
New States, who gravely took their place among
The elders of the nation, holding all
The rights and dignity of sovereign States.
Some had been bought by purchase, lib'ral made,
Of France and Spain—while Texas' wilds were gain'd
By hard fought battles with her neighbor rude,
Who yielded on compulsion, what in vain
Our country claimed as justly due to her.

THE THIRTEEN ORIGINAL STATES DELIBERATE UPON A NEW CONSTITUTION.

Our Constitution we have said was formed
By long deliberation of great men
Who came together to compare their views;
Each State then having name, was called upon
To give decision on the question vast.
"Shall we together stand—our Country save
By our united strength, and firm accord,
To hold our rightful place against the world;
Or, disintegrate, shall we be a prey

To foreign foemen, or domestic strife?
Some statesmen feared to delegate the power
To the head government, which might the States
Reduce, from sovereign to subordinate,—
But all at length perceived that only thus
Could stand America, a nation great—
So thoughtful maidens by affection urged,
To merge their future in another's weal,
Oft linger long, unwilling to resign
Their sovereign independence, for the state
Of partial subjugation—'tis question which
T'answer with due wisdom, must be resolved
By arguments derived from wise experience
Of what life is, what are its social claims—
Is standing singly, better than the strength
Which comes of Union? When the choice is made,
Why then abide by promise;—not free again
To choose, retract, or break the sacred bond.
Thus did our venerated Fathers choose
To join the Union in the greater strength
The Constitution to the Country gave;
Not for a term of years—their single life—
But for all time—in perpetuity,
The compact ran;—as well might men impeach
The tenure of the deeds by which they hold
The lands their fathers left them, as to break

The sacred compact of the several States
Our Fathers swore should ever be maintain'd.

SECESSION AND REBELLION.

It is but simply we attempt to urge
Our duties to our Country—yet 'tis meet
That all should know, and knowing seek to do.
That term *"Secession!"* what may it imply?
I ask of you fair friends, who boldly flaunt
The word, as if 'twere something newly found
T' express some virtue, hitherto unknown.
Hast thou reflected on its import well?
If language hath a sense, and words are ought
But idle breath, this hissing serpent-sound
Conveys an evil meaning—broken faith,
Destruction to the principle of life,
The very instrument which Satan wields
To gain man to his wicked purposes.
"Secede from God," the serpent lisp'd to Eve,
"Act for yourself," and you shall then be wise.
"Leave your paternal roof," the tempter says
To simple maiden trembling on the brink
Of the dark precipice, which before her yawns,—
To *leave, forsake, secede, all are but terms
Convertible*—though in the modern sense,

Secession means *rebellion to the laws*,
And deadly efforts to destroy the land
So dear unto our Fathers, who had deem'd
Their sons would cherish with their heart's best blood.
And why lay hand profane upon the ark
Of safety to the Country, th' united weal
Of all the States; would'st stab the parent's heart,
Stop the life-pulse which throbs within her veins?
Then dead were all the members, all depend
Upon one common life—then guard it well.
For such a parricidal act, what cause?
Was't fear of intermeddling with their rights
That caused the insurrection of the South?
Fear is not fact; far better 'twould have been
To wait for overt act, than thus to rush
To swift destruction from the mighty power
Of an indignant nation, firm resolved
To guard its rights, whate'er the cost might be.

LOOKING BACK.

How stood our Country when this war began?
The old world kingdoms saw our empire vast,
Attracting to its shores from every land
Those learn'd in science, great in intellect;
The mechanician and the artisan,
Gardeners and farmers, with domestics, all

Found here a sphere for study, or for work,
A place to exercise their various powers.
No longer Europeans proudly asked
Who ever read our books, for publishers
In London sought to fill their shelves
With works American—and to our shores
Their authors came, here finding, as they said,
Appreciative minds, more liberal men
To compensate for labors of the brain.
Our trade and commerce filled the world with wealth,
And proudly floated in the distant marts
The "Stars and Stripes," emblem of strength and power.
Thus did our Country flourish, far beyond
Whate'er the prophet seers of other days
Had dared imagine—for to them was hid
The great discoveries of the later times;
The Californian mines, the power of steam,
Electric influences, these changing all
The phases of man's life by magic art.
Peace dwelt within our borders, save that some
With *words* against their neighbors waged a war;
But in republics, words are freely changed,
They are not blows, nor should be met with such—
We were a happy people, following on,
As pleasure, interest, or instruction led.

We read of foreign wars, and pitied those
Whose lot had fallen in despotic lands.

AN EDUCATIONAL HOME.

But come with us, up yonder steep ascent,
Where crowning the hill's crest a mansion stands,
Massive its granite walls, and pillars firm
Support its Grecian portico. Around,
Hills rise o'er hills, while like a silvery thread,
Patapsco's waters add a varying charm.
That granite temple was erected there
By private liberality and zeal,
For better education of the young.
Let us approach the consecrated fane,
And view its inmates fair, who represent
The different parts of our republic vast—
For here assembled, in one common home,
Are daughters of the North and of the South;
From snowy climes to where the fervid sun
Kindles a deeper glow upon the cheek;
From the sun-rising to the verge extreme
Of Osage Mountains and Pacific's shore.
The great North-western region here has met
With old New England, parent of her sons,
And golden California too has brought
Her distant daughters to obtain for them

Treasures of intellect above all price.
As sisters, here all meet, all taught to love
The common country which protects their homes.
Hush, 'tis the hour of prayer! and reverent kneel
Those fair young maidens; then the organ swells
And gush of solemn music fills the air.
We see them next at recreation hour,
Wandering in pairs, or grouped as taste inclines,
'Mid perfumed paths, or seated 'neath the bowers
Where clematis with honeysuckle twines.
We do not find that, as companions, they,
Have chosen those who near them dwell at home,
But Southern Carolina loves full well
Her Massachusetts sister—thinking not
That enemies their brothers e'er will be—
They speak of future years, when school days o'er,
How happy they shall be, and sure to meet
Their dear companions in some beauteous spot,
Niagara, it may be, or perchance
At Newport, Philadelphia, or New York.
"My brother rare, you know he'll soon be free
From College rules, (he graduates at Yale,)
You sure must see him—and as you have taste,
And he has eyes, why—what will happen then?
Nous verrons—in our Southern home there's room
For a fair Northern sister—pleasant thought!"

THE CONTRAST.

The vision fades—and sundered far and wide
Are those fair girls;—widows and orphans now
Glide o'er the canvas, clad in weeds of woe,
Their homes deserted; wanderers o'er a land
Where hostile armies marching to and fro,
Threaten still further desolation in their train.
Young mothers, watching helpless infancy,
Deprived of comforts, such as in other days,
Were not from humblest menial e'er withheld.
Oh God! console the afflicted ones, and grant
Compassion to the victors; and though late,
Repentance to the erring who have caused
This suffering in our land—such our prayer;
Though feeble, 'tis sincere, and let none say
That pity is misplaced—alas, that e'er
In woman's breast should fell revenge be nursed,
Or love of country mixed with bitter hate
Of erring brethren, suffering for their crimes.

WEST POINT IN 1860.

One picture more we trace in peaceful times,
While treason yet lay slumb'ring in the hearts
Of those who dared mature the fiendish plan
A nation to disintegrate, the horrors brave

Of armed rebellion to the Country's laws.
The summer sun was cooled on Hudson's shore
By breezes from the lofty highlands near,
And West-Point, with its military school,
Ensconced amidst the smiling verdant hills
Call'd on the traveller to view awhile,
The country's training school for future men,
The nurse of her defenders. Fit it was
That here the patriotic heart should swell
With pride for what our country was, and what
It promis'd in the coming time to be;
First 'mong the nations, strong and well secured
From all attacks of intermeddling powers.
Not yet four rapid years have passed away
Since such our meditations as we scanned
The youthful soldiers, who, by vet'rans trained,
Shewed military ardor, ready for war;
Their country's proudest boast and sure defence.
There was a grand assemblage at West-Point,
For hither in the execution prompt,
Obedient to the call of government,
Had come great men, whose honored names were
    heard
With deep respect—"That's the War-Minister"—
"Jeff Davis' not a very handsome man,
But then his talents are to all well known,"

And when his Excellence, soon after this,
Honor'd our poor New England by a tour,
Visiting our war-ships, taking notes of all,
Surveying Forts, and scanning their weak points,
The foolish Yankees said—"How kind of him
To dine with us—How faithful, too, he is
To learn where is our weakness, that he may
The better know to remedy what's wrong,"
But to the "Military School"—others there
Sent by the War Department to report
How prospered all things at that famous post,
Demand our notice—Yonder is Beauregard,
Le preux chevalier, who bends him low,
And whispers nonsense in a lady's ear;
There martial Hardee in the mazy dance,
Proves th' omnipotence of beauty's sway
That thus can tame the lion in his den—
(For Hardee then commanded at this post;)
Others there were amid the brilliant throng
Whose names have since been famed in rebel hosts.
Yes, in that spot, lovely in nature's charms
Treason had entered faithless Arnold's soul
And bade him sell his country for reward.
But God be praised, that 'mong those traitors were
Men of stern courage, loyal and sincere,
Who yet had never dreamed a time would come

When they should meet such brethren in arms
Against the fostering country, whom all owed
For education, place, and maintenance.

OUR COUNTRY IN THE PRESENT.

Our Country in the Past
Was grand and glorious! and chiefly they,
Our Southern brethren drank of the full cup
Of national prosperity—but the gods,
As said the Ancients in their heathen lore,
"First make men mad, then they destroy themselves."
But let us rather say, as Christians should,
That God for sin hath justly chastened us.
The present is obscure, dimmed with the tears
Which fall from mourner's eyes throughout the land.
The mass of human suffering, who may tell!
Ask those who bent on Mercy's errand go
To battle-fields to seek the dying there,
The living mid the dead, what sights they see,
What words they hear! Oh God, can brethren dare
To mar Thine image thus—their hands imbrue
In brother's blood, by mad ambition urged!
But Mercy's Angel speeds her onward flight,
Bearing relief and consolation glad
To fainting, wounded, dying fellow men;
No question then of Southern sympathy,

Of rebel warfare, but to all alike
Gives comfort, aid and kindly word of cheer:
Not foreign accents as in wars abroad
Speak the combatants, but one Mother tongue,
Sons of the self-same nation, sworn alike
To her allegiance—moulded in one form
By education's hand, from the self-same books
Their duties taught, as citizens and men.
God help the suffering, wheresoe'er they be,
Whether they mourn for losses of the past,
Or fearful, tremble for the future stroke
Impending o'er the lov'd ones who afar
Meet the stern mandates of relentless war.
Our Country in the Present! would we trace
Rebellion's record, let us turn our eyes
To old Virginia's desolated homes,
To fair Kentucky's border, reeking still
With human gore—or Vicksburg's ruined mart,
New Orleans shrouded in her sable weeds;
To Gettysburg, where fell the serried hosts
Of our own country's sons, led on to fight
Against each other—bosom friends opposed—
Sad Chickamauga, Chattanooga, too,
Have witnessed horrors not to be described
Where late were happy homes of peaceful men.

THE FUTURE.

And is this all! Is yet the red cup full?
What mean these hostile armies in the field,
Waiting fair spring's return upon the earth?
Is this a signal to begin the strife
When God renews His bounties, and nature starts
To renovated life beneath His hand?
Oh may His word go forth that stays the sword,
And cries to the destroying fiend "enough."
And oh ye leaders in rebellion's van,
Can ye not see th' inevitable fate
Which must await the men who dared to brave
Their country's vengeance, by their mad attempt?
Then hasten far away—let not your blood
Be on your Country—in far distant lands
Live to repent you of the parricide
You would have wrought, had not your plans been
  foiled.
What plea can white-robed charity invent
To lessen the dark stain upon your names?
No! yours the damning sin which once in Heaven
Rebellion caused; the wish to reign supreme,
Not satisfied with highest honors given;
So Lucifer, son of the morning, fell,
And never more could he that place regain;

And now with seers of old, mine eager eye
Strains to behold the unknown hidden paths
Which lie before us.

      There is light beyond—
And dove-like peace with gentle wing descends;
See, as she comes the hideous bird of death
Flaps his dark plumage, shrieking as he flies
From fields whereon he looked for future prey.

Brethren, united as in former days,
Consult together for the common weal;
Chastened in spirit, more forbearing they,
Loving God better for their punishment,—
Columbia's Genius, smiling, looks abroad,
And cries, exultant, "ALL, AT LAST, IS SAFE."

APPENDIX.

UNITED STATES CHRISTIAN COMMISSION.

THE CHRISTIAN COMMISSION is one of the most active and useful agencies our present national crisis has developed. Its design is purely benevolent. It is that of relieving sufferings and other necessities occasioned by the casualties of the war. These sufferings and necessities appear in the camps, on board the vessels, and in the hospitals of the army and navy, and most of all in the terrific exhibition of the battle fields. They relate to both the temporal and spiritual requirements of the soldiers of the army and the marines of the navy; the officers in command, the men of the ranks; the disabled in the tents of the camp and in the wards of the hospital. The mission is that of love and mercy. It follows the good Samaritan to the spot where the sufferer lies, and without inquiring who he is, and how he was hurt, proceeds to the binding up of his wounds, and the use of the oil and the wine that are necessary for his relief and recovery.

FIRST MOVEMENT FOR THE RELIEF OF THE SICK AND DISABLED.

The first movement in the organization of an association for the purpose of ministering to the temporal and spiritual wants of the soldiers and sailors of the army and navy, was made in Baltimore City early in May, 1861. Before the idea of the camp and the hospital was fully disclosed, the necessities of the army upon its march, and the navy on board the war vessel, were realized. It was the supply of the Bible and the tract, and the devotional book to the man in health and upon the march and the voyage that was at first suggested. But this humane consideration was soon succeeded by the call from the camp, and the war vessel, and the hospital for the comforts and consolations of religion. There were but few chaplains for the camps, and none for the vessels and hospitals that were first ordered. The wards of the National Hospital on Camden Street, Baltimore, were well filled with the sick, many of whom had died before there was any official provision for the ministrations of religion to the sufferers. A number of the clergy of the city and of the members of the newly organized Relief Association, volunteered for the service, and for several months gave such attention as could be afforded to the sick, the dying, and the dead. So irregular was the service when it was first administered, that a number of the sick were neglected in their last hours, and the dead were buried without the ceremonies of religion. Notwithstanding this condition, complaint was made by surgeons of hospitals that the clergy and others visiting the wards were frequently in attendance in such numbers as to be hindrances to one another in the performance of their needed and desired offices. While the surgeons were complaining and desiring the discontinuance of such irregular visitations, intelligence of the fact was communicated to the President of the United States, who immediately proceeded to the inauguration of a measure which supplied each hospital with a chaplain. This is certainly one of the best features of the hospital service, and the honor of its establishment is due to the President, by whose promptness and energy of action it was accomplished.

The Baltimore Association was commenced by a few persons who agreed with each other to visit and minister to the sick and disabled of the hospitals and camps. While in the performance of their religious services, distributing Bibles, tracts and devotional books, and reading, conversing and praying with the subjects of their interest, they were induced to give attention to their temporal needs in the administration of such delicacies as are grateful to the sick and suffering. With his reading matter in one hand and his basket of conserves and nicely prepared nourishing food in the other, the member of the little band was frequently to be seen pursuing his way to the ward of his afflicted brother, to relieve the sufferings of his physical system, while he cheered his spirits with his conversation and consoled him with the assurances of religion and his prayers for his present comfort and everlasting safety.

Extension of the Field of Labor.

As the war progressed the work of the Association increased. Camps and hospitals were multiplied in and around the city. Additional laborers were required to furnish the necessary ministrations to the continually increasing numbers of the afflicted. As the field of labor extended, the necessary laborers were providentially supplied. The number was soon increased to fifty and subsequently to seventy men, all of whom are now actively and industriously engaged in the work. Monthly meetings for the recital and record of experience and reciprocal encouragement are held, and thus animated and animating each other with zeal in the good cause, the laborers of this department of the Lord's vineyard are doing the work of relief to thousands of their afflicted fellow men. Their services are rendered in assistance of the chaplains, by whose approval and under whose directions they appropriate their time and energies and means.

Establishment of Hospitals.

The first regular hospital was established in the buildings of the National Hotel, Camden Street, Baltimore. It was called the National Hospital, in consequence of its location. The first surgeon, who, when others were appointed, became chief, was afterwards chosen as the Surgeon General of the United States. It was under his auspices that the hospital system was inaugurated. So rapid was the progress of the war that in a few months it became necessary to establish a number of hospitals in Baltimore, Washington City, Alexandria and other places, in which large numbers of the sick and otherwise disabled, were placed.

Christian Associations.

The organization known as the Young Men's Christian Association, branches of which are established in every city of the United

States, manifested an early interest on behalf of the multitudes of their fellow citizens who volunteered their services to the cause of the Constitution and the Union. The subject of their privations and necessities was frequently and freely discussed, and methods of relief considered. Through this agency Bibles and other reading matter were supplied to the soldiers of the regiments as they passed through the several cities. In some instances the regiments were stopped for a time that refreshments consisting of biscuits, coffee &c., might be distributed among the men. It was in these ministrations that the sympathies of the soldiers on their way to the seat of war, and those of their friends that remained at home were intermingled, and the idea of mutual service developed. The defenders were followed in their expeditions of hardship and danger by the interests and prayers of the defended, and while away in pursuit of their patriotic enterprise, the defenders were remembered and cared for by their brethren, for the protection of whose liberties and laws and government, they had gone forth to imperil their lives. The consideration of such a topic under such circumstances could not be long continued without the resort to the most active and effective means possible for the protection and comfort of those on whose behalf it was suggested.

ORGANIZATION OF THE UNITED STATES CHRISTIAN COMMISSION.

The most active and energetic operator of all the branches of the Young Men's Christian Association, was Mr. GEORGE R. STUART, one of the most prominent and successful merchants of Philadelphia. It was at his instance that the proposition was considered of organizing a body of gentlemen for the management of a great benevolent and religious service for the army and navy. A convention composed of delegates from the several branches of the Young Men's Christian Association, was accordingly ordered. The convention assembled in the city of New York on the 16th of November, 1861. It was by this convention that the UNITED STATES CHRISTIAN COMMISSION was established. Measures were adopted by which the work was to be introduced into all the loyal States.

The object of the COMMISSION thus formed, was stated to be that of ministering to the temporal and spiritual welfare of the officers and men of the United States army and navy, in co-operation with chaplains and others. The gentlemen chosen as the United States Christian Commission were, Rev. Rollin H. Neal, D. D., of Boston; George H. Stuart, Esq., of Philadelphia; Charles Demond, Esq., of Boston; John P. Crozer, Esq., of Philadelphia; Rev. Bishop E. S. Janes, D. D., of New York; Rev. M. S. R. P. Thompson, D. D., of Cincinnati; Hon. Benj. F. Manniere, of New York; Col. Clinton B. Fisk, of St. Louis; Rev Benj. C. Cutter, D. D., of Brooklyn; John V. Farwell, Esq., of Chicago; Mitchell H. Muller, Esq., of Washington City, and John D. Hill, M. D., of Buffalo.

The members elect of the Commission met in Washington City a few days after their appointment, and selected George H. Stuart, Esq., President, Hon. B. F. Manniere, Secretary and Treasurer, and Messrs. Stuart, Janes, Cutter, Demond and Manniere the Executive Committee. The offices of Secretary and Treasurer were afterwards separated, and the Rev A. M. Morrison was appointed Secretary.

During the first year of the operations of the Commission, Messrs. Manniere and Cutter resigned their places and Jay Cooke, Esq., of Philadelphia, and the Rev. James Eells; D. D., of Brooklyn, were chosen to supply the vacancies. Joseph Patterson, Esq., of Philadelphia, was chosen Treasurer in the place of Mr. Manniere, and Messrs. Crozer and Cooke were appointed on the Executive Committee to fill the places vacated by Messrs. Cutter and Manniere. After a gratuitous service of several months Rev. A. Morrison resigned the office of Secretary, and the Rev. W. E. Boardman, of Philadelphia, was elected in his place.

The residence of the President being in Philadelphia, the head quarters of the Commission were removed from New York to that city.

The plan of operations prepared by the Commission was submitted to the President of the United States, and to several members of his Cabinet, by whom it was heartily approved and recommended. Encouraging letters were given by the President, by Secretaries Cameron, Stanton and Welles, by Postmaster General Blair, by Generals McClellan and Hooker, by Admiral Foote, and by Surgeon General Hammond, and other distinguished gentlemen.

APPENDIX.

DESIGN OF THE COMMISSION.

The design of the Christian Commission was declared on its organization to be the exciting of Christian Associations and the Christian men and women of the loyal States to action in the relief of the necessities of the officers and men of the army and navy. In carrying out this design the necessity was apparent of enlisting the services of volunteer laborers in the collection and distribution of money and hospital stores, with which to supply whatever necessities might be developed. This service appears as an extension of that contemplated by the Government in furnishing attendance and supplies to the inmates of the hospitals. Chaplains, surgeons and other attendants upon the hospitals were required to perform certain specified duties in ministering to the spiritual and temporal relief of their patients. Large assistance was soon rendered necessary in the supply of reading matter and delicacies to the sick and wounded. This assistance was furnished by the Christian Commission, and was gratefully received by the more humane among surgeons and others in charge of the camps and hospitals.

LABORS AND LABORERS OF THE COMMISSION.

The laborers of the Commission consist of such gentlemen and ladies as volunteer gratuitous services in places where they are desired. The services thus rendered consist in such ministrations as the sick and wounded of the camps and hospitals need. The most important part of the work is the preparation of the spirit for its departure from this to a future world. This work cannot always be performed successfully unless assistance and relief are afforded to the physical needs of the patients. The pains of the body must be relieved or mitigated before the mind can be sufficiently composed to admit of instruction and counsel in relation to the spiritual wants of the sufferer. In the performance of this part of the labor, large quantities of such delicacies as are grateful to the suffering, as well as of Bibles, Testaments, tracts and devotional books, have been provided and used. The delegates of the Commission, consisting of gentlemen of the various professions and pursuits, and ladies, all connected with the religious denominations, have rendered the needed services of waiting on the sufferers, and reading to them and counselling them in relation to their future safety. Chaplains and surgeons have acknowledged the services thus rendered with thankfulness, and the desire has been frequently expressed that they should be continued.

PROVISIONS BY GOVERNMENT FOR THE COMFORT OF THE DISABLED.

Very extensive provisions have been made by the Government for the comfort of the sick and disabled of the army and navy. Chaplains and surgeons in large numbers are employed, and they are laboring efficiently in the accomplishment of the object contemplated in their appointment. But it were impossible for the Government to do all that is required in this department of its operations. One Chaplain and one Surgeon are allowed to a regiment of a thousand men. For an army of men in health and engaged in active service upon the march and in the camp, this may be sufficient. Not so when the battle field appears, and when the epidemic attacks the camp. The need of attention in both the religious and medical departments is multiplied by these casualties. No estimate can be made of the necessities these casualties may produce until they actually occur. It is then that the emergency is met by the benevolent and gratuitous services of the Christian Commission. Hundreds of devoted men and women are held in reserve, whose names are registered upon the books of the Commission, and who may be called out at any moment. When the necessity arises the call is made, and the response thus far has been very nearly equal to the demand. The laborers go forth with cheerfulness to the fields, and in the camps and hospitals their Samaritan-like duties are performed. Thousands of the brave officers and men of the battle fields have acknowledged with gratitude the services these Christian men and women have administered, and many a valuable life has been saved through their agency. Thus it is seen that the reserve service which it were impossible for the Government to keep in continuous supply, is actually provided by the voluntary contributions of means and labors by the Christian Commission.

AID FOR THE COMMISSION SERVICE.

In aid of the service provided by the Christian Commission, a large number of the people of the loyal States have contributed. Associations of gentlemen and ladies have been organized in cities and towns of several of the States, for the supply of delegates and means for the work. Many self-sacrificing philanthropists have left their business and families for stated periods to undergo the privations of the march and the encampment, and to risk the dangers of the battle for the purpose of ministering to the necessities of those who have risked their all of property and their lives in the defence of their Government. In the performance of this labor there is generally no choice admitted in relation to locality or department of the army. The delegates are sent, as they are always willing to go, to such points as are most in need of their ministrations. Others have emptied their store-rooms of delicacies which they have provided for family use, and sent them in charge of the Commission to places of deposit from which they have been taken by the hands of the delegates and appropriated through them to the use of the sufferers that needed them.

GRATUITOUS SERVICES OF DELEGATES AND OTHERS ENGAGED IN THE WORK.

The laborers of the Commission consists of the members of the central body, and the committees of the same, which are distributed throughout the loyal States, the delegates who are sent out by the central body, the agents in charge of the stations, and the local committees, the "Relief" and "Aid" Associations which are in operation in every city and in almost every town and country place of any note in the loyal States. Besides these there are clerks and packers connected with the several places of deposit, whose services are necessary in the receiving and unpacking and re-packing and distributing the stores in transit from the residences of the donors to the places of their destination in the camps and hospitals.

Members of the Central Body.

The members of the Central Body, the head-quarters of which are in Philadelphia, the City in which the President resides, consist of George H. Stuart, Esq., *President, Philadelphia.* Rev. Rollin H. Neale, D. D., *Boston.* Charles Demond, Esq., *Boston.* Rev. Bishop E. S. Janes, D. D., *New York.* Rev. James Eells, D. D., *Brooklyn.* John P. Crozier, Esq., *Philadelphia.* Jay Cooke, Esq., *Philadelphia.* Mitchell H. Mullen, Esq., *Washington City.* Rev. M. S. R. P. Thompson, D. D., *Cincinnati.* Col. Clinton B. Fisk, *St. Louis.* John V. Farwell, Esq., *Chicago.* John D. Hill, M. D., *Buffalo.*

The Central Body is what its title imports, the centre of motion to the Commission. By it the various committees are appointed, and the entire work of the institution superintended. The President, with such other members of the Central Body as can find it convenient to accompany him, visits all the districts and stations of the Commission, and the battle-fields, and counsels with the committees, delegates and agents in relation to their work. His encouraging presence and conversation have been of great benefit to his co-laborers in this great and greatly needed service. The other officers of the Commission, at the present time, are as follows:

Joseph Patterson, *Treasurer, Western Bank, Philadelphia.*
Rev. W. E. Boardman, *Secretary,* 13 *Bank Street,* "
Executive Committee:—George H. Stuart, *Chairman, Philadelphia.* Rev. Bishop E. S. Janes, D. D., *New York.* Charles Demond, Esq., *Boston.* John P. Crozier, Esq., *Philadelphia.* Jay Cooke, Esq., *Philadelphia.*

Central Office.

At the Central Office, 13 Bank Street, Philadelphia, to the use of which Mr. Stuart has devoted the large room on the second floor of his warehouse, a very large proportion of the Commission stores are received. They are distributed from the Office to the offices of the committees and agents as they are needed. The use of Mr. Stuart's warehouse and the services of his clerks and porters are contributed to the Commission free of charge. Nearly the whole time of the president is appropriated gratuitously to the labors of the institutuion to which he is most ardently devoted, and which he has so faithfully served.

DISTRICT OFFICE OF MARYLAND.

The Office of the Maryland District, which is located in Baltimore, is appropriated and used in the same manner as the Central Office in Philadelphia. Mr. G. S. Griffith contributes the use of the second floor of his warehouse and the services of his clerks as they are required to the use of the Commission. Nearly the whole of his own time is devoted to the work.

At the office during and for some days after the battles of Antietam and Gettysburg, from fifteen to thirty voluntary laborers, consisting of clergymen, lawyers teachers and tradesmen, might be seen as hard at work as day laborers and as if they were to be paid for their services.

NO SABBATH ON THE DAY OF BATTLE.

As a period of rest there was no Sabbath to the Commission in Baltimore during and for days after the battles fought in Maryland and on its borders and in Pennsylvania. As the call was made from the field of carnage the response was echoed. When the call came on the Sabbath the warehouse of the merchant was visited and the purchase effected. The transmission to the office and packing were performed in as brief a period as possible when the service of the rail road company was brought into requisition. In each department the call was most heartily met, and ere the Sabbath closed the goods purchased and packed in the morning were in the evening ready for use in the wards of the hospitals.

The labor thus performed was appropriated in the spirit of the best of all teachers, who has told us that the Sabbath was made for man, and that it is right that we should do good on that day. It is not to be doubted that the blessing of Heaven was admitted upon those labors of faith and love and mercy.

DISTRICTS AND COMMITTEES OF THE COMMISSION.

For the purpose of facilitating the great work of the Commission the loyal States have been divided into Districts, and Committees have been appointed to labor in them, in the provision and distribution of hospital stores and reading matter. The duties of the Committees of several of the States, distant from the seat of the war, is that of providing and forwarding the necessary supplies, and procuring the services of delegates. In other States, those which are in proximity with the battle-fields, the Committees distribute, as well as gather, the supplies. They visit the camps, hospitals and battle-fields, and counsel with delegates and agents in relation to the arrangement of their plans and pursuit of their labors.

The States in which Committees are at work in the performance of their several services are Maine, Vermont, New Hampshire, Massachusetts, New York, Pennsylvania, Delaware and Maryland as one district, Kentucky, Tennessee, Illinois and the District of Columbia. In cities, towns and prominent country places there are Sub-Committees and Aid and Relief Associations, which are actively engaged in providing and forwarding stores to the Central and other offices. Through the agency of these bodies very large quantities of stores are in continual transmission, and the offices of the Commission are in their hourly receipt and use in the supply of the camps and hospitals.

Ladies' Relief Associations.

In connection with every hospital and with many of the camps there are Associations of ladies who operate in systematic arrangement in the preparation and application of the stores. These associations are divided into Committees of three, five, seven or more, according to the labor to be performed. One of the Committees is in attendance each day. These ladies, with their own hands, minister to the patients in their charge. Under the direction and advice of Surgeons, they prepare the supplies and convey them to the wards. They may be seen any and every day with their provisions of nice food and delicacies at the bedside of their patients, assisting them as their needs require in their use. In many instances, the wounded and those much weakened by sickness, are fed by them with spoons, and otherwise assisted in the effort to partake of the well provided meal.

No measure of relief, nor labor is spared by those angels of mercy in their attendance upon the sick and wounded soldiers, and sailors. They assist the cooks in preparation of the meals of the patients and supply them with water and wine as they need them. They are frequently commissioned by the Surgeons to administer their prescriptions to the patients. Without the visits and attention of these good Christian women, how cheerless and desolate would the wards of the hospital be to the afflicted and suffering soldiers? In their persons and ministrations, the presence of the mother and sister are more than half realized, and many of the comforts of home experienced. The eye of many a dying soldier has lingered in its languidness upon the form of his kind attendant, and with the vision of his home, in his view, his spirit has passed from its cot in the hospital ward to its place in the invisible world. The blessings of multitudes who have passed away, and of multitudes more who have been assisted in their recovery from sickness and disability through the agency of these gentle ministers of Heaven's will, have been invoked on their behalf.

CHRISTIAN ASSOCIATIONS.

Although the Christian Commission originated in a Convention composed of Delegates from the Young Men's Christian Associations, it is not conducted under their auspices, nor officially connected with them in any way. It is a distinct and independent organization. Great assistance however, in the provision of stores and reading matter, is rendered by the Young Men's Christian Associations. In some instances the rooms of those associations, are generally tendered, and used by the Commission, and the services of the Young Men are constantly applied in furtherance of its benevolent design.

The Christian Association of Baltimore City, is auxiliary to the Commission, and all its labors are rendered in connection with it. This body is not in the organization known as the Young Men's Christian Association. It is a body composed of clergyman and others, who devote themselves to the work systematically under a constitution, and make monthly reports and statements at meetings regularly appointed for the purpose.

By the members of this Association, and those of the Young

Men's Christian Associations, the ladies of the Relief Associations are frequently met at the bedside of the inmates of the hospitals, and in their joint labors and prayers, the subjects of their interest are revived and comforted.

OUTSIDE ASSISTANCE.

Outside of Christian Associations, and of any known organized bodies, a great interest on behalf of the Commission has been excited; and the public everywhere in the loyal States, has been aroused to action in the provision and transmission of stores and reading matter. Men and women in neighborhoods have banded together in small bodies, and gathered in, and prepared home delicacies for the needy objects of their consideration. With but little cost, and in the contribution of labor that was by no means oppressive, a vast amount of relief has, in this way, been afforded.

Under this head, may be mentioned the facilities and assistance afforded the Commission by Rail Road and Telegraph Companies. The number of miles of rail road travel that have been generally free to the use of the Commission in its transportation of delegates and stores, has been computed at twenty thousand; and nearly every Telegraph Company has given the use of its wires, free of charge, to the Commission. That there is patriotism in all the facilities and services thus appropriated, there can be no doubt. The service is more than patriotic; it is really religious in its character, and as such, will be owned and recorded by our Great Father in Heaven.

TRANSMISSION OF STORES TO MORE DISTANT FIELDS.

From Fredericksburg, in Virginia; Louisville, in Kentucky, and Murfreesboro and Nashville, in Tennessee, dispatches were transmitted to the Central office in the times of their emergency. Immediately, that is within two hours, delegates and stores were in transit, and reached their destination long before they were expected. In one instance, in an hour and an half, a large supply of goods was purchased, packed, invoiced, and carted three-quarters of a mile to the rail road depot, and reached in time to be sent off in the lightning train. The one instance thus alluded to, is mentioned not as an isolated one, for there were many of similar character; but to show how sure is the success of a laborious and difficult enterprise, when willing hearts and hands are engaged in it, and the blessing of Heaven is invoked and granted upon it.

LABORS OF THE COMMISSION.

The labors of the Commission are not limited, as some persons have supposed, to the supply of clergymen and religious services and books for sick and dying men. This is indeed the most important and necessary part of the service. But the Committees and Delegates of the Institution are not so ignorant and inexperienced as to suppose that the services of religion may be successfully performed in the view and on the behalf of mangled and suffering men, until their physical condition can be ameliorated and improved. No experienced Christian, unless it be in cases of extreme emergency, will ever attempt to impart religious instruction and spiritual counsel to the sufferer who is writhing in the pains of a bruised and bleeding body without sympathising with him in his trial, and the effort to relieve his bodily pain. The delegate of the Christian Commission bears with him to the battlefield, the camp, and ward of the hospital the means of his ministrations to the afflicted body, as well as that of his care for the needy soul. And he applies both as he finds opportunity. The haversack he carries contains refreshment for the suffering body, which is administered under the counsel and direction of the Surgeon, and when cheered by its application the reading of religious books, the conversation on religious subjects and the religious services are added, generally at the request of the patient.

CARE OF THE WOUNDED.

During and after battle, the wounded are removed to places of safety and delivered into the hands of such humane persons as may be near to receive them and minister to their necessities. The delegates of the Christian Commission are generally in attendance for the performance of this service. The provision of the hospital, the preparing of the wards, the removal of the patients, and the application of the assistance immediately required, are services that must be immediately performed. With astonishing rapidity have the wounded been borne from the field and placed under treatment by the delegates who have been in attendance, and prepared with every facility for the performance of the work. When in a place of safety, and refreshed and rendered comfortable, if such condition can be reached, the delegate begins his religious services, and continues them at the desire and request of the patient. In cases of great emergency, when death seems to be near neither the patient nor the delegate is willing to delay the services of religion; they are then performed as speedily as possible. There is but little danger of mistake in the manner of proceeding in nearly all such cases. The condition of humanity indicates the service it needs. The will of the sufferer is expressed in accordance with nature's dictates. In the later moments of its connection with the body, the spirit generally intimates its desire. The concern of the dying man, when fully realized, is less in regard to his bodily comfort than his soul's safety; and the course of the attendant may be directed by the patient's will. The Delegates of the Commission have been generally successful in the management of the cases committed to their care, and thousands that have departed, with other thousands that are living, have expressed their most profound gratitude in the receipt of their ministrations.

Preparation for the Service.

The Delegates of the Christian Commission are gentlemen who volunteer for certain periods to engage in the service. They are generally clergymen and other religious persons, who have been in the habit of attending upon the sick and dying. The names of Corps of these are registered upon the books of the Commission as they are kept by the Committees in charge of the several districts. When the emergency arises, but a moment's notice is necessary. The parties are in readiness, and hasten to the office where there are haversacks filled with such articles as are needed. Supplied with these, they generally proceed in the first train, and are soon at the field and at work. Boxes and trunks of stores are kept in readiness, and sent in the same trains with the delegates, so that the supplies and the laborers reach their destination at the same time. There never was a period of history, nor an occasion of war in which there were greater facilities for the necessary attendance upon the wounded of the battle-field. Nor was there ever a period nor an occasion in which the facilities afforded were half as promptly and as effectually used.

There must be distressing casualties when opposing armies meet each other for deadly conflict. In the meeting of such armies as are engaged in the present contest, the extent of the casualties is too great to be estimated. Notwithstanding this consideration, it may be safely asserted that but a small proportion of the suffering that could be reached has been left unrelieved. Delegates and stores have been on hand on almost every occasion in which they were needed, and labors and means have been most generously applied in its relief.

Liberality of the Service.

On all the occasions of battle, a greater or less number of the enemy has been left within our lines, and have been captured as prisoners. In clearing the battle-field of the wounded, these have shared our sympathies and care equally with the disabled of our own army. When the yet living form of the mangled and bleeding sufferer has been committed to the care of our delegates, the question has not been asked, is he a friend or an enemy. All have shared alike in the labors of the Commission, and there is now a large number of rebel officers and men who are indebted for the preservation of their lives to our Commission. This has been acknowledged with gratitude by many who are fully conscious of their obligations, and perfectly willing to admit it.

The Battles and the Commission.

It is not known that a single battle has taken place, near which and ready for their work, there were not the Delegates and Agents of the Commission. In many instances the Committee in charge of the districts have been present, and mingled their labors with those of the delegates in affording relief and comfort to the disabled. At Shiloh, the Delegates of the Commission were present with stores from Chicago, Illinois, having travelled over seven hundred miles to reach their destination. At Fredericksburg, Antietam and Gettysburg, the Committee of Maryland were present, and performed efficient service in the removal of the wounded and ministering to their necessities. At Chancellorville, Fair Oaks, Chattanooga, and at all the battle-fields, the needed ministrations were in readiness and promptly applied.

The Convalescent.

In many of the camps and hospitals, tents and rooms are set apart for religious worship. In these the convalescent are assembled for religious services, and when not so occupied they are the resort of the men for reading and meditation and conversation. The religious service with the convalescents consists in reading the scriptures, singing, prayer and preaching. Prayer meetings and experience meetings are held with them, and in which they mingle with more or less interest according to their temperament and disposition. It is a rule of the Commission to supply every soldier with a Testament, and much of the time of those who are able to leave their beds, is occupied in reading them. The Testaments and Bibles, when they can be provided, with devotional books, tracts, &c., are companions for the lonely hours that without them, must be spent by the patients in walking over the grounds, or in the listless and profitless expenditure of time in unoccupied thought, or in light and improper conversation and pursuits.

Reading Matter.

The reading matter distributed among the officers and soldiers of the army has been most gratefully received, and in most instances it has been used with great profit. It is as highly prized as the food of the mind and spirit as the usual hospital stores are esteemed as the food of the body. The soldier has carried the Testament into the battle, and returned with it, rejoicing in his preservation, or it has been found in his knapsack after his fall upon the field, with the evidences of its having been well used in the marks it has borne. Often has the wife's, and mother's, and sister's heart been cheered in its sorrow over the loss of the loved one, by the pencil traces, and other marks that have appeared upon the Bible or the Testament, or devotional book or tract. In large quantities, this portion of the property of deceased soldiers has been transmitted to their families and friends. They are now reserved as household treasures, bearing the record of the sacrifice to which they have submitted on behalf of their beloved country.

LIBERALITY OF BIBLE AND TRACT SOCIETIES, AND OF NEWSPAPER PUBLISHERS.

The American Bible Society has contributed nearly fifty thousand dollars worth of Bibles and Testaments to the service of the Christian Commission. The satisfaction afforded in the certainty of knowledge that the copies of the Scriptures thus distributed have performed a service the value of which cannot be estimated, affords a full remuneration for this immense outlay. The same may be said, in its degree and grade, in regard to the circulation of tracts and newspapers. In immense numbers these agencies of relief and enlightenment have been contributed. Their service has followed in the wake of the spiritual enlightenment opened by the Scriptures, and it has appeared as an important ally in the spiritual training of the subjects of its operations. The seed sown cannot be lost. It must spring up in the various qualities of the soil into which it has been placed, and it must bring forth its fruits, some thirty, some sixty, and some an hundred fold.

FUTURE BENEFIT OF THE COMMISSION'S SERVICES.

It has been argued that at the close of the war, and in the disbanding of the armies of the republic, there will be sent home to every city and town and village in the States, a band of men hardened in iniquity, and prepared for any sort of work of demoralization and wickedness. Such may have been the result in other countries and on other occasions of war. But the indications are different in the present prospect. If there is a speciality in the providence of the Christian Commission, it presents itself in its connection with this very subject. If the work of the Commission be successful, the disbanding of the army will not scatter broadcast over the land the corrupt and the vile. But it will scatter the morally and religiously enlightened and the morally and religiously disposed over all the face of our highly favored country. The distribution of more than five hundred thousand copies of the scriptures, nearly twenty-three million pages of tracts, and over three and a half millions of religious and other newspapers, must be effective, by the blessing of God, in counteracting the influences of evil, and in converting to the cause and service of Christianity, a large proportion of those in relation to whose vileness and corresponding degradation many fears have been entertained. Converted to the cause of religion in the camps and hospitals of the army, the multitudes that may be discharged and sent to their homes by the disbanding of the army, may be the means of doing much good in their respective localities. Through the agency of the Christian Commission, God may thus work His purpose in bringing good out of evil, and in constraining even the wrath of man to utter praises upon His name. In this consideration there is high encouragement for the labors of the Christian Commission in its membership and committees and delegates and agents. Not only the hope of our country's safety, but that of its future character and stability is in the issue, and it should animate every heart with zeal in the cause, and engage every hand for labor in its accomplishment.

STATISTICS OF THE CHRISTIAN COMMISSION SERVICE.

The following tabular statement exhibits a view of the means and labors expended in the great cause of relieving the necessities of the soldiers and sailors of the army and navy of the United States.

Bibles and Testaments distributed,..............................568,275
Soldiers' and Sailors' Hymn Books,........................502,556
Magazines and Pamphlets,..155,145
Books of various kinds,..1,410,061
Pages of Tracts,..22,930,428
Newspapers, &c.,..3,616,250
Delegates, Ministers, and others, sent to battle-fields,
  camps and hospitals,...1,563

VALUE OF STORES AND SERVICES.

Cash,..$ 398,399.58
Stores,...527,979.07
Bibles and Testaments,..46,749.20
Rail Road facilities,..44,210.00
Telegraph facilities,..9,390.00
Services of Delegates,...93,863.00

$1,120,590.85

THE UNITED STATES SANITARY COMMISSION.

THE best chapter in the history of any war, is that which exhibits how its horrors have been mitigated, and unavoidable sufferings relieved of their bitterest complexion. War is always, and necessarily, a great waster of human life. Its object is destruction—its aims, the infliction of suffering and death upon combatants—its purpose, to coerce by force, when reason fails to convince by persuasion. While the saddest feature of all is, that, like Saturn, it consumes its own children, outside even of the reach and influence of the enemy it has gone to combat.— Wherever it goes, a fatal imminence hovers over all its hosts, since, in carrying death unto others, they nurse the destroyer within themselves. Aside, therefore, from all moral speculation, it is a singular physical fact, that an army is always its own direst enemy; that the very gregariousness of a host constitutes its surest pre-disposition to destruction, unless science erect about it those safe-guards which shall prevent the incubation of all deadly agencies. Science being pre-vision, it follows that to her alone we can entrust the care of an army, in order to save it from that ingenerate consumption which, unheralded by trumpet or drum, daily mows its victims down with unrelenting and insatiable rapacity. This science, the best expression of a Christian and brotherly solicitude, is the science which is typified by the idea of a SANITARY COMMISSION.

Practically considered, however, the labors of this priesthood are not limited to pre-vision alone. But, and wherever the necessities of actual, as well as impending disease—suffering, or want, exhibit themselves either in hospitals, or on battle-fields—among enemies or friends, there the hand of relief is raised—the aid extended—the suffering mitigated—the anguish soothed. In this wider and more philanthropic sense, the duties performed by such an organization are as ample as the urgencies themselves, and embrace every thing which can give aid and comfort to the sick and wounded of an army. To compass this, a multitude of efforts of every name and nature must be made, and in all directions. The thousand items necessary to feed, clothe, lodge and tend the sick, which require varieties of workmen to supply them, and occasion diversities of occupation in communities, must be collected in special depots—the same articles being required in all with a difference only in their quantity. Foresight must always anticipate the wants which, simultaneously, and in all directions, ask to be supplied. All being equally beneficiaries, who wear the uniform of their country, none must be allowed to go unrelieved, for the claim of each is a sacred call upon the gratitude of the nation, not to be ignored. Lastly, transportation hither and yonder, at equal pace with a moving army—pushing on through obstacles of every kind to present the relief at the earliest possible moment—never to be out of material, and to be ready to supply all and everywhere upon a vast theatre of war—such are the daily necessities pressing upon a Sanitary Commission.

When the present war broke out, and the uprising of a whole nation placed an army of gigantic proportions in the field, it was felt by those who had read and pondered the bloody lessons left by preceding wars, that something must be done outside of established official departments, to aid in maintaining the integrity of such a host. From a small force of some ten thousand men, a few months saw us with an army of five hundred thousand, while at the same time no adequate provision for the sick or wounded could be immediately made by the Government. Left to the slow course of official routine, and in the hands of men accustomed to deal only with small bodies of troops, the wants of these great legions of warriors must, for a long while, have remained unanswered. Suffering and increased mortality, discouragement and despondency, would have been the consequence—our armies would have melted down, like those of England at Walcheren, or the Allies in the Crimea; and at this time, instead of presenting to the world the rare spectacle of an army never yet decimated by an epidemic, we should in all probability, have had to mourn the fate of thousands who had died of preventible disease. It will be remembered that the British Sanitary Commission to the East was only organized after the war had already progressed for over ten months, and when the sufferings of the troops had reached to such a degree, and their mortality risen so fearfully, as to seriously compromise their operations.*

Urged by these considerations, and the repeated lessons of past wars, a small number of gentlemen, at the very inception of our conflict, undertook to create a Sanitary Commission, which, as the representative of the intelligent interest, and sympathy of the people, with the army, should, in strict subordination to the rules of the War and Medical Departments, and as their assistant, endeavor to supplement those innumerable wants likely to arise in the course of their dealing with such hitherto untried masses. The spontaneous offers of assistance—the wealth of treasure proffered, and the universal desire expressed by all classes, in all communities, to take part in contributing towards the comfort of those whom the vicissitudes of war would soon cast as a burthen upon the Medical Department, revealed the necessity of organizing this magnificent outburst of patriotism, so as to render it both methodical as well as far-reaching in its benefactions. It was justly felt that, however kindly intentioned, the contributions of the people, whether in money or specific articles, in order best to fulfill the designs of the donors, and to help the general progress of the war, must be brought under some system of distribution which should co-ordinate itself with the discipline necessary to the efficiency of an army. A contrary course, as experience has everywhere shown, invariably tends to defeat its own purposes, by both wasting contributions, as well as diminishing the salutary influence of military rule. Ill-advised philanthropy, acting upon impulse alone and without judgment, might, nay, often does,

---

* According to Miss Nightingale, the mortality of the British Army during the first *seven* months of the Crimean War, was 60 *per cent.* That of our Army during the *year* 1862, was 50.4 per *thousand.*

defeat the object it most earnestly desires to accomplish, and in this way, good men, earnest Christians, zealous philanthropists, occasionally lay themselves open to rebuke, not for the noble spirit they profess, but for the thoughtless manner in which, in the ardor of their zeal, they seek to practice their humanity. In ordinary times no stringent lines of conduct need be drawn around such benefactions, nor are they, but it is far different in dealing with an army, the men of which are subjected to rules necessarily applied to them in the aggregate, and found to be essential to their well-being and corporate efficiency. Here the power which commands them, must control them, and he who would come to their aid for any purpose must approach them solely through that power.

Impressed with the conviction that the only true course to follow with regard both to the army and the people, was one, in entire parallelism with, and subordination to, the War and Medical Departments, a representative committee most fortunately selected among these gentlemen,* on the 18th day of May, 1861, addressed a communication to Mr. Cameron, then Secretary of War, upon the subject that was engrossing the attention of the country: already Relief and Aid Societies for the sick and wounded soldiers were springing up in all directions, though without any definite apprehension of the sphere in which their efforts could be made most available to the army. Full of good intentions, yet not knowing precisely how to turn them to the readiest use, the women of our country were taking the initiative in measures calculated to relieve suffering of every description, provided only they could reach it. Town, village, and ward committees were forming everywhere for similar purposes—money was lavishly bestowed—stores accumulated in profusion—personal services tendered by all classes, and still it remained an unsolved problem how this magnificent and multifarious philanthropy

---

* Drs. Bellows, Van Buren, Harris and Harsen, of New York, representing the Woman's Central Association of relief for the sick and wounded of the army—the Advisory Committee of the Boards of Physicians and Surgeons of the Hospitals of New York,—and the New York Medical Association for furnishing hospital supplies in aid of the Army.

should be organized into an enduring system of contributions, and an economical one of distribution, so as to extend the greatest good to the greatest number. It was plain at the outset that the necessities for supplies of this kind would never cease during the continuance of the war, and therefore, that the work of contributing must be divested of the character of a spasm of romance and brought within the purview of a stern, moral obligation. As the whole nation was interested in the health, comfort and success of the army, and stood ready to vindicate that interest by profusion of aid, so that aid to be most useful must be a feature constantly incorporated with the army—moving with it—attending to its wants, and acting as a supplementary department to the medical and quarter-master's.

The communication to Mr. Cameron explained in brief the advantage of methodizing the spontaneous benevolence of the country, and aiding the War Department with such supplies as were not included in the regulations of the army. The language used expressed most clearly the cogent reasons upon which it was founded, and left nothing to be desired in point of force, elegance or perspicuity. Like everything emanating from its accomplished author, it carried with it a weight of logic and a thorough appreciation of circumstances, which were unanswerable then, and have been since so well verified, as to impart to them almost a prophetic similitude. The effect of this letter was to elicit a note from the Acting Surgeon General of the Army to the Secretary of War, advising the institution of a "Commission of Inquiry and Advice in respect of the Sanitary Interests of the United States Forces." Coinciding heartily with the views set forth in this communication, Mr. Cameron, accordingly, and with the sanction of the President, appointed the following gentlemen a Board of Sanitary Commissioners, with power to add to their number, on the 13th day of June, 1861, viz: Rev. Henry W. Bellows, D. D.; Prof. A. D. Bache; Prof. Jeffries Wyman, M. D.; Prof. Wolcott Gibbs, M. D.; Wm. H. Van Buren, M. D.; Samuel G. Howe, M. D.; R. C. Wood, U. S. A.; G. W. Cullom, U. S. A.; A. E. Shiras, U. S. A. Such was the origin of the United States Sanitary Commission, which now numbers twenty-one executive members, and five hundred associates.*

As soon as this organization by the Government, of the Commission, as an advisory and supplemental branch of the War Department was effected, its Executive Committee proceeded without delay to carry out such plans as would most effectually accomplish those great objects which it had in view. Chief among these, and foremost in necessity of execution was that of securing a thorough Sanitary Inspection of Camps, Posts, and Hospitals. To accomplish this very important and delicate task—a task in which more or less seeming interference with the established discipline of such places would be manifested, a number of Medical Inspectors were appointed, whose duty it was made to point out to commanding officers causes of insalubrity in their midst, which, as laymen practically unacquainted with the principles of Hygiene, they were but too often found wholly blind to the existence of. And, as each inspection generally disclosed something that could be ameliorated—and as often the stronger fact, that this amelioration could not be secured through the regular official channels, so the Commission found itself constantly called upon to supplement the Hygienic wants of our troops. What these thousand wants, repeated daily and in different directions, were,

---

* The following gentlemen now constitute the Sanitary Commission, viz:—
H. W. Bellows, D. D., New York. A. D. Bache, LL. D. Washington, D. C.
F. L. Olmsted. George T. Strong, Esq., New York. Elisha Harris, M. D.,
New York. W. H. Van Buren, M. D., New York. G. W. Cullom, U. S. A.
A. E. Shiras, U. S. A. R. C. Wood, Assistant Surgeon General, U. S. A.
Wolcott Gibbs, M. D., New York. S. G Howe, M. D., Boston, Mass. C. R.
Agnew, M. D., New York. J. S. Newberry, M. D., Cleveland, Ohio. Rt.
Rev. T. M Clarke, Providence, R. I. Hon. R. W. Burnett, Cincinnati, Ohio.
Hon. Mark Skinner, Chicago, Ill. Hon. Joseph Holt, Washington. D. C.
Horace Binney, Jr., Philadelphia, Penn. Rev. J. H. Heywood, Louisville, Ky.
J. Huntington Wolcott, Boston, Mass. Prof. Fairman Rogers, Philadelphia.
Penn.

OFFICERS:—H. W. Bellows, D. D. President. A. D. Bache, LL. D., Vice-President. George T. Strong, Treasurer. J. Foster Jenkins, M. D., General Secretary. J. S. Newberry, M. D, Associate Secretary. J. H. Douglas, M.D, Associate Secretary. F. N. Knapp, Associate Secretary.

it would require too much space to enumerate. They embraced almost everything relating to Diet, Clothing, Cooking, Tents, Camp-grounds, Transports, Hospitals, and Camp-police. And of the benefits present and future secured by this intelligent prevision of an army's necessities and contingencies, no single illustration will serve better to teach us, than the fact of furnishing *immediately*, when wanted in a season of great peril in 1861, vaccine virus for thousands of men, at a time, when the regular Medical Bureau of the Army could supply but a *tenth* part of what was needed, and that only after a *fortnight's* delay. What would have happened to the troops but for this timely succor it is not difficult to foresee, and it is saying little to assert that it would have been unsafe to place bodies of men upon transports, where, of necessity they must be crowded, with such a certainty of small-pox before them, and consequently great delays must have ensued in collecting a force at any distant point.

The next step to prevention in the matter of disease or suffering, is that of relief applied to it when existing. Here the Commission found a field commensurate with that of the theatre of war. It established agencies in most of the principal cities and towns, and created depots of supplies—some stationary, some moveable at all the principal points occupied by the army. With every army corps there have gone one or more relief agents* who, anticipating the wants both extraordinary, as well as ordinary, of the troops, have never failed to supply them in the movements of their most pressing need. It would hardly be believed possible, were it not well authenticated, that, for *forty-eight* hours after the battle of Antietam, thousands of wounded men, received all their supplies of medicine (opiates, stimulants, chloroform) diet, bedding and clothing, chiefly from the Sanitary Commission. The regular Government supplies did not reach the field of action for *two* days. Need it be asked what would have become of the wounded but for this

---

* Each great division of the army has a Chief Sanitary Inspector, and a Superintendent of Field Relief, and when a force is stationary, a Lodge is established near its head-quarters. If the force is in motion supplies are issued from wagon trains, or from steamboats, of which the Commission has three.

timely foresight and energy in transportation of hospital materials, or how great was the number of lives saved by this appreciation of the necessties of an impending battle

"For want of timely aid, thousands die of medicable wounds."

This sad truth so often repeating itself, and yet so constantly disregarded, the Sanitary Commission have never lost sight of, and hence, whether at Vicksburg, Murfreesboro', Chancellorsville, Chattanooga, Chickamauga, Fredericksburg, or Gettysburg, their depots have ever been prepared to distribute, even during the hottest of the fight, those grateful supplies whose value as life-saving agents depends so much upon their timely administration. Those only who have been in the habit of considering the difficulties attendant upon transporting the *material* of an army, with all the assistance even which official position can command, will be able to appreciate the energy manifested by the Commission, and the efficient use made of the little means placed at its control in transporting, by independent routes from the army, yet always keeping pace with it, even in an enemy's country, those supplies destined to relieve its direst necessities. But for this never-tiring energy our battle-fields would have had little mitigation to their horrors, and many a life now of use to the country must inevitably have been sacrificed to the insatiate monarch of war.

In another way, and with a delicacy which silences all criticism, the Commission has rendered great service to the Medical Staff of the Army, by issuing a series of medical monographs upon subjects of the gravest importance in Military Surgery. Prepared as these have been by some of our most eminent Physicians and Surgeons, they carry with them a weight of authority which renders them most valuable contributions to the Medical literature of our country, while especially addressed to our Surgeons on the field, who cannot carry libraries with them, obtain the assistance of consultations, nor devote much time to the periodical publications of their own profession, they furnish invaluable suggestions and instruction in practical medicine. Some nineteen of these monographs have already been published, and thousands of copies distributed among our army Surgeons.

35*

Another great work executed by the Commission in obedience to that spirit of solicitude with which it has always watched over the soldier, has been the special Inspection of Hospitals. This duty, committed to gentlemen of the highest standing in the Medical Profession, occupied some six months for its performance, and resulted in the recommendation of many forms of improvement in our present Hospital system. Over two hundred of these establishments were critically examined, and an inquiry of the most thorough character made into the condition of every one, and every thing in them. The report of these inspections would make a large volume, and add valuable information to the history of such institutions. All the suggestions combined in it have been laid before the proper authorities, and will, we doubt not, find their ultimate realization at an early day.

Second only in importance to the system of general relief for the Army, while in the field, of which we have already spoken, has been that department of Special Relief, which, from its very inception, almost, the Commission has been called upon by daily admonitions of experience, to organize. This department deals with soldiers singly and disconnected from all military rule. It picks up stragglers from regiments who have lost their way—* sick and discharged soldiers going home without money—applicants for pensions, or waiting for back-pay—men who are hungry, and those who want a night's lodging, and dispenses to all, the most christian charity of relief suited to each particular want.

---

* At points like Washington or Nashville, for example, there may be daily found scores or hundreds of men separated from their regiments and anxious to rejoin them, but unable to obtain transportation, and without legal title mean while to quarters or rations, or any kind of recognition or aid from any Government officer within reach. Some are returning after a furlough, but find that their regiment has moved. Their little stock of money has given out, and they must beg through the streets for aught that any official has the power to do for them. Others are sick, but no Hospital can admit them without a breach of regulations. Others are waiting to get their back pay, but there is some technical defect in their papers for which they are not responsible, and they must wait a week for a letter to reach their regiment and be answered, before they can draw a dollar from the Paymaster, and subsist as they can meanwhile.

San. Comm. Doc. 69, *p.* 31.

Such a department as this does every thing by turns. It furnishes a home to the homeless—shelter to the lost wanderer—food to the hungry—medicine to the sick—helps men to get to their distant homes—sends some one with them whenever they are too sick to go alone, and *plays the part of a Good Samaritan to all.*

The chief objects sought to be accomplished by this department are as follows, viz:

First.—To supply the sick of newly arrived regiments such medicines, food, and care as their officers are, under the circumstances, unable to give them. The men thus aided are chiefly those not sick enough to have a claim on a general hospital, but who nevertheless need immediate care to prevent serious illness.

Second.—To furnish suitable food, lodging, care, and assistance to men who are honorably discharged as unfit for further service, but who are often obliged to wait for several days before they obtain their papers and pay, or to sell their claims to speculators at a sacrifice.

Third.—To communicate with distant regiments in behalf of men whose certificates of disability or descriptive lists on which to draw their pay prove to be defective—the invalid soldiers meantime being cared for, and not exposed to the fatigue and risk of going in person to their regiments to have their papers corrected.

Fourth.—To act as the unpaid agent or attorney of soldiers who are too feeble or too utterly disabled to present their own claim at the Paymaster's office.

Fifth.—To look into the condition of discharged and furloughed men who seem without means to pay the expense of going to their homes, and to furnish the necessary means where the man is found to be true and the need real.

Sixth.—To secure to soldiers going home on sick leave railroad tickets at reduced rates, and through an agent at the railroad station to see that they are not robbed or imposed upon.

Seventh.—To see that all men who are discharged and paid off do at once leave the city at which they receive their discharge, for their homes, or in cases where they have been induced by evil companions to remain behind, to endeavor to rescue them, and see them started homeward with through tickets.

Eighth.—To make men going home discharged, or on sick leave, reasonably clean and comfortable before their departure.

Ninth.—To be prepared to meet, at once, with food or other aid, such immediate necessities as arise when sick men arrive in large numbers from battle fields or distant hospitals.

In order the better to carry out the designs of this Department, *Homes* have been established in many of our principal cities, where assistance of every kind is afforded to soldiers. That these homes have, by their very successful and beneficent operation, proved the wisdom of their founders, none will dispute, after reading the subjoined report of their benefactions, brought up to the 1st of October, 1863.

	Number of Persons Received.	Night's Lodging Furnished.	Meals Given.
"Home," Washington, D. C.,	7,287	26,533	65,621
Lodges 2, 3, 4, 5, Washington,		23,590	184,995
"Home," Cleveland, Ohio,		2,569	12,227
Lodge, Memphis, Tenn		2,850	14,780
Lodge, Nashville, Tenn		4,821	11,909
Home, Louisville, Ky		17,785	52,080
" " "			at R. R. Sta. 49,933
Home, Cairo, Ill		79,550	170,150
Home, Cincinnati, Ohio,		40,017	10,000
Lodge, Alexandria, Va		604	5,980
Home, Boston, Mass		1,407	4,129
Home for Nurses and Soldiers' wives and mothers, Washington,		1,583	3,640
Home, for Nurses, Annapolis, Md		569	2,847
Home, Chicago, Ill		3,109	11,325

AGGREGATE.
Of Lodgings Furnished, 206,570.
Of Meals given, 602,656.

In addition to these many provisions for the sick and wounded soldiers, and the comfort of all classes of the military in their individual as well as their collective capacity, the Commission, consulting the feelings of the community at large, has caused to be maintained, for over a year past, a *Hospital Directory*, by means of which the friends of any soldier could ascertain whether or not he was in hospital. A man might be too sick, or too severely wounded to be able to write to his friends, and inform them of his condition. The Directory comes at once to their aid, and supplies them with the needed information. Although in one sense this can not be considered a Sanitary measure, having nothing to do with the protection of health, yet the very satisfactory manner in which the undertaking has flourished, and the interest manifested in it by all classes, shows plainly enough that it has subserved a want of the most universal character. And since the Commission are only the Trustees of the people for the employment of a large fund, intended to benefit the Army, they have felt that, in whatever way that fund could be applied so as to reach the soldier even remotely, it was still but carrying out the intentions of the people to direct it in such way.

The Directory Books have been kept in four places, viz: Washington, New York, Philadelphia and Louisville, and the following table illustrating the number of recorded names will show how widely extended must be the circle of people interested in knowing the whereabouts and condition of their several relatives or friends in the Army.

	Names.
Washington Office to Oct. 1st, 1863, contained	169,007
New York " " " "	27,320
Philadelphia " " " "	24,513
Louisville " " " "	186,433
	407,273

These reports are corrected daily—they give the name, regiment, company—and nature of disease or wound, of every man admitted into a General Hospital, and go on further to tell the names of those dying, or discharged, and if so, what ultimate disposition has been made of them, or in other words, whether they have rejoined their regiments, or been discharged for permanent disability.

Besides all this regularly appointed work which the Commission, as the Trustee of a great charitable fund, is daily carrying on, there are extra calls constantly being made upon it to meet the wants of sudden emergencies. These calls, generally un-anticipated, are always pressing in their nature, and must be attended to at once. They come like a thief in the night, or the sound of a fire-bell, to startle the country, and appall us by the sufferings they threaten. Not to be able to meet and master them in their very cradle would be to stand by, and see suffering go unrelieved by those who do not themselves share the danger. But relief, unless methodized, is good only for a day. It can not be depended upon for a long siege, and a combination of wants. It becomes simply an aggravation to those in whom its ephemeral appearance has created hope and expectation. Fortunately, the expansive character of a system, like that adopted by the Commission, and the assurance of hearty support from the loyal public behind, enables it to do all that is ever required of it, *and a little more.* It always has a margin to its relief-work wide enough to embrace something else not yet classified in the multifarious category of its achievements. Thus every flag-of-truce boat that has ascended the James River for the reception of exchanged prisoners, has carried such stores of food and medicine as were most indispensable to men in the debilitated and starved condition of those who have been confined in Confederate prisons. And, in addition to this itinerant benefaction, it sent from November 17th, to December 3d, a space of fifteen days, $28,000 worth of supplies to Richmond for the use of our imprisoned soldiers there. Such, without a more special enumeration of hundreds of particular instances which will never figure in reports because of their lesser importance, has been the course of Christian philanthropy, pursued by the Commission in its generous, yet economic distribution of the bounties which the patriotism of the nation has poured into its Treasury. And perhaps the happiest feature in this connection, and that which most symbolizes the unity and harmony of action everywhere actuating the country, is the fact, that all classes, from the poorest of the poor, to the richest of the rich, have alike contributed to its resources. And if we may believe that the offerings of the poor, made in a spirit of self-sacrifice and true charity, have a double blessing accorded them, we can entertain no doubt that the labors of the Commission, so signally favored in the past, will still receive the invisible, yet everywhere revealed signs of Divine approbation.

The following "Roll of Honor" will tell for itself, and in tones louder than any human emphasis can give it, the interest which the loyal American people, in whatever lands living, and however far from home, feel in their Sanitary Commission.

SANITARY COMMISSION.

Contributions received by the Treasurer of the Commission from June, 1861, to December 7th, 1863.

From Maine,	$17,720	33
" New Hampshire,	1,701	44
" Vermont,	2,035	15
" Massachusetts,	48,548	86
" Connecticut,	5,181	35
" Rhode Island,	8,068	30
" New England, (States not discriminated,)	6,683	75
" New York,	160,042	58
" New Jersey,	3,170	88
" Pennsylvania,	11,699	18
" Delaware,	765	00
" Maryland,	1,733	00
" Washington, D. C.,	2,333	08
" Ohio,	2,700	00
" Michigan,	578	00
" Illinois,	546	25
" Kentucky,	6,166	45
" Indiana,	500	00
" Minnesota,	45	00
" Nevada Territory,	54,144	75
" California,	526,909	61
" Oregon,	26,450	78
" Washington Territory,	7,258	97
" Idaho,	2,110	46
" Van-Couver's and San Juan Islands,	2,552	68
" Honolulu,	4,085	00
" Santiago de Chili,	3,688	84
" Peru,	2,002	00
" Newfoundland,	150	00
" Canada,	439	48
" England and Scotland,	1,150	00
" France,	2,750	00
" Turkey,	50	00
" China,	2,303	93
" Cuba,	23	00
" Unknown Sources,	3,192	88
Total,	$919,580	98

This does not include the various amounts raised by Branches of the Commission for their own use, and expended in the purchase of *Hospital stores, clothing*, &c., &c. No enumeration of the supplies furnished by thousands of sewing circles, churches and individuals to these branches is at present possible, and outside of their contributions to its Central Treasury. Could this sum be ascertained, it would probably be found reaching to millions of dollars.

That an institution of this kind—so universal in its benefactions, and so prolific in resources, should require for its maintenance a constant stream of contributions, none can wonder who have followed the foregoing brief outline of its labors. It has become so habitual too, to look to the Sanitary Commission as a sort of tutelar saint who is always ready for any call however great or urgent, that the public mind has certainly relieved itself of the burthen of much uneasiness by a confidence in its almost omnipotent character. Knowing that through its hundreds of agents it is omnipresent in the fields of danger—and experience having shown its capacity to meet every necessity of every occasion, there is reason to fear lest public sympathy with it, may lose that earnest, vivifying character, which has heretofore been so manifest, and dwindle into a feeling of personal indifference to the work ahead, because of the very successful manner in which the Commission has acquitted itself. But when the following monthly exhibit of its expenditures* is read, and a look taken at the map of our restored possessions, it will be seen that the work of relief now embracing so large a field, and upon which, both Government and Army have learned to depend, cannot be retrenched, but on the contrary, must go on increasing. And yet, alarming as is the statement, the fact is nevertheless true, that the Commission at present is gnawing its treasury down to the very bone, and unless assistance of the most ample kind soon reaches it, must suspend its operations. It is so painful to contemplate a possibility of this kind, even in imagination, that one does not like to dwell upon

* The disbursements of the Central Treasury for the *eight* months ending December 1st, 1863, were as follows:

April,	$29,142.57
May,	36,315.09
June,	54,623.21
July,	92,020.86
August,	40,507.07
September,	28,470.35
October,	30,191.81
November,	49,845.87
	$361,116.83

Making an average of over $45,000 a month!

it long enough to conjecture what, and how disastrous to the courage and moral tone of our army, would be its consequences. It is asserting little to say that the consciousness of an institution like the Sanitary Commission, is an element of strength to the soldier, to the officer, and to the Government. It is the guardian and protector of the former—the counsel and assistant of the latter. It inspires the soldier with courage, because he knows from experience, that he can depend upon its strong arm, as an ever present help in sickness—suffering or poverty—that he never appeals to it in vain, and never suffers injustice at his hands—but that like a kind, yet stern guardian, it acts in the place of parents, as it also does by their authority, implied through its creation and maintenance by them.

When it is remembered too that the Commission has labored in the most catholic spirit towards *all* soldiers, from whatever region, or nationality coming, looking only to the *uniform* as the guarantee of their devotion to the one cause of our common country, and insisting upon ignoring that disposition so common at the outbreak of the war; but now, and mainly through its efforts, happily abandoned, of discriminating in the distribution of supplies, between the soldiers of different States—a custom at once inhuman and mischievous in its tendency, and calculated to destroy the national character of our army, by surrounding even the comforts for the sick and wounded, with certain conditions and limitations; when these things are remembered in connection with the direct aid it affords the Government, through the better health of the troops it secures—the decreased mortality in hospitals, and after battles, which its ready help and abundant provisions and comforts for the sick insures, thereby keeping our army up to a higher standard of efficiency than it could otherwise possibly be— surely, when those things are called to mind, and the record of past good work proves it all by inexorable statistics, can there be any reason why the people should not permanently adopt it as an offspring of their own—nurse it in the depths of their keenest sympathies—and place it in the front rank of those instrumentalities which, under God's good grace, and in the fulness of His time, will restore us our Union—extinguish the last ember of sedition, and perpetuate, as a new order of things among the nations, the ability of a Republic to sustain its integrity against the most violent and disruptive of internal commotions.

The wisdom exhibited by the Executive Committee in their management of the delicate trust confided to their hands, has elicited the admiration of all who have paused to reflect upon the perplexities which ever surround, and hamper, undertakings of so vast, and various a character. Without any precedents whatever to guide them — for the labors of the British Sanitary Commission to the East, were infantile when compared with our own— and starting with ill-concealed apprehensions on the part of some of our highest executive officers, lest the Commission should be managed in the interests alone of sentimental philosophy, they have shown an ability to grapple with emergencies, and a skill commensurate with the difficulties of every problem, whether sanitary or social, together with a fertility of resource such, as has not been surpassed by any department of the Government. Indeed, some of the most valuable suggestions upon subjects only collaterally related to Sanitary science, but all tending to increase the efficiency of the Army, and which have commanded the attention of the War Department, are emanations from this many-headed and far-sighted Commission. Could all be known of the good work done through pen and speech, and personal persuasion by the various members of the Executive Committee who have met daily, and almost nightly, too, in addition, for the past two and a half years, it would present a record of statesmen-like discussions—far-sighted anticipations of coming events—preparations for circumstances undreamed of by the masses—inquisitions into subjects of the largest import to the future well-being of our country, the whole tempered by a spirit of broad and liberal concession to the law of public opinion while marching in advance of it—such, as could only flourish in the atmosphere of pure and un-sectarian patriots. And where all have labored with equal zeal, and lent their best efforts to the common cause, deeming no sacrifice of time or personal comfort too great to him whose country is travailing in the throes of civil convulsion, it would be inviduous to mention names, or call attention to persons already filling so large a space in the grateful remembrance of their countrymen. With an ever-present sense of duty well performed, and a consciousness of the rectitude of purpose animating them, they can point to the thousand happy homes made happier for their labors, and the ten thousand lives saved to the Republic in the day of her direst necessity. It is a beautiful thing to blend the virtues of the patriot, with the wisdom of the statesman, and the graces of a Christian philanthropy, but far more beautiful still to lay them upon the altar of one's country in humility and faith, believing that all manner of invisible agencies are working in harmony with the truthful and earnest laborer, and bringing Heaven nearer to him according as he follows its golden intuitions. For, in the noble imagery of Bacon, "certainly, it is Heaven upon earth to have a man's mind move in charity, rest in Providence, and turn upon the poles of truth."

THE END.

www.ingramcontent.com/pod-product-compliance
Lightning Source LLC
Chambersburg PA
CBHW051737300426
44115CB00007B/597